FOLEY & LARDNER

Attorneys AT Law

1842-1992

COMMITTED TO EXCELLENCE · SINCE 1842 ·

150 YEARS

FOLEY &
LARDNER
Attorneys AT Law
1842-1992

ELLEN D. LANGILL

THE STATE HISTORICAL SOCIETY OF WISCONSIN, Madison

Published by the State Historical Society of Wisconsin
Madison, Wisconsin

Copyright © 1992 by Foley & Lardner
All rights reserved
Printed in the United States of America

First Edition, 1992

The paper used in this publication meets the minimum requirements of American National Standard for Information Sciences—Permanence of Paper for Printed Library Materials, ANSI Z39.48-1984.

Library of Congress Cataloging-in-Publication Data

Langill, Ellen.
  Foley & Lardner: Attorneys at law, 1842–1992 /
by Ellen D. Langill.
      p.   cm.
  Includes bibliographical references and index.
  ISBN 0-87020-267-7 (hardcover)
  1. Foley & Lardner—History.   2. Law firms—Wisconsin—History.
I. State Historical Society of Wisconsin.   II. Title.
KF354.W5L36   1992
340'.06'0775—dc20   92-20157
                                                       CIP

ACKNOWLEDGMENTS
Design
Lesiak/Crampton Design Inc
Chicago, Illinois

Editorial Development
The Wheetley Company, Inc.
Skokie, Illinois

Photography acknowledgments appear on page 245.

◄ Contents ►

Preface		*vii*
Foreword		*xv*
1	Beginnings, 1833–1842	1
2	Finch & Lynde: Early Partnership, 1842–1848	12
3	Political Life in the Wisconsin Territory, 1842–1848	21
4	Law and Early Statehood, 1848–1857	34
5	Finches, Lynde & Miller, 1857–1860	48
6	Milwaukee and the War Years, 1861–1865	61
7	Practicing Law in the Gilded Age, 1866–1873	70
8	The End of an Era, 1874–1885	83
9	The Miller Years, 1886–1890	94
10	Expanding the Partnership, 1890–1905	107
11	Miller, Mack & Fairchild, 1906–1917	120
12	World War I and the Decade of Prosperity, 1917–1931	134
13	Legal Changes in the Depression Era, 1932–1940	142
14	Partners in Wartime, 1941–1945	154
15	Postwar Growth and New Directions, 1945–1973	163
16	Epilogue: A National Law Firm, 1974–1992	177
	Appendixes	
	I Firm Names	187
	II Partners	189
	III Mergers	199
	IV Foley & Lardner Offices	201
	Notes	203
	Index	227
	Photographs	following pages 69, 119, 167

❧ Preface ❧

The 150-year history of an organization such as a law firm provides a unique research opportunity for a historian. The charge presented to me by Foley & Lardner as I took a leave from teaching academic history was to research and write the story of the firm, one of the oldest in the country. The members of the firm's book committee supported my vision of the project, which was to set the firm's story into the context of the economic, social, cultural, and legal history of the city of Milwaukee, the state of Wisconsin, and the nation as a whole. The materials further presented the opportunity to study changes in the practice of law and turning points in American legal history, as reflected in the experience of this enduring partnership.

Several office moves by the firm resulted in a very sparse archival collection, and the research task became a daunting one. Fortunately, the earliest records of the territorial and state courts in Milwaukee are preserved in the collection of the Milwaukee County Historical Society, where I was able to read all of the cases that the firm handled from Finch's arrival in 1839. Although there are no extant Finch papers, the Lynde collection in Milwaukee and at the State Historical Society of Wisconsin in Madison provided valuable materials, as did letter collections of other early Milwaukee attorneys, such as John H. Tweedy.

In reviewing the nineteenth-century materials I posed several initial questions: What kind of a man became a successful lawyer on the early midwestern frontier? What economic and social concerns led to the enormous amount of litigation in territorial Wisconsin? What other activities did lawyers pursue—in business or politics or land investments? What qualities allowed two such different men as Asahel Finch and William P. Lynde to succeed and to continue their partnership for four decades? What subsequent loyalties have cemented their affiliation into an unbroken partnership spanning a century and a half?

In studying the characters of Finch and Lynde and the flavor of early politics, other questions became central to the work. How did the history of the firm reflect significant changes in the law itself over these decades as tort and contract law matured prior to 1900? What forces shaped, or resisted, the many changes in the relationship of government to utilities, corporations, taxation, and regulation in the twentieth century? And on a more basic level, how has the nature of practicing law changed from the old one-room, two-man office of the 1840s to the large, technologically sophisticated firms of today with hundreds of partners and multiple offices across the country? What was it actually like to practice law in a day and age when legal forms were scarce, when electricity was unknown, and when an appearance at the Supreme Court in Madison involved a tortuous two-day ride in a coach over dirt roads?

Working with these and other themes, the history of the law firm became a mirror in which to study reflections of these many changes in the law and the practice of the law. The backdrop of the original Finch & Lynde partnership agreement is the story of a primitive frontier village, with mud streets, frame stores, primitive wharves, and cattle roaming the byways. As the law firm matured in its first decade, so did Milwaukee, becoming a city in 1846 and a leading commercial and industrial center by 1860.

The cross currents of temperance, antislavery, and political strife between Republicans and Democrats caught both Finch and Lynde in their grasp. The two men were on opposite sides of many issues, even ran against each other for Congress, and yet remained steadfast partners and lifelong friends.

The survival of the firm after the deaths of Finch and Lynde in the early 1880s was largely due to Benjamin Kurtz Miller, Sr., who had become a partner, along with Finch's nephew, before the Civil War. During the regime of B. K. Miller, Sr., and his son and heir, George Miller, the law firm's record of guiding and defending the state and city's major corporations continued. However, with the industrial age came the birth of utilities and the changes in law practice that took lawyers out of the courtroom and into the boardrooms of many corporate clients. The firm's focus shifted to counseling and negotiating business agreements, contracts, taxation problems, labor matters, and compliance with the growing amount of government regulation in the twentieth century. Much of the firm's work as business counselor was, of course, confidential, and unless a matter went to court there is no usable record. The public record of the firm's activities through its litigation, which supported all of these areas, survives as a valuable research tool. The firm handled many cases that challenged public rate control of streetcars and gas, telephone, and electric companies, key taxation questions, antitrust claims, libel issues, and matters of contested wills and estates.

During the 1890s several other law partnerships that survive today were established in Milwaukee. The partnership of Winkler, Flanders, Bottum, Smith & Vilas (today's Michael, Best & Friedrich) was one such active partnership that actually had its roots in the 1850s. Churchill & von Briesen (today's von Briesen & Purtell) was another firm with which Miller, Noyes & Miller worked on several matters. Other firms with historic roots in the 1890s include today's Quarles & Brady, which grew from the partnerships of Wood, Warner, Tyrrell & Bruce; Olwell & Brady; and Lines, Spooner & Quarles. Both B. K. Miller, Sr., and George Miller were friends of brothers Joseph V. and Charles Quarles, and Asahel Finch had known Willet Spooner's grandfather, Senator John C. Spooner, from Republican politics and work on street railway matters. Edgar L. Wood and Lawrence A. Olwell each came to Milwaukee from law school to practice law in 1892, one year before Edwin Mack joined Miller, Noyes & Miller and six years before the death of B. K. Miller, Sr. Before the turn of the century, William Kaumheimer also opened a law office, the forerunner of today's Reinhart, Boerner, Van Deuren, Norris & Rieselbach.

These new law partnerships, as well as the firm of Miller, Noyes & Miller, prospered with the general economic growth of the late nineteenth and early twentieth centuries. A Jewish partner and outstanding scholar, Edwin Mack, joined George Miller in 1906, possibly one of the earliest Jewish partners in a Yankee law firm in the country. Under the firm name of Miller, Mack & Fairchild from 1906 to 1951, the firm's reputation rested on the expertise of its business advice, its litigation successes, and its partners' involvement in the charities and clubs of the community. The list of corporate and individual clients contains the names of many leaders in the Milwaukee area, prominent families, and major corporations. The firm's partners have traditionally served on the boards of key nonprofit agencies as well as on corporate, bank, and utility boards.

Following the deaths of George Miller and Edwin Mack in 1931 and 1942, the firm struggled through the manpower shortage of World War II, with plenty of business and a shortage of lawyers to do it. One associate during this period of scarcity was a young woman attorney, the first in a major Milwaukee firm, but she left in 1947 without attaining partnership. The success of the firm throughout the war years depended on the strength and leadership of Arthur Fairchild, a partner since 1906.

It is after World War II, however, that many significant changes occurred which created the firm style of today. New recruitment tactics took the firm into competition with eastern firms for top legal talent from eastern law schools. The firm grew from only eight partners before World War II to 255 partners five decades later. Keeping the partnership intact throughout these changes demanded the strong leadership of Leon Foley and Lynford Lardner, and the talent and commitment of partners who joined the firm in the postwar years. On the retirement of Foley and the death of Lardner, control of the firm was modernized to the new structure of a Management Committee, with an administrative partner to oversee daily operations.

The suddenness of Lardner's death in 1973 forced this change on the firm at a time when the younger partners had become dissatisfied with the system of one-man rule. The firm's responsiveness to this leadership crisis in October 1973 and the ability to overhaul its management system with a broad consensus were pivotal to the partnership's continued survival. Through this Management Committee rule, with the team system coordinating matters in areas of specialization, the expansion of the firm into a national law firm with offices in Madison, Chicago, Washington, D.C., and Florida was successful during the 1970s and 1980s. We have de-emphasized the contributions of living partners and former partners, and do not include their photographs.

My work on this project has been aided by the valuable insights of James Willard Hurst, who read and commented on the manuscript in draft form and who graciously agreed to write the Foreword. The assistance of Judy Simonson and the staff at the Milwaukee County Historical Society has been vital, as has the research work of Scott Latus and Tim Evans. The staff at the firm library has been of great help on numerous occasions, as has the pioneer work on the firm's history begun by partner Gilbert Hardgrove and organized by librarian Noreen Link. Frederick I. Olson, professor emeritus at University of Wisconsin,

Milwaukee, and Paul Hass of the State Historical Society of Wisconsin provided valuable comments on the historical narrative, as well as encouragement throughout the process. Further assistance has come from various historical societies in New York, in Michigan, and especially from the State Historical Society of Wisconsin, whose director, H. Nicholas Muller III, supported the society's role as publisher.

The support and advice of the firm book committee, led by Allen Taylor, has been both stimulating and challenging. The comments from many partners on the last two chapters, as well as their willingness to give oral interviews of their days with the firm, have also been pointed and helpful. As the author and academic historian, I have been granted access to all information available in the firm's records. The historical conclusions in the narrative are mine alone. I want to particularly thank Vernon Swanson, George Chester, Steven Keane, Richard Mooney, James P. Brody, and the late Joseph Barnett and Theodore Bolliger for sharing their time and memories with me. Many other firm members provided suggestions and corrections, including David Beckwith, Ted Wiley, Harry Wallace, Paul Barnes, Harold McComas, Jere McGaffey, Bernard Kubale, Tom Shriner, Mike Bowen, and Jim Huston, who supervised the project throughout. Janice Feldstein contributed editorial polish and substantial shrinkage to the original manuscript and steady support to its author. My work on this project was assisted on a daily basis by the willing and cheerful assistance of the firm's librarians and many support staff, particularly Connie Pemrich and Karen Szyszko. The meticulous proofreading of Susan Wineke and the patience and encouragement of Ross, Kjersten, and Kari Langill have also been invaluable.

The story of Milwaukee's legal, political, and economic history could be multivolumed. Distilled from an original manuscript of threefold magnitude, the book tells the essence of the firm's historic saga. This is the story of a long and successful partnership, a story which I hope will capture the interest of readers, both lawyers and nonlawyers, and will add to existing knowledge of Milwaukee's and Wisconsin's colorful past, as well as of American legal history in the years between 1842 and 1992.

Ellen D. Langill

To my parents
for their unending support and encouragement

❧ Foreword ❧

No law firm in Wisconsin, and no more than a handful in the United States, can match Milwaukee-based Foley & Lardner for its 150-year lineage. Lawyers are not noted as archivists. Much of what they do for clients yields no printed records. Practical pressures lead to periodic culling of files, and proper regard for client confidentiality limits what under different circumstances would be published. What remains is often only formal or barebones evidence of the planning, counseling, negotiation, and give-and-take of controversy that fleshed out dealings among clients, opposing or cooperating lawyers, accountants, witnesses, political groups, and public officials. However, enough is available from the long chain of lawyers that leads up to the late-twentieth-century Foley & Lardner to provide us rewarding insights into strands of continuity and change in the roles of lawyers in the profession and in the society in which they practice.

Historians have been slow to treat the bar as an active agent in legal history. Long focused on courts and judges, when legal historians broadened their scope to deal with legislatures and executive or administrative officers they still bounded their subject by the activity of formally constituted official agencies. Yet in substantial measure, what public policy spelled in practical impact on people's lives depended on what went on in lawyers' offices. As clients brought their concerns to the law firm, lawyers helped structure business dealings, helped translate generalities of statutes or regulations into their particular impress on private action, helped bring policy issues into focus by framing claims that might stimulate, qualify, or resist official action. After the Civil War, people's activities become more complex and interlocked, with increased divisions of labor and a greater scale of operations. Accordingly, there was more need to take account of longer-run consequences of public and private action. There was need, too, for more conscious effort to plan and manage affairs and better to account for gains and costs. These pressures for more deliberate action by private actors meant that what went on in lawyers' offices became relevant to what went on in legislative or executive halls. Lawyers thus figured among the lawmakers.

The long continuity of the Foley & Lardner lineage allows us to see, in the course of this firm's practice, reflections of major currents in lawyers' business, the nature of their clients, and the play between public and private concerns. Just as the work of lawyers in many ways brings general propositions of law to particular definition, so what stays the same and what changes in the practice of such a law firm can help us see patterns in the otherwise bewildering variety of social experience.

Four features especially stand out in the 150-year record of this twentieth-century law firm to explain its unusual survival and success. Most obvious is the evolution from individual or small-partnership law practice to group practice, involving an increasing number of associated lawyers, backed from about the 1920s on by a growing support staff within the office and need of larger capital investment in library and equipment. Most lawyers always operated on a smaller scale. But the twentieth-century Foley & Lardner demonstrated what became the standard type of the large law firm in major metropolitan centers.

Changes in the scale and form of the firm responded to changes in the nature of clients and their affairs. One relatively constant character of this firm's lawyers from the 1840s into the later twentieth century was their main focus on matters arising from clients' marketplace activities. The firm's lawyers were never materially in the fields of criminal law, domestic relations, or personal-injury torts. In the first nineteenth-century generation, particular matters of property and contract law bulked largest in the docket. The later nineteenth century saw the firm drawn not only into episodic problems but more and more into continuing representation in its clients' flow of transactions. Marketplace activity developed with increasing variety and complexity, matched by more diverse government action and regulation. From the early years of the twentieth century, a firm with a large business clientele thus felt pressure to recruit more lawyers of specialized legal or business knowledge and skill.

A second trend in law practice reflected in the role of Foley & Lardner was a major shift from litigation as the principal activity to a prime focus on in-office activity. These lawyers tended to give more and more of their client-caretaking efforts to counseling and negotiation in matters where shrewd assessment of business concerns might count as much as treatment of law. This new emphasis was especially marked where the extended reach and intricacy of tax law introduced unfamiliar complications into structuring business transactions and transferring property among generations. From an earlier stage in which lawyers seemed typically to appear only when relationships had seriously broken down, they now spent more time in planning, negotiating, and arranging affairs to prevent or limit breakdown. The goal became to forestall trouble, rather than to salvage what could be saved from the debris of a broken relationship. A strong firm still needed to serve clients by going to court on proper occasions, but out-of-court dealing took on a greater role than earlier.

A third feature of the evolving practice was the growing prominence of business corporations in the roster of clients, including banks, public utilities, and manufacturing and commercial enterprises. Such companies typically operated on a larger scale—both in assets and in the reach and complexity of transactions—than businesses the firm had served in the nineteenth century. Their affairs drew lawyers into recommending forms of business organization, helping recruit high-level management, and advising on patterns of supply, distribution, and customer relations. Government at all levels responded in varying ways to this greater range and complexity of marketplace activity. Thus the firm's practice led it more often to represent clients in dealings with legislators and with executive and administrative officials.

Finally, all these elements in the 150-year Foley & Lardner experience also entered into the character of the lawyers' relations with the community of which they were part. In the first generation, partners were sometimes publicly identified with partisan politics. The founders of the firm repeatedly sought and sometimes won elective office. But from the turn of the century, as the lawyers became more and more engrossed with the affairs of corporate clients, conspicuous participation in politics was rare. In its place another type of community involvement loomed, as the firm's lawyers advised or sat on the boards of local educational and philanthropic bodies. But the dominant character of the practice—service and support for the legal needs of corporate business—emerged early in the twentieth century, and has remained.

James Willard Hurst
Madison, Wisconsin, 1992

FOLEY & LARDNER

Attorneys AT *Law*

1842-1992

1

Beginnings
1833–1842

On September 8, 1842, Asahel Finch and William Pitt Lynde became partners in the practice of law. Their office was in the frontier settlement of Milwaukee in the territory of Wisconsin. Although the thirty-three-year-old Finch and the twenty-five-year-old Lynde were men of vastly different backgrounds, legal training, and personal styles, they forged a lifelong bond of personal loyalty and professional respect. More than that, they founded a law partnership that has endured for a century and a half.

When Finch and Lynde founded their firm, the frontier village of Milwaukee was a settlement of 2,500 people bustling with the fever of economic growth. Its streets were unpaved. Wooden storefronts along board sidewalks were crude. Livestock still roamed the streets. East of the Milwaukee River, small clapboard homes fronted on north-south streets such as Jefferson, Jackson, and Van Buren. East Wisconsin Avenue was the main artery running east from the river wharf at East Water Street. The dozens of new settlers who arrived each week during the season of navigation bought or built homes, invested in land, and opened new businesses. Besides Finch and Lynde, there were sixteen other lawyers in Milwaukee then. All were kept busy.

Asahel Finch was born on February 14, 1809, in Genoa, Cayuga County, New York. His parents were merchants who had migrated in the 1770s from Pennsylvania to the Finger Lakes area of New York. At the age of fourteen Asahel became a boarding student at Middlebury Academy in the western New York county of Genesee. After completing his four-year high-school course, he entered the business world in nearby Buffalo, where he met and married Mary deForest Bristol, a native of Connecticut.[1]

After a short time the Finches decided to move westward to the prosperous territory of Michigan. In 1830 they boarded a steamer at Buffalo, disembarked in Detroit, and continued one day's ride southwest to Tecumseh in the adjacent county of Lenawee. The air was said to be more healthful there—Detroit was suffering a cholera epidemic—and business opportunities were more favorable. Finch opened a dry-goods store but moved the following year to Adrian, Tecumseh's rival for business and later the new seat of county government.[2]

There Asahel opened another store, this time with two partners—Abel Whitney, also a native New Yorker, and Nelson D. Skeeles. The county records show that the store carried a general inventory that included "dry goods, crockery, hardware, and groceries." Though the business prospered, the firm dissolved in the following year "at the suggestion of Mr. Finch." The reasons for his suggestion are not clear.

Finch then turned his attention to land investments and banking. From the beginning, though, he demonstrated what was to be a lifelong interest in public affairs. In 1834, he drafted and was the first to sign a petition from the citizens of Adrian to the territorial legislature, asking that a road be built extending westward about sixty miles. Town citizens hoped the road would draw business from the hinterlands and make Adrian a commercial center.

In 1835 Finch and Whitney embarked on two more enterprises: the opening of Adrian's first drugstore and the purchase of some lots nearby. On one of them, in the center of the town, they built the Hance School Building, which housed their pharmacy on the ground floor. By the end of the year, however, Whitney decided to move west to pursue land investments, and Finch bought him out.

In the fall Finch's career took a new and decisive turn. Orange Butler, a lawyer who had served with distinction in the western part of New York as a district attorney, came to town to practice law. Butler quickly established a flourishing law practice in Lenawee County, partly because of the reputation he had earned in New York. A graduate of Union College and a former classics teacher, Butler had followed the dream of many Americans in the 1830s and moved west to seek greater opportunities.[3]

The great demand for lawyers in eastern Michigan provided such an opportunity for Butler and gave him the incentive to seek a legal apprentice. Finch joined Butler's office as a clerk, while still maintaining his other business interests. Butler's invitation opened the door of opportunity for Finch, who had no formal education beyond his commercial high-school course.

Reading law in such an apprenticeship was the customary path to the legal profession in the nineteenth century.[4] Even by 1850, there were only fifteen law schools in the country, and they were largely clustered in the eastern states. The University of Michigan Law School was not founded until 1859; Wisconsin's opened in 1868. Twenty years after Finch had gained admittance to the Michigan bar, Abraham Lincoln wrote that the "cheapest, quickest, and best way" into the world of law was to "read Blackstone's *Commentaries,* Chitty's *Pleadings,* Greenleaf's *Evidence,* Story's *Equity,* and Story's *Pleadings.*"[5]

As Finch was starting his legal education, Lenawee County became embroiled in a dispute over its southern border with Ohio. Inaccurate surveys done when the Northwest Ordinance was drawn up in 1787 were the source of the problem. As a young leader in the area, Finch was asked to serve as moderator of a rump session of citizens that assembled in 1836 to settle the border issue. The resulting compromise gave Ohio the port of Toledo and gave Michigan the peninsula above Lake Michigan. The boundary was finally surveyed, and Michigan became a state in 1836. Wisconsin, diminished by the loss of the Upper Peninsula, became a separate territory in the process.[6]

Immediately after Michigan became a state, the reputation that Finch had gained for his efforts in the boundary dispute helped him win election to the state legislature. Orange Butler also won a seat. The first session convened in January 1837. Butler was appointed to the committee on elections; Finch, to the committees on banking and incorporations, accounts, and the state prison.[7]

After the January session adjourned, Finch returned to reading law, investing in real estate, and working as a cashier at the newly created Farmers' and Mechanics' Bank of Homer, a day's ride from Adrian.[8] In June a special session was called. Finch took an active role in the creation of a new committee on currency.

In the early nineteenth century, banks could print and issue their own notes. The federal government did not assume the exclusive right to print and control paper money until the Civil War. Paper money from frontier banks came to be called "wildcat" money, because its value was not based on gold or on federal treasury notes. Wildcat banks backed their notes with investments in land, in the optimistic belief that they would increase in credibility as the frontier prospered. Finch's bank, the Farmers' and Mechanics' Bank of Homer, was just such a wildcat bank. Finch, bank officers, and Homer residents all believed that land was a safe investment in the 1830s. The westward migration and the entrepreneurial spirit of the Jacksonian age were grounded in that unbounded optimism.

By early 1838 Finch was not only named president of the bank but was also ready to apply for membership in the Michigan bar. What was required in those days was a sponsored petition to the state Supreme Court. Finch had complied with the simple require-ments: He had lived in the Michigan territory for a year and had read law for three years with a member of the state bar.[9]

Upon his admission to the state bar in 1838, Finch settled into what seemed a secure and productive life in a small American community. He helped establish the First Presbyterian Society of Homer and the Democratic party of Lenawee County, and he bought an interest in a textile mill with Skeeles, his former dry-goods partner.

But 1837–1838 brought economic catastrophe. A short-lived period of expansion in 1836 and early 1837 collapsed in a panic, caused by President Jackson's ill-advised war on established eastern banks. Loans were called, bankruptcies proliferated, currency was devalued, and banks failed. Finch lost his faith as a Jacksonian Democrat.

In Homer the collapse came in 1838. The bank tried desperately to call in its outstanding notes, found its debtors unable to pay, and was forced to default and close its doors. Finch and many other bankers like him could not have foreseen the precipitous collapse in currency; faith in prosperity and in land values had proved to be totally ill-founded.

Some settlers elected to pack up and return east. Others, like Finch, looked west for another chance. After paying off what debts he could, he boarded a steamer with his wife Mary and their two daughters for the frontier settlement of Milwaukee in the territory of Wisconsin.

Arriving in Milwaukee in October 1839, Finch brought with him his most valued possession, his seal of admission to the Michigan bar, which was honored in Wisconsin. Within a month he was able to enter a law office and start anew. Many Milwaukee residents were embroiled in controversies resulting from the Panic of 1837 and the depression that followed, and the dozen lawyers in town were much in demand.[10]

Finch promptly joined the Plymouth Church, a union of Presbyterians and Congregationalists on the frontier. He and Mary joined the choir. He pawned his gold watch to buy lumber for the church building. He turned to the new and very active Whig party, which had been organized to contest the Jacksonian Democrats. Through those institutions, Finch met the small corps of lawyers and professional men in town and forged new relationships. He also joined two movements that were sweeping the Midwest by 1840: active opposition to alcohol and to slavery.

Through these associations he met attorney Charles Lynde, the elder brother of William Pitt Lynde, the man who was later to become his partner. Finch began to practice law with Hans Crocker and Horatio N. Wells in Milwaukee's preeminent firm, which needed a third lawyer because Wells was increasing his role in public affairs.

Finch's first case was filed in the district court under the partnership name of Wells, Crocker & Finch. *Blanchard v. Lelands* was typical of the cases that the firm handled in those days. It was a matter of a debt unpaid, a promissory note held by the firm's client, plaintiff Hiram Blanchard, from Lelands and his partner, Byron Kilbourn. Finch won judgment for the face value of the note, $149.15, and costs of $14.06.[11]

Wells, Crocker & Finch handled dozens of such collection cases, appearing usually as counsel for the creditors. Two of the larger cases that Finch took during this period involved clients Solomon Juneau, founder and first mayor of Milwaukee, and his partner from

Green Bay, Morgan Martin. After the 1837 panic, Juneau and Martin brought many cases in the district court.

In one of the most important, they sued Rufus Parks, one of the directors of the Bank of Milwaukee. The bank had failed in 1838, and many of the directors sued each other over their significant financial losses. The case against Parks brought an award of $1,209 to Juneau, who held his note. Parks appealed, but eventually lost.[12]

Shortly after starting this case for Juneau and Martin, the firm took on a much larger claim *against* Martin for the Farmers' and Mechanics' Bank of Detroit. Martin had signed a note to the bank in 1837 to finance his own land speculations with Juneau in Milwaukee. The crash came before Martin had repaid his $35,000 debt.[13] The firm's reasons for representing the Michigan bank against its former client are not recorded, but the engagement may have resulted from Finch's earlier connections in Michigan. Frontier lawyers found it highly profitable to represent out-of-state creditors because they usually retained a percentage of the collection as their fee. The firm was known as a creditors' firm, seldom representing debtors. It was a pattern that Finch would later continue.

Martin was not as successful in his land speculations as many others in Wisconsin were, and several times he was brought near bankruptcy as creditors called in his outstanding notes. He never completely recovered, although litigation against him dragged on in the courts for many years.

Such enterprises as flour milling, warehousing, match production, bricklaying, and carpentry flourished in Milwaukee in the 1840s. John Plankinton and Frederick Layton (who later became clients of Finch's firm) began a meat-packing business. The *Milwaukee Sentinel* estimated that four million board feet of lumber arrived on Milwaukee's wharves to feed the building boom in 1842 alone. Retailers—including Finch's father and brother, who had followed him west from Michigan—imported such items as fruit, cloth, nails, powder kegs, whiskey, and iron stoves for Milwaukee's new settlers. The firm's clients included many who were engaged in importing and retailing.[14]

Records of the cases handled by Finch in those early Wisconsin years show a distinctively polished handwriting, a smooth writing style, and an ease with Latin phrases. But the rough-and-tumble life of the Milwaukee frontier shines through, too. In *Clark v. Aldrich,*

Finch appeared for the plaintiff Clark, who had ridden to Milwaukee in May 1840 from Indiana on his "chestnut, sorrel horse," to look at land and business opportunities. As Clark prepared to leave Milwaukee a month later, he allegedly neglected to pay the full bill at his boarding establishment. Not to be cheated, the owner quickly summoned Milwaukee sheriff Owen Aldrich, who confiscated Clark's horse, saddle, and bridle until the matter could be settled.

Clark found his way, on foot, to the door of Wells, Crocker & Finch. Finch took his case and sued to recover the horse, saddle, and bridle, or their $90 value. The court considered affidavits from Indiana witnesses who swore to the ownership and value of the horse. A scrap of paper evidenced Clark's full payment of his boarding bill. Clark won his $90 judgment.[15]

It is difficult to find records of the fees paid to lawyers for cases either as large as Juneau's and Martin's or as small as Clark's. Few lawyers kept account books in those years. Not even case ledger books have survived. Legal fees were neither standardized nor publicized. Even standard legal forms had to be imported from printers in the East until Milwaukee had its own capable printing shop. Often the court records contain evidence written on scraps of torn paper, and the lawyers' pleadings were submitted on simple lined sheets, wrapped crudely and sealed with wax. Occasionally fees are recorded on similar scraps: $2 for drafting a pleading or $10 for a court appearance. In the early 1840s, butter cost 50 cents a pound in Milwaukee. Pork cost 25 cents a pound, potatoes 50 cents a bushel, and flour $18 a barrel. A lawyer in a firm like Wells, Crocker & Finch could make a comfortable living.[16]

In his two years with Wells and Crocker, Finch became an established and respected member of the Milwaukee bar. He purchased a lot in Juneautown, on Milwaukee's east side, two blocks from Courthouse Square (bounded by Biddle, Oneida, Jefferson, and Jackson streets, now Kilbourn, Wells, Jefferson, and Jackson). His handsome frame house on the southwest corner of Mason and Van Buren streets stood across from the home of his friend, Charles Lynde.

The courthouse, which measured 51 by 42 feet and housed the courtroom on the second floor and four jury rooms on the first, was built in a "Tuscan style with four columns" and was completed in 1837 at a cost of $5,000. Juneau and Martin built it with help from east-side contributors who were anxious to keep the seat of government on their side of the Milwaukee River. Most of Milwaukee's lawyers lived and maintained offices nearby, primarily along East Water Street (now Water Street) and Spring Street (East Wisconsin Avenue).

By the end of 1840 the Wells, Crocker & Finch firm was flourishing. With the return of prosperity there were a large number of cases to handle. To facilitate the work, Finch became a justice of the peace and a notary public, notarizing documents and certifying witnesses for his own cases and for those of other attorneys as well.

But the partnership survived less than two years. In the summer of 1841, Crocker left to join a man named John Tweedy, leaving Wells and Finch to continue alone. Finch was the dominant partner in that relationship. Personally unstable, Wells was given to heavy bouts of drinking that hampered his productivity. The contrast with his partner was sharp, for Finch urged and practiced temperance and was personally somber and industrious. "He walks slow," said one observer of Finch, "his eyes cast upon the ground, as if in deep thought; gives you a quick searching glance in passing, and if an acquaintance, a nod of recognition." Yet Wells, with his "ready wit and bright sayings," helped enhance the firm's roster of clients.[17]

After Crocker's departure, Wells and Finch continued to represent many clients from Michigan and other states to the east who were attempting to recover funds owed them by Wisconsin residents. In their first case *against* Juneau they appeared in behalf of Samuel Hinman, a native New Yorker and a director of the New York and Wisconsin Land Company. The judgment of $24 against Juneau was appealed by his attorneys—Tweedy & Crocker.[18] In another case a client of theirs, George Bailey, was successful in a suit against Juneau and the other owners of the steamboat *Milwaukee* for failure to pay dockage fees of $800.[19]

Yet in this same June term of 1842 Wells & Finch also appeared in at least two cases on Juneau's behalf. There was a shortage of able lawyers in the 1840s, and the myriad business interests in which Juneau was involved made it necessary for him to engage many of Milwaukee's most prominent professionals. In *Whitney v. Hathaway* Wells & Finch represented Juneau and his partner George Smith in a complex of land partition cases that found that Hathaway's survey was erroneous.[20]

By the summer of 1842, however, the Wells & Finch partnership was beginning to show some strain. Finch began to resent Wells's erratic work habits and sought other assistance with his growing caseload. He invited William Pitt Lynde (pronounced "lined"), the younger brother of his friend Charles Lynde, to join him and Wells as an associate.

Finch and Charles Lynde had become close after Charles's arrival in Milwaukee in 1840. Both were elders in the First Presbyterian Church. Both actively promoted the temperance cause. Delegates to the Territorial Temperance Convention held in Kenosha in August 1840 included Finch, Charles Lynde, the Reverend Stephen Peet, and Harrison Reed, editor of the *Sentinel*. Despite their sharply contrasting family backgrounds, Charles Lynde greatly respected Finch as a self-made man of scant formal education.[21]

The Lynde family dated back to colonial Massachusetts in the 1670s.[22] Several family members had attended Yale in its first classes, and two of the Lynde ancestors had served as chief justices of the Supreme Judicial Court of Massachusetts. William Pitt's father, Judge Tilly Lynde, had migrated from Massachusetts to New York, where he practiced law and became a member of the New York Legislature. He also speculated in Wisconsin land.

Charles attended Hamilton College in 1834 before transferring to Yale, from which he received a B.A. in 1838. He studied at the Law School of the University of the City of New York in 1839 and 1840 before heading west. He was admitted to the Wisconsin bar immediately after his arrival. In addition to his church and temperance activities, he was one of the founders of the Milwaukee Lyceum, a group of young men who gathered to hear lectures, share books and ideas, and enrich their cultural life in a frontier settlement.

Charles encouraged friends from the east to join him in the Wisconsin territory. In December 1840 he wrote to John K. Bartlet, M.D., in New Haven:

> My business is pretty good, notwithstanding we have *eighteen lawyers here!* . . . Everything is new, everything is rapidly improving. We are all young, and all enthusiasm. Come John, come early, as soon as may be, the sooner the better.
>
> Milwaukee is the "Empire village." . . . the largest steamboats can pass up these rivers above our village. . . . All admit that this place is speedily destined to become a city of no ordinary magni-

tude. . . . It is no common occurrence for our steamboats from Buffalo (of which one arrives every other day during the season of navigation) to leave here from twenty to fifty to one hundred emigrants. . . .

A tolerable house is worth $100 a year, but you can build here as cheap as at the East and then you could save rent. Rents are so high because every house is full and emigrants are constantly coming in, and must have room and will pay well for it. I shall complete my house by spring.[23]

Like his brother Charles, William Pitt Lynde (called "Pitt" by his friends) was well educated and well prepared in the law. Born in 1817, he, too, began college at Hamilton but transferred to Yale in his sophomore year. He graduated in 1838 with highest honors and gave the valedictory address. He excelled as a student of ancient languages and was especially proficient in Greek.

Pitt studied law for one year at the University of the City of New York, where he took courses from Benjamin F. Butler, a former law partner of Martin Van Buren and later a famed Civil War general and governor of Louisiana during the Reconstruction, and David Graham and Chancellor Kent, noted jurists and teachers.

He then entered Harvard Law School, where he had the opportunity to study under Joseph Story, a justice of the Supreme Court, and Simon Greenleaf, author of the leading treatise on *Evidence*. Story held a chair endowed by Nathan Dane, for whom Dane County in Wisconsin was later named.

Immediately after William graduated from law school and was admitted to the New York bar, Charles wrote to a friend, obviously in response to an expression of interest on his brother's part: "Pitt wrote me about a month since, and requested that I would receive him into partnership with myself in the spring and I wrote him back to 'come on.' . . . If young married men are in any danger of losing their 'energy' at the east, let them come to the west and they must be nerveless indeed if they do not catch something of the life, and buoyancy of feeling here exhibited."[24]

As a graduate of the nation's preeminent law school, William Pitt Lynde could undoubtedly have had his choice of legal possibilities in the East. But his own restlessness and imagination and his brother Charles's enthusiasm about life and opportunities in the Midwest propelled him westward. He arrived in Milwaukee with his bride, Mary Blanchard Lynde, in May 1841, where he joined his brothers Charles and Watts in the practice of law.

Their dream of a family law firm was short-lived. Charles and Watts returned to western New York that summer to visit relatives. On August 16, shortly after they embarked on the steamboat *Erie* to return to Milwaukee, the ship exploded off Buffalo. Both brothers died. In the wake of the family tragedy, Pitt and Mary Lynde went back home to New York for the winter of 1841. But they decided to return to Milwaukee in the spring, there to make their lives. Lynde may already have considered his choice of legal partners in Milwaukee, for he joined Wells & Finch as a legal assistant shortly afterward.

Lynde found Asahel Finch to be a superb mentor, and it was not long before the two young attorneys realized that they worked well together. They formed their partnership on September 8, 1842, four years before Milwaukee became a city and six years before Wisconsin became a state. The contrasts between these two men were dramatic—in education, family background, personality, political beliefs, and style. Yet these very differences enriched their partnership. Each remained in the firm until he died four decades later. Through their successors, the firm they founded flourished for 150 years.

2

Finch & Lynde: Early Partnership
1842–1848

Finch and Lynde founded their firm in a decade of renewed economic growth and swift political change. During the
1840s Milwaukee became a city, and Wisconsin became a state. Like
other lawyers in the territory, Finch and Lynde did more than represent their clients in matters of daily life and commerce. Lawyers
also wrote city charters, drafted state constitutions, and debated
questions of social reform and public policy. Though Finch was a
devout Whig and Lynde an active Democrat, their mutual respect
outweighed party differences, and their partnership prospered.

Early in 1842, realizing that a well-functioning port was vitally
necessary if Milwaukee was to become a leading commercial center,
the village petitioned the federal government for funds to improve
the harbor. The resulting $30,000 subsidy was spent for a harbor
cut, dredging the Milwaukee River, and constructing a better lighthouse and wharves. It was the infrastructure merchants needed to
bring in supplies for the growing hinterland and to ship the grain and
lead that were produced farther west. Two million pounds of lead
left the port in 1843, and during the next decade Milwaukee became
the largest shipper of wheat in the nation.

Milwaukee had 800 buildings and 50 stores in 1843. Its streets were still unpaved, but hopes were high. The Milwaukee *Courier* exulted: "The stores of our merchants are well supplied with as fine assortments of goods as can be found in the west, and our streets are thronged day after day with teams from the interior, bringing to market the produce of the country."

Except when winter closed down lake navigation, the piers constituted the main passenger and commercial depot. Hotel runners met the new arrivals, and travelers could choose temporary lodging in one of a dozen boarding hotels. Many only passed through Milwaukee en route to farms and towns farther west. Lynde's wife Mary was struck by the crudeness of this frontier settlement when she arrived in May 1841. Cowbells made the first sounds she heard, for cows wandered the village streets. There were other shocks, too, such as the need to walk along dirt (or mud) streets from the wharf to her brother-in-law's home because, as he informed her, "We haven't any carriages here."

By 1843, immigrants from Germany and Ireland had helped swell Milwaukee's population to 3,000. Chicago was slightly larger, but Milwaukee's population was growing faster. During the 1840s, the village became a diocese of the Roman Catholic church, the first Masonic order was established, and an enterprising German string quartet gave a few concerts. The community was beginning to establish its own institutions and its own culture.[1]

The eighteen lawyers in town were much in demand. Many of the new settlers brought with them the baggage of unresolved financial entanglements that needed to be sorted out. The main business of lawyers was land—buying and selling it for their clients, searching titles, and making deeds.

Collections were another staple of lawyers' practices. The frontier was a litigious place: The Milwaukee district court alone considered several hundred civil suits each year in the early 1840s, a ratio of one lawsuit to every ten residents of the village. Here, lawyers could make a comfortable living.[2]

The district court in Milwaukee was established after Wisconsin became a territory in 1836, under an act that created a Supreme Court, three district courts, and three probate courts. The Milwaukee district extended north to Green Bay and south to the Illinois border. The three districts were of equal population initially, but Milwaukee's population grew until the duties of its judge far exceeded those of the other two. Judge Andrew Galbraith Miller handled everything except probate matters and claims of less than $50. District court decisions could be appealed to the territorial Supreme Court in Madison. Before statehood in 1848 and court reform in 1853, appeals were heard by the district judges sitting as a body.

The cases that Finch and Lynde handled in the early years of the partnership reflected the struggles to recover defaulted debts and establish property ownership that preoccupied those who lived on the frontier. Finch and Lynde's connections in the East brought them clients who had grievances against men who had neglected to settle their debts before sailing west from Buffalo or who had failed to pay on notes to partners in land investments.

Nineteenth-century creditors large and small had every expectation that their grievances could be redressed in court with the help of a sympathetic, trustworthy, and not unduly costly attorney. For one such client, Finch & Lynde solicited affidavits from several New York residents to prove that the defendant, a newcomer to Milwaukee, had not paid a Buffalo merchant's $131 bill for a rocking chair, writing table, bedstead, and mattress.[3] In another case a New York client was able to recover possession of his schooner, unjustly detained by a defendant who had not paid the $1,200 charter fee.[4] The firm successfully defended another claim involving a charge of theft and trespass: In *Whipple v. Putnam,* the defendant was accused of cutting several choice trees on Whipple's land. Finch & Lynde called nine witnesses to testify that the tree stumps were on Putnam's side of the unfenced boundary.[5] Such cases were the stuff of life to those who lived in the Wisconsin territory.

Finch & Lynde gained a reputation for thoroughness that was attractive to clients. Throughout his legal career, Finch did what Timothy Walker had recommended in his 1830 valedictory address at the Cincinnati College of Law: "The most learned lawyer in the world would not get business, if he did not attend to it. The question with the client is, not who knows the most law, but who will manage a cause best."[6]

As early as the 1840s efficient United States mails made it possible for frontier lawyers to do legal work for eastern clients. Letters were addressed simply:

Finch & Lynde
Counselors at Law
Milwaukee,
Wisconsin Territory

Postage from New York City cost as much as eighteen cents, and delivery usually took one or two weeks.[7] Occasionally, the firm had to retain an eastern lawyer to collect its fees. If delinquent clients owned land in Wisconsin, the lawyers could get writs of attachment here.

Lynde's handwriting and his wordy prose appear infrequently in the records of early cases. As the junior partner, Lynde learned conciseness from his mentor. There is more evidence of Finch's work than of Lynde's, but it appears that by 1843 the men worked together on most matters.

One of the firm's early clients was Charles Dewey, the builder of Milwaukee's first two-story brick commercial building and a leading developer. Dewey knew Finch and Lynde through their involvement in the First Presbyterian Church, where Finch was an elder. The firm defended Dewey in suits by men who had hauled, sold, or laid bricks for his building or had performed other services for him. Dewey was masterful at finding reasons not to pay in full, or not to pay at all, and it was difficult for his lawyers to prepare a defense against the claims that were brought against him.

Before long, Finch and Lynde themselves fell victim to their client's delinquency. In July 1844 they retained Levi Hubbell, a young attorney who had recently come to town from a successful practice in New York, to represent them. The complaint cited Dewey's failure to pay for "work and labor, care and diligence . . . performed and bestowed." The charges mentioned in the bill of particulars give us some idea of the fees that were typical of the time: "$41.00 for drawing an appeal bond, $10 for the lawsuit against Richardson," and $10 to $20 each for a number of subsequent matters. Hubbell won a judgment for Finch & Lynde, for which he charged them $300.[8]

The firm had a more satisfactory relationship with another major client, George Dousman. Dousman was a respected warehouse owner, developer, public official, gentleman farmer, and treasurer of Milwaukee County for several terms, and was known for his personal and fiscal integrity. He became involved in a number of suits over land claims and the estates of his relatives. Dousman first came to Finch & Lynde with a matter involving land warrants. Frequently litigated on the frontier, warrants redeemable in land were available to settlers who lived on and improved forty or more acres. Warrants were transferable to investors. Some $16,000 in warrants were at issue in the suit against Dousman. Finch & Lynde used affidavits from the land office in Washington, D.C., to prove Dousman's ownership.[9]

Joshua Gifford retained the firm to handle an appeal after a Washington County justice of the peace fined him for selling liquor without a license. In his testimony Gifford cited his belief that the justice was biased because he was "a cold water man" who believed "that no man ought to use liquor in any case and that therefore justice would not be done or obtained." Perhaps Gifford hoped Finch's well-known stance for temperance would help his case. But it didn't. Gifford lost the appeal and had to pay a $25 fine and $11 costs.[10]

Women were seldom direct clients of the firm, for married women and minors had to be represented in court and other legal matters by a husband or legal guardian. In a defamation case Finch & Lynde represented Elizabeth Van Houten and her husband John in a $3,000 suit against Israel and Abigail Smith. Mrs. Smith was accused of shouting out in public that Mrs. Van Houten was "no better than a whore!" During the trial, Israel Smith escalated the verbal war by threatening to "take Mrs. Van Houten into the woods even though it was sugar-making time." There is no record of how the case was resolved.[11]

Although divorce was rare in the nineteenth century, the firm defended Milwaukeean Hiram Barber against an alimony claim brought by his ex-wife, a New Yorker. Their New York divorce decree had ordered quarterly alimony payments. The case was settled while an appeal to the Wisconsin Supreme Court was pending.[12]

When Judge Miller convened his district court in June 1843, the partnership of Finch & Lynde represented more clients than any other firm in town. But in the summer of 1843 a series of allegations threatened to harm Finch's and Lynde's professional and personal reputations. The difficulties arose in litigation involving a large Michigan land transaction and disputed credits for drygoods. The firm's client, Oliver Hyde, had sued his partners Linus Cady and Leonard Farwell (later governor of Wisconsin). After an out-of-court settlement, Cady and Farwell sued Hyde for slander. During the litigation, Finch took some sealed answers to interrogatories from the post office and said he had delivered them to the court. At that point, the answers were lost.

Attorneys Yates, Tweedy and Crocker charged that Finch & Lynde had intentionally destroyed the answers because they were harmful to their client. However, the assistant clerk of court testified that Finch had actually delivered the answers to the court. Judge Miller ruled there had been no fraud on the court and ordered the interrogatories to be sent out again.

Next, the plaintiffs' attorneys charged that Finch and Hyde had tried to influence the Michigan appraisers. Finch's former partner, Hans Crocker, may have known of Finch's earlier financial difficulties in Michigan. Yates, Tweedy & Crocker issued a new series of interrogatories about Finch's reputation among men in Adrian, Michigan, and nearby towns. The majority of the answers were damning to Finch, asserting that his sworn testimony was not worthy of belief. These were crushing statements, and made for trying times for Finch personally and for a law partnership that had worked hard to establish a reputation for probity as well as for legal skill.

With help from Lynde, his steadfast partner, Finch was able to show that only two of the eleven men who impugned his character had had direct encounters with him. The others admitted they knew only hearsay about Finch's use of unfair tactics in the 1837 election for state representative. The failure of the bank in Homer no doubt also had hurt Finch's reputation. Altogether, Finch's record in eastern Michigan had raised many doubts about his character. Finch would have had a difficult time putting all this to rest but for another revelation, namely, that Cady himself had tried to influence the appraisers in his own behalf. Shortly afterward, the suit was dismissed.[13]

The firm weathered the difficulties of the *Hyde* case, although the strain of the litigation and the death of Finch's one-year-old daughter took a noticeable toll, clearly evident in Finch's cramped handwriting during this period. Finch, the stern Presbyterian deacon, also faced the challenge of controlling his temper. One adversary, James Holliday, had been warned by other attorneys about Finch's occasional outbursts in court. When Finch called Holliday a liar, Holliday responded with a blow to the jaw that knocked Finch to the floor. Judge Miller fined both men $50 and the trial continued.[14]

Breach of contract cases were a courtroom staple, then as now. In *Chapin v. Jewell,* Levi Hubbell represented Chapin, who alleged that Jewell and Daniel Newhall had not paid the $1,000 price for 400 barrels of apples bought from Chapin's store. Representing the defendants, Finch & Lynde proved that the apples on the bottoms of all 400 barrels had been rotten and that the contract with Chapin had specifically stated "good apples." They found a witness, James Smith, who had been a clerk in Chapin's store but had since moved several times around Wisconsin and Illinois. Judge Miller approved two motions for a delay until Smith could be deposed. Smith testified that Chapin had told him to put all of the rotten apples on the bottoms of the barrels and to cover them with good ones. The contract was thereupon canceled. Chapin had to pay $11.60 court costs, which included the cost of searching for Mr. Smith.[15]

Judge Miller sometimes set up arbitration panels to resolve contract disputes. Arbitration panels of one sort or another had been in use by American courts since colonial times. Several of the firm's cases in November 1845 were handled by a panel consisting of three justices of the peace who heard the disputed facts and returned their findings to the court.[16]

As Milwaukee's trade in wheat grew, the firm represented several clients in cases involving its sale, storage, milling, and exporting. Daniel Newhall, the former groceryman, became the biggest grain dealer in the Northwest, with twenty sailing vessels and the capacity to ship 15,000 bushels a day. Finch & Lynde continued to represent Newhall's interests as well as those of George Dousman, who had also turned to grain warehousing and storage.[17]

The 1840s also witnessed growth in the marine insurance business. Understandably, Milwaukee became a marine insurance center because lake shipping was its merchants' lifeblood. Lynde particularly developed an expertise in marine cases. In 1846 the firm managed a successful suit against the owners of the schooner

Sylvester Marvin for failure to deliver four loads of lumber from Twin Rivers, Wisconsin, to Milwaukee.[18]

In 1844 the firm's growing caseload and the increasing commitment of both partners to participation in public life made it necessary for them to seek additional help. They turned to Levi Hubbell, who had represented them in their collection suit against Dewey. Hubbell was a man of great self-assurance, who had achieved a measure of prominence in a New York legal practice before coming to Milwaukee. He came to Milwaukee in June 1844 and quickly established himself. Hubbell had strong political aspirations and obviously considered Milwaukee to be a promising venue in which to pursue them. He asked that the firm name be changed to Hubbell, Finch & Lynde, and his new partners concurred.

Hubbell proved to be an adept lawyer and a hard worker. However, the partnership soon became strained. Finch found the tripartite relationship difficult and unsatisfying and missed the collegiality of his one-on-one work with Lynde. He found it frustrating to work with Hubbell, who wanted to handle cases alone. Hubbell's ego proved impossible to deal with. When he began signing documents "Hubbell, F & L," the abbreviation, even if innocent, was certainly not pleasing to "Mr. F." or "Mr. L." Hubbell remained in the partnership for only one year, until August 1845, when he left (or was invited to leave) to practice law alone and to pursue his political ambitions.

Several years later, Finch ran against Hubbell for a judgeship. Still later, Finch testified against him when Hubbell was tried after being impeached as a judge. In the fall of 1845, however, Hubbell's departure from the firm received little notice.

Three years later Finch and Lynde decided to bring in legal assistants to do research and help with drafting documents. They hired three men during the last two years of the decade. None was ever made a partner. The first, Edward G. Ryan, joined the firm for several months before going into practice on his own. Ryan had been a key leader in Wisconsin's first constitutional convention in 1847. Later he became chief justice of the Wisconsin Supreme Court.[19]

After Ryan's departure, two younger men, John C. Starkweather and Gabriel Bouck, joined the office for a time. Starkweather, a native of Cooperstown, New York, and a graduate of Union College, joined Finch & Lynde in 1848 to serve a one-year apprenticeship. He was admitted to the Wisconsin bar three years later and practiced law in Milwaukee until 1861, when he received a commission as colonel of the First Regiment of Wisconsin Volunteers, organized for the Civil War. Wounded in 1863 at the Battle of Chickamauga, Starkweather served through the war and retired in 1865 as a brigadier general. He returned to Wisconsin to settle for a while in Oconomowoc as a farmer, before ending his career as a lawyer in Washington, D.C.

Bouck was the son of a New York governor and a graduate of Union College. He migrated to Wisconsin in 1848 and immediately joined Finch & Lynde. After his admittance to the bar in 1849 Bouck moved to Oshkosh to practice law. During the Civil War, Bouck was commissioned as captain of the Second Regiment of Wisconsin Volunteers, serving with the Army of the Potomac and in the Battle of Shiloh. Later he began a political career, winning posts as state attorney general, Wisconsin assemblyman and speaker of the assembly, and Democratic congressman in 1876 and 1878.[20]

With the assistance of these three men, Finch and Lynde were able to keep up their thriving practice and also pursue their continuing political ambitions. The mid-nineteenth century was a time of highly charged issues. There was the prospect of statehood, the issues of slavery and western expansion, and the consequent realignment of political parties. Finch and Lynde were thoroughly engaged in the issues of the day.

⚜ 3 ⚜

Political Life in the
Wisconsin Territory
1842–1848

Beyond their partnership in the practice of law, Lynde and
Finch shared a keen interest in politics and political issues. Lynde
was as active a Democrat as Finch was a Whig. Lynde had remained
in the party of Andrew Jackson, which was so powerful in his home
state of New York. In Milwaukee the Democrats opposed banks, favored hard money, and wanted limits on federal spending for internal improvements such as harbors, canals, and roads. Led on the
state level by Henry Dodge, territorial governor for eight years and
then delegate to Congress, the Democratic party dominated politics
in Milwaukee and in the territory throughout the 1840s.[1]

Political conservatives were split into several factions. There
were some Conservative Democrats, but more important were the
Whigs; the Free Soilers, who were committed to stopping the spread
of slavery; and the Liberty party, with which Finch affiliated for a
short time until it came to be dominated by abolitionists.

Lawyers were drawn to politics for many reasons. The visibility
of political life helped attract clients. The kinds of issues that concerned politicians were extensions of the pragmatic, everyday matters that were brought to the lawyer's office. Drafting laws, crafting

social policy, and balancing conflicting interests at several government levels were activities that attracted the imaginations and engaged the energies of lawyers. It was not so much that governing
required their special gifts and experience. Rather, it was an arena
that naturally fascinated them.

Public service took both Finch and Lynde into community
work, as it did many attorneys in early Milwaukee. Finch became
one of Milwaukee's first school commissioners. He worked to charter the city's first medical college and the Normal Institute, which
later became Downer Seminary and College. The father of two
daughters, Finch supported education for women and girls. Lynde
also served on the Downer board for many years.[2]

Many lawyers on the frontier had political ambitions, and Finch
and Lynde were not exceptions. In early 1844 Lynde ran unsuccessfully for trustee of the village of Milwaukee from the First Ward. After
his defeat, Lynde joined a committee to draft a city charter. The
following year he was appointed by Democratic Governor Nathaniel
Tallmadge to be attorney general of the Wisconsin Territory. When
Tallmadge switched to the Whig party, newly elected Democratic
President James Polk named Henry Dodge to replace Tallmadge as
territorial governor. As attorney general, Lynde, with whom Dodge
was friendly, became embroiled in a controversy over charges that
federal funds allocated to the territorial government during Dodge's
earlier term as governor had been misused by several men in his
administration. Charged with playing politics, Lynde was accused of
being less than arduous in pursuit of Dodge's cronies.

In summer 1845 Lynde resigned his position as attorney general
to accept a more prestigious appointment as United States district
attorney for the territory. Again he faced a storm of criticism, this
time led by the Milwaukee *Sentinel and Gazette,* published by
Rufus King, a Whig. The paper called for Lynde's removal for his
weak handling of the alleged corruption in the Dodge administration.[3] Lynde managed to ride out the political storm and was never
charged formally. By winter, the community turned its attention to
other issues.

Under the village charter, each of Milwaukee's three wards operated independently. The system was unwieldy. It was difficult to
coordinate basic services such as fire protection, road maintenance,
boardwalk construction, or relief to disappointed immigrants who

were in desperate circumstances. It was impossible to enforce prohibitions against rowdyism in the streets or even to control the livestock that was running wild. The veneer of civilization was not thick
enough for drunkenness and gunslinging to be controlled. Random
shots struck Finch's home on several occasions. Once a bullet barely
missed Finch's wife and daughter as they sat in the parlor.

Similarly, Milwaukee was not ready when smallpox hit in 1843
and 1845. Finch's daughter died in the 1843 epidemic. In 1845 the
village faced another upheaval when rivalry between the east and
west sides erupted in the notorious "Bridge War," in which a mob
tore down the Chestnut Street and Spring Street bridges. The violence was short-lived, but it served to increase the determination of
leading citizens to end the three-part division and seek a unified
city.[4]

Milwaukee achieved city status on January 31, 1846. Solomon
Juneau, the community's foremost landowner and developer and a
major client of the firm of Finch & Lynde, was elected as the first
mayor. Milwaukee had grown to a settlement of 10,000. Its prime
location on Lake Michigan made it a natural venue for entrepreneurs
who wanted to capitalize on the opportunity to build canals and railroads that would provide access to the hinterland to the west.

The heated issue of the expansion of slavery had far-
reaching political consequences in Wisconsin and in the nation in
the 1840s and the succeeding decade and a half. In 1846, during
the Mexican War, Congress proposed but failed to pass the Wilmot
Proviso, a controversial rider to an appropriations bill, which would
have outlawed the expansion of slavery to any territory gained as a
result of the conflict. When the war ended in 1848, the divisive
slavery question resurfaced. Lynde's party, the Democrats, wrestled
with the issue of slavery's expansion for the next twelve years.

Although Lynde opposed slavery, he remained cautious in his
public statements. Finch was more outspoken, criticizing the pursuit
of runaway slaves by their former masters into Wisconsin, but he
never embraced the radical posture of the abolitionists and never
broke his Whig ties. Moderate antislavery men parted from radical
abolitionists over the question of the federal government's right to
end slavery in the South. Like Finch, many who hated slavery and
believed it unjust still did not believe that the government had the
legal and constitutional right to deprive slaveowners of their prop-

erty. Finch's church—the Union of Presbyterian and Congregational Churches in Wisconsin—had declared slavery to be a sin in 1841. Founded in 1801 as a cooperative effort on the frontier, the denominational union split in the 1850s over the issue of slavery.

When the Wisconsin Territorial Anti-slavery Society was organized in 1842, Finch became an active member. He opposed the spread of slavery into free territories, but did not call for its forced abolition in the slave states. He joined the executive committee of the Liberty Party Joint Stock Association in 1844, when the group solicited shares to fund its own antislavery newspaper, the *Freeman*. Lynde also bought stock in the Liberty Association to help the new publication get started, but he avoided taking a public stand against slavery.[5]

By 1847 the antislavery movement in Wisconsin became the subject of further agitation. With the arrival from New York of Sherman M. Booth, a fiery abolitionist, the *Freeman* changed hands, and Finch withdrew his support. Both Finch and Lynde, like many other politically involved men of the period, abhorred slavery but deplored abolitionist calls for radical, even violent, measures against it.

In the summer of 1842 Finch became directly involved in an effort to help a runaway slave. Sixteen-year-old Caroline Quarles arrived in Milwaukee en route from her home in Missouri, a slave state. She was temporarily sheltered at a boardinghouse until slave catchers reached the city and began searching every hostelry. When her recapture seemed imminent, a protector sought aid from Horatio N. Wells at the boardinghouse where Quarles was hiding. Although Wells himself refused to get involved, he referred the man to Finch, Well's former partner. Finch immediately got Quarles out of the boardinghouse and hid her in a large empty barrel at a site across the river from his law office. During the night, Quarles was taken from the barrel and driven in the hollowed-out bottom of a wagon to Prairieville (now Waukesha), where she was harbored until her eventual escape to Canada.[6]

In an embellished account of Finch's heroism, the *Evening Wisconsin* wrote at the time of his death that he had aided Quarles by "bringing her food, clothing, and drink, and finally, when . . . the southern slave officers began to press close upon her tracks, sat cramped with her in a sugar hogshead during a long day of terrible heat and at night delivered her safely over to the late Samuel Brown, father of ex-mayor Brown, who carried her to Lyman Goodnow, near Waukesha." The editorial continued, "Slave hunters never were able to catch a single fugitive trusted to the plans and care of Asahel Finch, for his great heart was in the work of breaking the shackles of slavery." [7]

The extent of Lynde's involvement in Quarles's escape is unclear. Northern Democrats found the issue of abolitionism divisive. Some left the party to become "Barnburners," or radical reformers. Others joined the Liberty party, a splinter group that also included northern Whigs. Lynde remained a faithful Democrat.

Although Finch had been briefly active in the Liberty party in the early 1840s, he remained a staunch Whig who supported gradual emancipation and "free soil," not abolitionism. His conversion to the Whig party from his earlier affiliation with the Jacksonian Democrats in Michigan sprang not only from the losses he suffered from Jackson's banking fiascos but also from his realization that the Whig party was based on more conservative economic principles than the Democratic party. He considered it an excellent forum for causes to which he had become devoutly committed—temperance and opposition to slavery.

But being a Whig was a disadvantage in Democratic Milwaukee. Finch's 1846 campaign for probate judge was unsuccessful. But he was elected city attorney in 1847, the same year his former partner Horatio Wells was elected Milwaukee's second mayor. In this post, Finch was called upon to prosecute matters such as disorderly conduct, failure to pay taxes, and other misdemeanors. In reality, the job of city attorney demanded very little time. Finch was fortunate to be able to devote most of his energies to the growing demands of his private law practice. By 1847 Lynde's two terms as a public official had come to an end, and he was once again able to carry his full share of the work.

Finch and Lynde again took opposite positions in 1846, when voters began to debate a proposed state constitution. The Wisconsin Territory had reached the 60,000 population required for statehood in 1840, only four years after its separation from Michigan. At once, Governor Henry Dodge began to lobby for statehood. In 1841 Finch drafted a Whig petition that called for a territorial convention. Voters of the territory turned down the statehood proposition four times, but by the time Iowa became a state in 1846, Wisconsin citizens decided they, too, were ready.[8]

Despite the bitterness between the Whigs and Democrats, they agreed on one issue: Wisconsin was being deprived of significant pieces of territory—the Upper Peninsula, which had been transferred to Michigan in 1836 (an action in which Finch had played a role); the land extending to the southern tip of Lake Michigan, which had gone to Illinois; and the land around the western tip of Lake Superior, which had been added to the territory of Minnesota. Although none of these territorial claims was ultimately successful, the grievances provided politicians with material for impassioned speeches.

Wisconsin's first constitutional convention met in Madison in 1846 and completed a draft that was influenced by the strong anti-banking views of the Democrats. It was largely based on New York's revised constitution of 1846, a copy of which had been rushed to Madison for use as a model. Although Finch expressed an interest in being a member of the convention, only one Whig from Milwaukee was elected. Lynde was familiar with the New York convention reform movement, but his job as district attorney precluded his being a delegate. Two issues in particular aroused controversy: a clause favoring an elected judiciary, which precipitated hot debate among lawyers across the state, and an even more controversial plank, which not only outlawed banks but also forbade both issuing and circulating bank notes.

Once the convention adjourned on December 16, 1846, voters had four months to read and debate the constitutional draft before the vote on April 6, 1847. At a courthouse rally on March 8, 1847, Lynde and other Democrats defended the banking prohibitions, the planks favoring lien laws for workers and mechanics, the bankruptcy clauses, and the clause permitting married women to own property. The Whigs, led by John H. Tweedy and Finch, alleged foul play and public deception by the Democrats. They charged that the Democratic promises of a fair lien law were false. The Whigs argued for sound banks and for bank notes instead of hard money.[9]

Though their work together as lawyers and partners continued undisturbed, Finch and Lynde were active on opposite sides of the constitutional referendum. On February 24, 1847, Lynde convened a meeting at the Milwaukee House Hotel, at which he presided over a series of speeches by leading Democrats, including his former partner, Levi Hubbell. He described the desirability of the antibanking clause, spoke ardently for hard money as the true circulating medium, and aroused the gathering to an enthusiastic endorsement of the constitution.

Finch continued to work actively with the Whig committee in Milwaukee, countering speeches by men who shared Lynde's beliefs with tracts and letters of his own. Although Milwaukee had elected only one Whig delegate to the convention, local Whigs rallied to defeat the first draft of the constitution when it was submitted to the voters. On March 30, 1847, just before the vote, Finch helped draft a final appeal in opposition. In language typical of the fervor of the day, he wrote, "Awake from your lethargy and arouse to earnest, persevering, determined action! . . . Omit no exertion to secure a full and fair expression of the popular voice. Erect your standards; assume your stations; marshal your ranks; do your duty; and a glorious victory will crown and consecrate your efforts." [10]

The Whig appeals prevailed. By a total of 20,231 to 14,116, Wisconsin citizens rejected the proposed first draft of the constitution. Statehood was delayed until a second convention met in the fall and winter of 1847–1848 to consider the elimination of the most controversial clauses. Under a new draft, the judicial power of the state was to be vested in a Supreme Court, circuit courts, courts of probate, and justices of the peace, all to be elective. Submitted to the voters in March 1848, it was approved by a vote of 16,759 to 6,384. The debate was less passionate than the previous year's.

Just before the second proposed constitution was submitted for approval, Lynde reminded Tweedy, who was serving as territorial delegate to Congress, of the vital need for a clause in the statehood bill that would give the United States Supreme Court jurisdiction over cases pending during the transition from territorial to state government. This issue was especially significant to Wisconsin, because the state courts were not officially organized immediately after statehood. It was also of crucial importance to Finch and Lynde, who had several cases pending at that time. In general, however, this was not a period of great judicial activity. In anticipation of the reorganization of the territorial courts into state courts and the addition of the new federal court, the judges of the territorial courts handed down very few decisions from late 1847 throughout

1848. Despite Lynde's plea, to which Tweedy responded, the federal courts did not step in; cases were simply delayed until the new system was put into place in early 1849.[11]

Wisconsin's voters were jubilant at the passage of the constitution. Territorial Governor Dodge proclaimed that Wisconsin was officially ready to apply to Congress for statehood, and the approved constitution was sent to Washington in early May. Sponsored in Congress by Nathan Dane, the Wisconsin statehood bill passed on May 19. President Polk signed it on May 29, 1848, the same day the Mexican War ended.

Certain that the statehood bill would pass, Wisconsin territorial leaders had scheduled elections for state officers (to fill out the 1848–1849 term) on the second Monday in May. Voters in the First Congressional District, which included most of southeastern Wisconsin, elected Lynde, a rising star in the Democratic party, as one of the state's first two delegates to the House of Representatives, to serve until March 3, 1849. The other was Mason C. Darling, a Democrat from Fond du Lac.

Being a member of Congress in those early decades was not a full-time job. Congress traditionally met for one three- or four-month session each year, from December to March, unless a special session, such as the one held in 1848, was needed. For service in the United States House of Representatives in the 1840s, a congressman received $8 per day, plus reimbursement for travel from his district.[12] With the Thirtieth Congress still in session, Lynde and Darling wasted no time in going to Washington. They took the standard route: a lake steamer to Buffalo, a packet boat on the Erie Canal to Albany, a steamer down to New York, and thence on to Washington. The journey took almost three weeks.

In the fall Lynde returned to Milwaukee to campaign for a full congressional term. He was opposed by his own partner Finch, the Whig candidate, and by Charles Durkee of Southport (now Kenosha) who ran on a strictly abolitionist platform. Durkee had been Finch's associate in the early years of the Wisconsin Anti-slavery Society and Liberty party. By the middle of the 1840s, however, Finch and other moderates had left the splinter group to return to the Whig fold. The issue of the spread of slavery to new territories and Durkee's more extreme stand on abolishing slavery in the South became two of the deciding issues in the 1848 campaign. Finch sought the middle ground. As a moderate antislavery Whig, he hoped for the support of voters who opposed the radical stand of the abolitionists and of those who were wary of the compromises that the Democrats were making with the "slavocracy" in the South.

Finch had sought public office ever since his unsuccessful race for probate judge in 1846. In April 1848, as statehood became a near certainty, he ran for a seat in Wisconsin's new state assembly from Milwaukee's First Ward. He was narrowly defeated in the April election, just one month before Lynde's successful run to represent Wisconsin in Congress. But he still cherished the dream of reentering public life.

The *Sentinel* ascribed Finch's two defeats to the Democratic hold on the German · ote. It urged the Whigs to appeal to the German "Forty-Eighters" to vote in accordance with the freethinking social-reform tradition that had brought them to America. However, Finch's reputation as a strong temperance advocate alienated most of the German electorate.

The Whigs hoped that 1848 would be a good year for their party. At the national level Zachary Taylor, the victorious general of the Mexican War, was a presidential contender. At the state level the Whigs had been victorious in the debate over the constitution. As he campaigned for himself, Finch spoke at many Milwaukee rallies for Zach Taylor and at "Rough and Ready Club" meetings around southeastern Wisconsin. Because he had tasted little local political success, the nomination for a national post brought Finch great satisfaction. The only downside to his running for Congress was the fact that he had to oppose his partner Lynde. To be selected as the Wisconsin Whig party's first nominee for Congress after statehood was a high honor. Furthermore, Finch received the nomination over many other powerful Whigs and several fellow attorneys, including men like Rufus King (editor of the *Sentinel* and later a strong supporter of Finch), John H. Tweedy, and Jonathan Arnold.

In challenging his friend and law partner in this congressional race, Finch risked more than political defeat. The bitterness of the 1848 race tested their personal relationship and the solidarity of their partnership. Some analysts have suggested that Finch ran only to draw reform votes away from Durkee, thus allowing Lynde to win a second term. But the evidence from all contemporary accounts is convincing that Finch and the Whigs ran an all-out campaign against Lynde, as they did against Durkee.

The three-way campaign quickly became heated, with charges flying between the contenders and the newspapers that championed them. The pro-Whig *Sentinel,* published by Rufus King, and the pro-Lynde, pro-Democrat, *Evening Wisconsin* battled bitterly over Lynde's record in the Thirtieth Congress. The *Sentinel* assailed Lynde for upholding President Polk's veto of a rivers and harbors bill that would have funded substantial internal improvements in Milwaukee. In his own defense Lynde replied that he had voted *for* the bill when it came to the House of Representatives, but had not opposed the head of his own party, President Polk, when he chose to veto it for economic reasons.

Finch and Lynde never debated each other publicly or confronted Durkee directly, but their positions were fought out by the rival newspapers. Besides opposing each other for the congressional seat, each partner actively supported the rival presidential candidates. Lynde appeared at a rally for the Democratic nominee for president, Lewis Cass, on September 11; three days later Finch spoke eloquently at a Rough and Ready Club rally for Taylor.

Finch found it expedient to distance himself from the radicals of both the Democratic and the Free Soil parties. Like many who hated slavery, he feared that the abolitionists' call for direct federal action to end slavery in the South could destroy the Union. Like Abraham Lincoln and moderate Republicans of 1860, Finch declared himself opposed to the extreme position of the Durkee group.

Finch continued to sound the call to Whigs to stay true to the principles of their founder, Henry Clay, whose conservative economic policy supported federal aid to internal improvements but abhorred governmental interference in the free-market economy or on the issue of slavery. Lynde opposed Whig economic principles, challenged Finch's call for aid to harbors and roads and stricter regulation of banking and currency, and maintained his own cautious position on slavery.

The campaign also turned on issues other than slavery or abolitionism, specifically matters relating to the exemption of forty acres of land from a foreclosure or bankruptcy sale and the recommendation to limit a workingman's day to ten hours. Lynde called the ten-hour limit a measure that would "tend to elevate the moral and intellectual character of the working man." Finch strongly disagreed. He agreed that humane employers would not require more than ten hours of work, but argued that government attempts to regulate working hours would violate freedom of contract. Finch also opposed the land reforms that reflected the antispeculator sentiment of the Democrats.[13]

A free-market economy without government restrictions or regulations was a sacred canon of the conservative Whigs, but not for many of the city's immigrant Germans, who had worked unsuccessfully in their homeland for economic and social reforms. The banner of economic conservatism was raised in a circular signed by several key Whig leaders, including Finch, E. G. Ryan, and Daniel Wells. Finch's father, a gentleman farmer in Waukesha, and many others also joined in. In response, the German-language newspaper, *Volksfreund,* urged all good Germans to vote for Lynde and the Democratic ticket. The fact that Finch and many other prominent Whigs were known to be ardent temperance men remained a mark against them in the German community.

One last issue raised in the campaign was a charge that Finch had worked for Lynde's congressional candidacy six months earlier in the special election. Finch once again responded with a public letter on the matter. He wrote the editor of the *Sentinel* that in May he had supported and voted for Lynde's Whig opponent, E. V. Whiton. "I did what I could to secure his election not, however, on the ground of any ill-feeling towards Mr. Lynde, for I knew him to be worthy of confidence and an honest man, but because Mr. Whiton was a Whig and the exponent of Whig principles."[14]

In a final effort to promote Finch on the eve of the election, the *Sentinel* urged Whig voters to stay true to their party. "Mr. Finch is as firm an opponent of Slavery Extension, as warm an Advocate of River and Harbor improvements, as zealous a champion of the rights and interests of Wisconsin as Mr. Durkee. What is more, Mr. Finch is a *Whig* and can necessarily have more weight in the next Congress . . . than either of his competitors can hope to have."[15]

As an incumbent, Lynde had already enjoyed a taste of Washington politics. Finch had little real hope of winning in the largely Democratic district and was still handling most of the firm's casework. The firm's two new legal assistants, Bouck and Starkweather, helped. In a campaign letter written shortly before the election,

Finch told his supporters: "I have been under the necessity of embodying my views in this communication in great haste being pressed with many cares, and business engagements, for which I trust you will make due allowance."[16]

Lynde carried Democratic Milwaukee County, as expected, but lost the election to Durkee. Finch finished last. The vote was Durkee 5,038; Lynde 4,436; and Finch 3,615. The results proved to be the first indication of the strength of the Liberty party in southeastern Wisconsin and the passion aroused by the issue of slavery, which was Durkee's sole campaign issue.

Nationally, it was a Whig year. General Taylor defeated the Democrat Lewis Cass for the presidency. Votes for the third-party (Free Soil) candidate, Martin Van Buren, took the election from the Democrats and gave Taylor, the Whig, the presidency. Free Soilers, Northern Whigs, Barnburner Democrats, and other disaffected voters would soon change the map of American politics by making slavery and the Republican party the key issues during the next decade.

Two days after the election Lynde left for Washington to serve out the remainder of the term he had been elected to in May 1848. The session began on December 3, 1848, and ended on March 3, 1849. His prompt departure gave the partners little time to rehash the election or heal any wounds created by the campaign. However, there is no indication that feelings were ever sour between the two men or their families over the campaign. Finch, with the assistance of Bouck and Starkweather, carried on the casework and held the practice together until Lynde returned in May 1849.

Finch appeared on November 17 at a Whig victory rally for Taylor, staged in Waukesha by the Rough and Ready Club. He and his wife Mary also prepared to celebrate the upcoming marriage of their seventeen-year-old (and eldest) daughter Mary to Christopher Papendiek on December 14, 1848. Papendiek and his brother George were German immigrants. George Papendiek headed a firm called The Banking House near the Finch & Lynde law office at 210 East Water Street. Christopher worked in banking with his brother and also served as the consul to Wisconsin, Michigan, Iowa, Illinois, Indiana, and Minnesota from the German kingdom of Hanover. This tie to Milwaukee's prosperous German community brought new clients who might otherwise have avoided a Yankee firm.

Following the wedding, the newlyweds boarded for several years with the Finches in their home at 18 Mason Street. During this time the Papendiek banking house suffered bankruptcy, an event with which Finch could personally identify. Mary and her husband became parents of a son, George, in December, but he died at age five in 1854. (The death in 1860 of Finch's only other child, Delia, born in Michigan in 1833, left Mary as the sole heir and Finch without grandchildren.)

The Lyndes, too, had lost their infant daughter Fanny in 1847. Still in mourning, Mary Lynde did not accompany her husband to Washington until December 1848, when she recorded in her memoirs that she "met Mrs. James Madison and Mrs. Alexander Hamilton." During his final four months in Congress, Lynde opposed the abolition of slavery in the District of Columbia and gained admission as an "Attorney and Counselor" to the Supreme Court of the United States. In one of his last acts as a congressman, Lynde mailed letters and documents home to his district during these final months, including "valuable work on California . . . a good map of the overland route to the Gold Diggings!" [17]

When the Lynde family returned to Wisconsin on May 19, 1849, on the steamer *Niagara,* the country was swept up in California gold fever. In Milwaukee leading businessmen had organized the city's first Board of Trade to promote its wheat exports and the produce of the city's thirty-nine factories and breweries. In 1849 Milwaukee was on the verge of a period of industrial growth that would demand new kinds of legal expertise. As for the law partnership of Finch & Lynde, it had survived many challenges and one near catastrophe in its first six years from 1842 to 1848. In their private lives, both men had dealt with the stress of political conflict and searing personal losses. With the return of Lynde in May 1849, they resumed a close relationship and continued their work in the areas of commercial and corporate law.

❈ 4 ❈

Law and Early Statehood
1848–1857

Wisconsin became the thirtieth state when President
James K. Polk signed the statehood bill on May 29, 1848. As Milwaukee's economy expanded in the following decade, Finch &
Lynde represented clients in the areas of manufacturing, transportation, banking, insurance, and utilities. By the end of the 1850s, the
firm counted many of Milwaukee's new industrial concerns among
its clients. As a result, the partners focused less on land issues, bankruptcies, and collection work. Finch and Lynde acted not only as
attorneys but also as investors and fellow entrepreneurs in Milwaukee's industrial and commercial growth. That pattern became a tradition for later partners.

In August 1848 the new state of Wisconsin scheduled judicial
elections for the five new circuit courts. Although the districts were
supposed to be roughly equal in territory and population, the Second Circuit comprised Milwaukee, Waukesha, Jefferson, and Dane
counties and was much larger than the other four. Until the constitutional revision of 1852, the Supreme Court consisted of the
judges of the five circuit courts meeting once a year *en banc* to hear
appeals. That system soon proved unworkable.

Wisconsin also was designated as a single judicial district of
the United States. Initially, the federal court in Wisconsin was not

attached to any other circuit, and its decisions were subject to review only by the Supreme Court of the United States.[1] President Polk appointed Andrew G. Miller, who had served on the territorial bench since 1838, as the new federal judge for Wisconsin. Both Finch and Lynde had become close personal friends of Miller in their nearly ten years of association, and Judge Miller later steered his son Benjamin K. Miller to Finch & Lynde for legal training.

The elective state courts quickly became partisan battlegrounds, despite expectations to the contrary by those who had drafted the state constitution. The first elections for circuit court judges were set for August 1848. Levi Hubbell, Finch's and Lynde's former partner, who had sought political office after his departure from the firm, won a judgeship in the hotly contested second district.[2]

On January 8, 1849, the new state Supreme Court convened in Madison for the first time to elect a chief justice and to draw lots for judicial terms. The terms were staggered: One justice was to serve a term of one year; others, from two to five years, respectively. Hubbell drew a term of three years, thereby assuring the Milwaukee electorate of a new judicial election in 1851. At this first Supreme Court session, the five justices adopted a rule admitting all attorneys from the territorial courts into practice before the new state courts "on taking the official oath." Other persons "entitled to admission were to pay [a] fee to the clerk of three dollars."[3]

In 1850, when the demands on these first five justices became overwhelming, the legislature created a sixth circuit for the state. The establishment of a separate appellate body in 1852 eliminated the conflicts that had often arisen earlier, when circuit judges sat on the appellate bench of the Supreme Court to hear appeals from their own decisions.

Finch's position as city attorney was considered a political plum because many of the men who had occupied it had moved on to judgeships or high offices. Before statehood and the creation of a distinct county court system, the city attorney also served as the county prosecutor. The city attorney was paid a small salary plus a stipend for each case he prosecuted. Prosecution for crime was rare because Milwaukee had no organized police force until 1852. Consequently, the job demanded very little time or attention. Finch therefore had no difficulty in maintaining a very lucrative private practice in the circuit court while appearing in the same court as a prosecutor. In the mid-nineteenth century, even the job of mayor demanded only several hours a week.[4]

During his one-year term as city attorney Finch handled only a few criminal cases, most of them involving assault and battery. Many of the lesser cases derived from the need to uphold local ordinances. Convictions usually resulted only in fines or, less commonly, in a short jail term in the small block of cells attached to the courthouse. Judge Hubbell was especially interested in prosecuting "laws prohibiting gambling, private lotteries, unauthorized banking and the selling of liquor to the Indians."[5]

In contrast to the city attorney's light load, the demands on a circuit judge were great indeed. Hubbell maintained an exhausting schedule. He convened three court terms per year in Milwaukee, beginning on the first Mondays of February and May, and on the third Monday in September. In addition, he held court for two terms each in Waukesha, Jefferson, and Dane counties. His burden was somewhat reduced in 1850 when Milwaukee County established its own separate court to handle minor civil cases and probate matters. Hubbell also traveled to Madison to sit on the Supreme Court for a two- to four-week session each year. With his regular practice in Hubbell's court, Finch knew its burdens, but his ambition was not dampened. In 1851, he decided to challenge Hubbell for the judgeship.

Hubbell's partisanship when he first campaigned for judge in 1848 prompted critics to accuse him of "staining his ermine." Consequently, men from many political factions rallied around Finch when Hubbell faced reelection in 1851. Members of the state bar met in Madison and vowed to "oppose the reelection of Judge Hubbell and to support any fair man against him." The campaign between former law partners became one of the most bitter in Wisconsin history. Eventually, one newspaper called for an end to the constant "vituperative and personal abuse."

Although a Democrat, Lynde did not support Hubbell. He undertook the lion's share of the firm's caseload in the summer of 1851, relieving Finch to campaign. The returns on September 29 were close: Finch lost by 900 votes out of a total of 8,300, winning in most of the Yankee areas but losing in the Irish and German parts of the judicial district.[6]

Two years later, many of the detractors who could not defeat Hubbell at the polls brought formal charges of misconduct in the legislature. He was impeached, and Finch testified against Hubbell in the 1853 impeachment trial in the state Senate. Finch's former associate (and later Supreme Court chief justice) Edward G. Ryan served as prosecutor. An eloquent Ryan called Hubbell's conduct "judicial harlotry," but the Senate narrowly acquitted him. After retiring from the bench in 1856, Hubbell remained active in Milwaukee politics and in the law, maintaining an office adjacent to that of Finch & Lynde for many years.[7]

Milwaukee's expanding economy demanded more sophisticated legal skills. In 1848 Milwaukee's four flour mills processed 800 barrels daily, and the first paper mill was opened by Nelson and Harrison Ludington. In January the first telegraph line reached the city. This new electric system of high-speed communication stimulated economic growth.[8] Between 1840 and 1850 Milwaukee grew faster than any other American city, including Chicago.[9]

Lumbering flourished with the increasing demand for factories, breweries, stores, and homes. Among Milwaukee lumber barons who became clients of Finch & Lynde were brothers Nelson and Harrison Ludington and Elisha Eldred and his son Anson. The Eldreds owned hundreds of acres of Wisconsin forest near the mouth of the Oconto River. They pioneered in the use of band saws in their mill.[10] Earlier, Finch & Lynde had handled many collection cases for Eldred, including several against the Ludingtons. By the 1850s their legal services focused more on the operation of the lumber business itself.

Elisha and Anson Eldred shipped lumber to Milwaukee and Chicago on a variety of boats, and the fate of these vessels and their cargo was a constant source of litigation. When one vessel failed to deliver 129,000 board feet of lumber to Milwaukee in the spring of 1849, the Eldreds took its owners to court. Just as the case was being heard, the vessel appeared with its cargo of lumber worth $903, and the matter was dropped at the plaintiff's expense.[11] Shipping caused endless litigation, and many lumbermen soon found it expedient to purchase their own lake vessels rather than rely on the commercial shipping companies.

The industry was also beset with conflicting claims of land ownership. In the unmarked forests of northern Wisconsin, unscrupulous lumbermen or even misguided lumberjacks could end up cutting thousands of board feet from the wrong timber plot, with lawsuits an inevitable result. Wrongfully cutting timber from United

States lands might mark only the beginning of a lumberman's legal problems. In 1852, for example, the firm began to defend its clients against a claim that they had converted $11,000 worth of lumber that the Brown County sheriff had seized. The litigation turned on fine points of jurisdiction, attachment, and the amending of writs. Over the next ten years, the firm twice lost in the lower courts and twice won reversals in the Supreme Court. The final resolution is not known.[12]

With the economic development of the 1850s came a revolution in transportation. Investors and developers turned to canals, plank roads, waterways, and railroads to transport raw materials and a growing number of manufactured products. Canal fever swept the country after the financial success of New York's Erie Canal in the 1820s and 1830s. Many immigrants to Wisconsin, including both Finch and Lynde, had traveled to Buffalo by packet boat along the canal.

Even before statehood, Byron Kilbourn had promoted a canal from Milwaukee to the Wisconsin River. Despite initial public support, however, only a mile-long strip along the west bank of the Milwaukee River was completed before Kilbourn's dream collapsed. State funds were withdrawn from the canal company, and Kilbourn was fired as canal commissioner. Many lawsuits over water rights and canal land were brought during the next fifteen years. Finch & Lynde often appeared for investors who, after work was suspended, refused to pay the balance due for the bonds they had pledged to buy. The canal segment lay idle until the 1880s when the city filled it to create Commerce Street.[13] The only revenue the canal ever generated was derived from the water power of a dam built on the lower Milwaukee River. The power supported a number of small industries, including five flour mills, a woolen mill, two iron foundries and a half-dozen woodworking factories.

It was not considered unethical for a firm to represent both sides of a controversy. In a suit by Kilbourn against the other directors of the canal company after his ouster, Lynde represented Kilbourn and Finch represented the canal company.[14]

As the firm practice grew in complexity, Lynde, in particular, concentrated on shipping or mercantile law and the water rights along navigable rivers. He represented George Walker, a former mayor of Milwaukee, in a suit to enjoin Milwaukee from building a new wharf that would interfere with Walker's privately built docks.

Lynde argued in the Wisconsin Supreme Court that the Northwest Ordinance of 1787 and the Wisconsin Constitution forbade "any obstruction to a navigable stream as a public nuisance." Walker's rights to use a navigable river as a common highway, "forever free," could not be abridged, Lynde contended. The circuit court had ruled against the city on the pleadings and the Supreme Court affirmed, but whether that ended the litigation is not known.[15]

As the transportation revolution continued in southeastern Wisconsin, Finch & Lynde became involved in representing both plank road and railroad companies. Wooden or corduroy roads proved more feasible financially than the canal, and several companies built plank roads northward and westward from the city. Although split logs laid flat side up made roads that were passable in all seasons, the ride was rough. A fellow passenger on one of Finch's coach trips to appear in the Supreme Court in Madison recalled that Finch's "long beard bounced with each lurch of the coach" for two uncomfortable days. Tollhouses were located every five miles with turnpikes, or large horizontal spokes, that turned to let wagons or riders through. Tolls were five to ten cents per axle for wagons and less for a horse and rider (except on Sundays, when churchgoers could use the roads at no charge).[16]

These privately constructed plank roads that connected Milwaukee to adjacent agricultural counties were of primary importance to the city's growth as a shipping and manufacturing center. Road companies were private enterprises that hoped for large profits from toll-paying traffic. Usable public roads and highways were still far in the future. The Milwaukee and Watertown Plank Road Company, a client of Finch & Lynde, collected tolls of $1,300 each week. Such companies needed legal assistance in both their building phase and their ongoing operations, though they were subject to fewer legal entanglements than the canals or the railroads.[17]

Plank roads that covered lengthy routes between markets, such as the road built by the Janesville Road Company, were soon destroyed by competition from the railroads, whereas the shorter roads survived. The 150 miles of plank roads leading to Milwaukee in 1852 helped stimulate the city's business growth. The cost of building plank roads, although sizable, was modest compared with railroad construction. They provided routes and access to markets that railroads could not serve.

Finch & Lynde began to take an active role in handling the tangled legal issues revolving around the new railroad lines in Milwaukee and southeastern Wisconsin at the beginning of the 1850s. It was clear to the leaders of the young city that if Milwaukee did not become a rail center, it might lose much of its overland commerce to Chicago, its nearest competitor. By December 1849, Milwaukee's thirty-nine factories were producing $1,700,000 in goods annually, but this manufacturing output was still far overshadowed by the city's enormous trade in wheat and flour.

The first railroad company chartered in Wisconsin, the Milwaukee and Waukesha, was established in 1847. Almost immediately (even before any track could be laid down), it became involved in lawsuits over its proposed route, the fair price for acquisition of land, and stock subscriptions to finance construction costs. The railroad retained Finch & Lynde during its first months of existence when a Brookfield farmer, Andrew Eble, sued to win a higher price for his land. Following Eble's lead, many other farmers took the railroad to court to appeal the valuation decisions of an independent board of commissioners. However, like Eble, they were largely unsuccessful.[18]

In 1851 Finch & Lynde defended several disgruntled bondholders who were sued by the railroad because they had not paid for the bonds they had promised to buy. They counterclaimed, charging the railroad with fiscal doubledealing in secretly favoring certain investors, a policy the courts held to be a violation of trust. The firm's clients recovered their investments. Later investors were less fortunate, however, as fiscal mismanagement of several railroads worsened over the next two decades.[19]

Finch's victory in these cases impressed the railroad, and he was invited to join the Milwaukee and Mississippi's board of directors and to serve as the railroad's attorney in May 1852. He also joined the board of the Milwaukee, Fond du Lac, and Green Bay Railroad, which became the Milwaukee and La Crosse in 1853. The firm defended against several suits by farmers who complained of damage to their wheat, corn, or turnip crops along the track.[20] Some claims were resolved by mediation panels, although Finch & Lynde usually appealed sizable mediation awards to circuit court.[21]

Railroad building began in earnest in the 1850s. The Milwaukee and Waukesha Railroad Company changed its name to the Milwaukee and Mississippi Railroad and laid its first track in September 1850. Tracks reached Waukesha in 1851 and Madison in 1854. Finch rode the first ceremonial train to Madison, where he made an "eloquent reply" to the welcoming speeches of state officials. As railroad fever escalated, farmers eagerly signed up to mortgage their farms at 8 percent interest and buy railroad bonds that promised to pay them 10 percent. Milwaukee even used tax funds to finance construction. In May 1851 the city reported a municipal debt of $400,000, of which $234,000 was in credits extended to railroads. Although some reformers advised caution in this mounting indebtedness, voters remained fervently prorailroad. George Walker, who had promised continued support to the railroads, was elected mayor.[22]

The industrial revolution in general and railroads in particular fostered changes in suits to recover for civil wrongs or torts, for these new machines could injure livestock, damage tangible property, and worst of all, "had a marvelous capacity for smashing the human body."[23] Courts and advocates had to write new legal rules for the new circumstances created by the railroads. Finch & Lynde defended the Milwaukee and Mississippi in two suits brought to recover the value of cattle killed by a train on a line in Crawford County. They argued, first, that cattle had no right to feed on grass growing between the ties of a railroad track; second, that the plaintiff had been negligent in allowing cows to graze on the track; and third, that there could be no recovery since the cattle were trespassers. The defense was successful. In many agricultural states, however, legislation forcing the railroads to pay for injuring livestock was enacted long before they were forced to pay for loss to human life and limb. Other states began to demand that locomotives ring a bell at each crossing and eventually required that crossings be marked by warning signs.[24]

In 1856 Finch & Lynde defended the Milwaukee and Mississippi Railroad in a suit by a youth who had lost his arm when he was thrown from the top of a freight train. The central issue was whether the boy was a railroad employee or a passenger pressed into service to handle the brake. A Milwaukee jury decided he was a passenger and awarded him $7,500, but the trial court recognized its own faulty jury instruction and ordered a new trial. The Supreme Court affirmed the order, and the plaintiff won $6,200 in his second trial four years later.[25]

Railroads and other employers were likely to prevail when employees' injuries could be blamed on the victims' own negligence or on that of fellow employees. The rule that employees assumed the risk of injury when they took dangerous jobs—the "fellow-servant rule"—was a powerful defense. A public enthusiastic for modern transportation accepted the legal rules that made it difficult for injured employees to win damages.[26]

Railroads were often involved in contract litigation, too. Contractors often found it difficult to collect from the cash-poor lines. Finch & Lynde represented railroads in a number of cases where payment had been withheld from construction companies because the rails were not laid correctly or the roadbed was graded too steeply.

From 1853 to 1857, when railroad fever was at its height, approximately 6,000 Wisconsin farmers mortgaged their homesteads to purchase railroad stock. When the Panic of 1857 forced Wisconsin's railroads into bankruptcy, the farmers found that their mortgages had been transferred to eastern creditors and that their railroad stocks were virtually worthless. Charges that railroads received unfair tax breaks, that they were callous about dangerous working conditions, and that they had cheated investors eventually erupted in massive farm protests. The Grange Movement of the 1870s finally succeeded in generating federal regulations to control many such railroad abuses.

The negativism about railroads that mounted to a crescendo by the close of 1857 was in sharp contrast to the overwhelming enthusiasm of Wisconsin's citizens toward the arrival of the railroads only six years earlier. In the early 1850s men who served on a railroad board or as railroad attorneys were hailed as heroes working for the public good. The arrival of a railroad at a farming village or commercial center was an occasion for great celebration. Subscribing to stocks that would bring track close to one's farm or city became an all-consuming fever for Wisconsinites during the 1850s. But then the bubble burst, and bitter recrimination replaced enthusiasm.

Finch & Lynde handled legal business from out-of-state railroads as well. The firm represented the New York and Erie Railroad Company (predecessor of the New York Central) in several suits brought by Wisconsin businesses that sought to recover for missing shipments from suppliers in the East. In two of these suits, Finch &

Lynde filed a petition to move the matter to the federal district court, arguing that it alone had jurisdiction to decide such disputes. Both petitions were denied.[27]

Other new businesses occupied Finch & Lynde, too. By the mid-1850s an extensive German immigration had brought a number of brewers to Milwaukee. Valentin Blatz had come from Munich, where he had been a foreman in several breweries owned by his father. He married the widow of brewer John Braun in 1851, and set about increasing Braun's beer production a hundredfold, from 150 barrels to 15,366 in 1868. Finch & Lynde successfully defended him in a collection case by proving his signature had been forged on a promissory note.[28]

The insurance business was a by-product of the threat of fire that accompanied city development. Most buildings were frame, built close together, and heated with woodburning stoves. Finch himself had lost a barn to fire shortly after his move to a twenty-one-acre parcel of land on the west side. One of Milwaukee's worst fires occurred in 1854, when $400,000 worth of property was destroyed, including the United States Hotel, the Mitchell Block stores, and thirty other buildings in the downtown area. The building housing the law offices of Finch & Lynde on Wisconsin Avenue narrowly escaped. Finch lost $1,000 worth of furniture that was stored in Milwaukee's largest warehouse, the Wall auction room on the northwest corner of Water and Wisconsin. His son-in-law George Papendiek also lost $2,000 worth of property, insured by the Aetna Company, a Connecticut insurer. As litigation over insured losses proliferated, the firm represented Aetna and other distant insurers, such as the American Mutual Insurance Company and the Rensselaer Insurance Company of Rensselaer, both based in New York.[29]

Collision policies for moving vehicles were not being written yet. Finch & Lynde handled the defense for a prominent stagecoach company, Frink, Walker and Davis (for which it had done work since the territorial years), in a case that resulted from the collision of a wagon with its stagecoach in 1850. The owner of the wagon, a local doctor, sued for his medical expenses and the value of his wagon. The jury awarded the doctor only the cost of his wagon. When the stagecoach company decided to appeal even that limited award, Finch & Lynde suggested that it obtain other counsel.[30]

Far more controversial than insurance claims, banking and currency remained active issues throughout the early years after statehood. Although Alexander Mitchell's Wisconsin Marine and Fire Insurance Company had been chartered in 1839 as an insurance company, Mitchell and his Chicago partner, George Smith, actually turned the business into a thriving bank under the guise of doing only insurance work. Despite the constitutional provision outlawing banks, the Marine received money on deposit and issued notes that served as a stable medium of circulation in early Milwaukee. What came to be called "George Smith's money" was good as gold on the cash-starved midwestern frontier. The need for such a financial institution, even one that sidestepped the law, is demonstrated by the growth of the Marine's circulation, from $387,000 in 1848 to $1,470,235 by 1852.

Another profitable sideline took the Marine into making advances that farmers repaid when they harvested and sold their crops. It was a good business, for Wisconsin experienced a 500 percent increase in wheat production between 1850 and 1860, even during the bad years of 1857 and 1858.[31] The certificates of deposit issued by Mitchell and Smith became a favored currency in the lower Lake Michigan area in the hiatus between the Panic of 1837 and the renewal of legal banking services in 1852. These certificates were always redeemed at face value. Among the personal papers of the Lynde family are a number of such notes written and drawn on the Wisconsin Marine and Fire Insurance Company. The law firm also used Mitchell's quasi-bank as its depository. Finch & Lynde had occasionally represented Mitchell personally in the 1840s. By 1850 it was also handling an increasing number of cases for the Marine, such as an 1853 matter involving disputed loans to the Little River Mills in Oconto.[32]

In 1851 the state legislature responded to a change in political climate and voter demand to legalize banking in the now stable economy. What came to be called the Free Banking Law of 1852 permitted banking under the supervision of an elected state bank comptroller. Voters approved it by a margin of nearly four to one, 31,219 to 9,126. Free banking meant that any group that complied with the rules of deposit could establish a legal bank without the cumbersome procedure of applying for a specific state charter. Under its provisions, which later proved to be faulty, each bank was required to deposit United States bonds, bonds of various states, or railroad bonds with the bank comptroller before it could open its door to depositors or issue its own bank notes.[33]

Passage of the 1852 act drew Finch and Lynde more deeply into their relationship with the business of banking. The Marine became the first bank in Milwaukee to receive approval as a state institution. In 1853 the Farmers and Millers Bank (later the First Wisconsin National Bank) was established in Milwaukee, with Finch serving on its first board. Five more banks were established in Milwaukee during the next two years.

Despite the many banking disasters of only fifteen years earlier, the public still believed its money could be safely entrusted to banks. Finch, who had suffered so badly during the 1837 disaster as a bank president in Michigan, once again became the president of a new banking house, the Globe Bank of Milwaukee, on May 27, 1857. Lynde became a major shareholder. The Globe Bank located its offices on the southwest corner of Michigan Street and Broadway in the newly built Albany Building, where Finch & Lynde moved in the same year.

But Finch's timing was poor again. Though for a while the banking business shared in the general prosperity, the Panic of 1857 wiped out many banks in Milwaukee and elsewhere in the state. The panic was caused by many factors, among them, a failure in southern cotton prices, a faulty bank deposit system, and the ongoing cycle of boom and bust that had also brought the enormous growth in Wisconsin's economy in the nine years since statehood in 1848. The Globe Bank was able to collect sufficient capital from its outstanding loans to pay off outside investors and close without the ignominy that had shadowed Finch's first banking catastrophe twenty years earlier. Thereafter, Finch served as bank attorney, but not as a banker or major investor.[34]

Part of the capital that was raised for Wisconsin banks had come from bonds or unregulated currency from southern states. William E. Cramer, the owner of the *Evening Wisconsin,* warned his readers in 1853 that Milwaukeeans should be wary of the flood of notes circulated by unstable southern banks such as the Atlanta Bank in Georgia, which were being distributed by the Wisconsin Marine Bank. After Cramer called these notes from Atlanta "trash," Finch & Lynde was asked to defend the Milwaukee newspaper in the resulting libel suit brought by the Atlanta Bank. The suit was settled after a long trial with abundant testimony from other newspaper-men who supported Cramer, but the terms of the settlement are not known. In another libel case, Lynde appealed on Cramer's behalf after a jury found the *Daily Wisconsin* had libeled Josiah Noonan, a publisher and postmaster, and a Democratic party leader. The Supreme Court held the Racine County judge had incorrectly in-structed the jury about libel per se and remanded for a new trial.[35]

In the years before the Panic of 1857 and the disasters of the Civil War, Finch and Lynde became attorneys for other new business enterprises springing up in Milwaukee and directors of some of them. On November 23, 1852, Milwaukee was lit by gaslights for the first time, an occasion that prompted a great public celebration. Within five years, seven miles of gas pipe were laid throughout the city, bringing the benefits of streetlighting to more and more neigh-borhoods.[36] Lynde was one of the incorporators of the Milwaukee Gas Light Company in March 1852. Both Finch and Lynde served for many years on its board, and Finch later became its president.

Finch's judicial campaign early in the decade had placed a heavy burden on Lynde. In addition, Finch took several months away from the firm after the sudden death in July 1855 of his forty-three-year-old wife Mary. Following her death, Finch left Milwaukee for a while and traveled extensively throughout the East, visiting family, friends, and business associates in New York. He did not return to his home at 381 Broadway until early the following year. For several months, Lynde received some assistance from Henry L. Palmer, an attorney new to Milwaukee, who later became president of the Northwestern Mutual Life Insurance Company and Democratic speaker of the Wisconsin Assembly and Senate.[37]

At this same time, in the middle of the 1850s, Finch and Lynde decided to hire two assistants to help with the caseload. They brought in Finch's nephew, Henry Martyn (Matt) Finch, and the son of Federal Judge Andrew G. Miller, Benjamin Kurtz Miller, who con-tinued to act as clerk of his father's federal court for five years while also working with Finch & Lynde. By 1856 these two associates had proven themselves invaluable, and in December Finch & Lynde officially invited them to join the firm. The addition of Matt Finch and B. K. Miller was the first expansion of the fifteen-year-old part-nership since the unsuccessful relationship with Hubbell ten years earlier.

The new partners were announced on January 1, 1857, and the firm name was changed to Finches, Lynde & Miller. The partnership moved into larger offices in the newly constructed Albany Building. For the first time, the firm occupied a suite of offices, instead of one or two small rooms.

The four partners faced a challenge in handling the flood of litigation that resulted from bankruptcies among Wisconsin's railroads and disasters to its financial institutions. Beginning in 1857 and throughout the Civil War (1861–1865), Finches, Lynde & Miller would handle hundreds of cases arising from the economic morass and the dislocations of war. In the decade of prosperity following statehood and in the years of economic chaos that followed, transportation, industrial, banking, and insurance companies turned increasingly to Finches, Lynde & Miller. The firm's capacity to serve as business as well as legal advisers to Milwaukee's growing corporate community was well-established as the partnership attained its fifteenth anniversary on September 8, 1857.

⧉ 5 ⧉

Finches, Lynde & Miller
1857–1860

The four years before the outbreak of the Civil War were litigious, as the Panic of 1857 began to take its toll on railroads, banks, and other Wisconsin businesses. Judge Arthur McArthur, successor to Alexander W. Randall and Levi Hubbell on the second circuit bench, doubled the number of court terms. McArthur presided over his courtroom with a professionalism and dignity not seen since Andrew Miller's promotion in 1848 to federal district judge. Judge McArthur's son Arthur was a Civil War hero, and his grandson was General Douglas MacArthur, the Supreme Commander of Allied forces in the southwest Pacific during World War II. The new judge brought a welcome change for the better in ethics and judicial professionalism from the Hubbell years.[1]

In McArthur's courtroom, Finches, Lynde & Miller, as well as smaller law firms, worked to bring order out of the banking and currency problems of the late 1850s and to establish the troubled railroads on a solid new footing. In the four court terms of 1857, the newly expanded firm managed 700 cases arising out of the economic chaos. The addition of Matt Finch and B. K. Miller proved propitious as the demands on all four men multiplied even in the first year of their partnership.

Asahel Finch's nephew Matt had come west to Wisconsin in 1850 at the age of twenty-one. Born in New York, he had migrated first to Michigan and then to Milwaukee in the trail of his pioneering uncle. At first he joined his uncle Cullen Finch in business as a Madison merchant. Soon afterwards, he returned to Milwaukee to learn the printer's trade by working at the *Evening Wisconsin*. He was drawn to the law in 1850 and began to read law as an apprentice with Abram D. Smith and Henry Lewis Palmer, two Milwaukee lawyers who were friends of Asahel Finch and Lynde. He completed his apprenticeship and was admitted to the bar in 1853. He practiced on his own in Janesville for a short while, then returned to Milwaukee at his uncle's invitation to join Finch & Lynde as an associate. For four years he handled collections and many other routine matters, freeing the senior attorneys to work on more complicated cases.

By 1853, procedures for collections had been streamlined in the circuit court by the use of printed legal forms. Matt Finch became expert in these routines, and handled almost 1,000 such cases in the Milwaukee circuit court in the 1850s. His work helped Lynde through difficult years when the senior Finch was away from the office. After a four-year term as an associate, Matt Finch entered into full partnership on January 1, 1857.[2]

Like his uncle, Matt Finch had no formal education beyond high school. His companion as a junior partner in the firm had some. Born in Gettysburg, Pennsylvania, on May 6, 1830, Benjamin Kurtz Miller was named after his maternal grandfather, a leader in the Lutheran church in America. He came to Wisconsin in 1839 when his father, Andrew Galbraith Miller, was named territorial judge. Miller returned to Pennsylvania in 1846 to enter the freshman class at Washington College, his father's alma mater. After three years of classical education, being too poor to continue, he returned to Milwaukee to pursue a legal apprenticeship in law in his father's new federal courtroom. On August 1, 1848, Miller was named deputy clerk of the newly created federal district court. The federal court was located on the fourth floor of Martin's Block on the southeast corner of Wisconsin and East Water streets, just across from the post office and the adjacent law offices of Finch & Lynde at 18 Wisconsin Street.

Miller's work earned him the respect of the Milwaukee legal community, even among those who had misgivings about a son's serving as clerk to his father's court. He was admitted to the bar on May 6, 1851, his twenty-first birthday. Three months later, he was promoted to clerk of the district court upon the recommendation of "the ablest lawyers then in practice" (among whom was Asahel Finch). He also began to work for Finch & Lynde when the court was not in session. Since Miller's limited time made it necessary for him to confine his work in the firm to small matters, the bulk of associate responsibilities fell on Matt Finch. Like Matt Finch, B. K. Miller joined the partnership on January 1, 1857.

During his five years as clerk of court, Miller became a leader of a second generation of rising young professionals. He and Matt Finch reflected the diverse personal styles of the firm's founders. Like his uncle, the reticent Matt Finch centered his social life around the church. Miller was a popular young man-about-town, active in the bicycling club and a leader of the Young Men's Association, which created the first public library collection in the city. Matt Finch was a Whig and then a Republican, like his uncle. Like Lynde, Miller was an active Democrat, who had witnessed his father's unpopularity for applying the fugitive slave law against Wisconsin abolitionist Sherman M. Booth, on trial in his federal court.[3]

In Miller and Matt Finch, the law firm had found young men of energy and talent to continue the work of the partnership. From its earliest expansion, the firm did not distinguish between new and senior partners. All four drew equal incomes. One study of their office described an egalitarian atmosphere where matters of workload, fees, rental space, purchases, partner income, and the use of support personnel were settled by general discussion.[4]

It was fortunate that, unlike the firm's founders, neither Matt Finch nor Miller entertained political ambitions. The firm was flooded with cases. There was a rush of new businesses in Milwaukee and a realignment of banks and railroads. The firm needed all of the young men's time and energy.

As it moved into its new quarters on the southwest corner of Michigan and Broadway in January 1857, the firm listed itself in the city directory as "Finch, Lynde & Miller, attys., 6 and 8 Albany Building." Within the first year, the directory was corrected to read,

"Finches, Lynde & Miller," the name that would remain in use until 1890, even after the deaths of Lynde and both Finches.[5]

The Panic of 1857, which created economic havoc across the country, was caused by the sudden collapse in the price of southern cotton as well as by the overexpansion of banking and railroad indebtedness during the fifties. Many Milwaukee banks fought for their survival or retained counsel to carry out an orderly dissolution in the face of the financial crisis. Asahel Finch had long been involved in banking and had served as an adviser to many financial institutions in Milwaukee. Not the least of them was the Germania Bank, owned and operated by his son-in-law Christopher Papendiek and Christopher's brother, George.

In 1854, on the death of their only son, Mary Finch Papendiek and her husband decided to dissolve the Germania Bank and to leave Milwaukee. The hazards of banking were brought home to the extended Finch-Papendiek family firsthand when a bitter depositor stormed into the bank's offices and demanded enough money to pay a note on his home. When George Papendiek did not produce the money, the man fired a double-barreled pistol at him. He missed George Papendiek, but killed a bank clerk. The resulting trial became one of the most celebrated murder trials in early Milwaukee. With many citizens angry at banks, the killer became a not entirely unsympathetic figure.[6]

While Finch and Lynde did not get involved in the murder trial, they did wrap up the affairs of the Germania Bank, paid the depositors, resolved matters with its creditors, and settled the Papendieks' personal business affairs, a process that dragged on for almost a decade. Much of this work by the firm was done with a minimal charge to the assets of the bank. The personal business, in fact, had to be taken care of with no compensation at all, since Finch's daughter and son-in-law had left the state on the verge of bankruptcy.

Just before entering the partnership, B. K. Miller had married Isabella Peckham, the daughter of the prominent Milwaukee banker, George W. Peckham. Peckham's Bank of Commerce engaged the firm to recover as many assets as possible when it closed its doors in 1856. Representing banks such as Peckham's and the Germania helped the firm to develop its expertise in the specialty of banking law and brought many other bankers to the door as litigation multiplied in the bleak days of 1857.

As the city's oldest law firm and the only four-man partnership, Finches, Lynde & Miller increased its load from 700 cases in 1857 to 1,000 the following year. Until the last quarter of the nineteenth century, litigation remained the core of the firm's business. Firms of more than three partners were rare before the Civil War. The addition of two new partners, moreover, allowed the firm of Finches, Lynde & Miller to move more quickly than smaller firms into specialized areas such as banking and currency, utilities, and corporate organization.

Another young associate, Walter S. Carter, joined the firm for a short time in 1858, but did not stay to become a partner. Three years younger than Miller, Carter had come to Milwaukee in March 1858 on the advice of legal mentors in New York and Connecticut, who suggested that he seek training and opportunities in the West. After working in the firm for ten months, Carter entered the office of Levi Hubbell, just down the hall in the Albany Building, to clerk for the former judge for two more years. Beginning in 1860, Carter practiced law in Milwaukee alone or with one partner for nine more years before moving to Chicago in 1869 to establish his own firm, a predecessor of MacChesney & Becker. Reversing the westward movement typical of the era, Carter then moved back to New York City in 1873. Carter and Miller remained close friends all their lives. The two traveled together to Europe with their families several times. Carter's Chicago and New York ties became valuable connections for Finches, Lynde & Miller.[7]

In 1858, the firm represented the American Express Company, the leading package and money-transfer business before the Civil War, after $8,000 in cash and securities had been stolen from its office safe in Madison. The company had tried to deliver the packages to the State Bank at Madison shortly after 5 o'clock the afternoon before the theft. The bank had rejected the delivery because its banking hours had ended at 4 and its cashier had left for tea, taking the keys to the safe with him. Lynde argued, and the Supreme Court agreed, that the company's extraordinary duties as a common carrier ended when it made a reasonable offer of delivery, and that it was thereafter liable only for gross negligence.[8]

The firm also handled an increasing number of probate matters. Finch had remained the attorney of record on a great many wills drawn for early settlers during the years of his partnership with Wells and Crocker. The wills of many of Milwaukee's earliest settlers came to probate in the late 1850s. Michael Dousman, a client of Finch's since 1839, died in Milwaukee in 1854, leaving a fortune in land to his children. Finches, Lynde & Miller represented the estate and Dousman's sons Hercules, Talbot, and George against a challenge by their father's second wife and young daughter. The decision in probate court ultimately turned on the question of Dousman's domicile. Had it been Wisconsin or Michigan? Asahel Finch submitted an affidavit swearing that he had traveled to Mackinaw, Michigan in 1848 to redraw Dousman's will. Although Dousman's Michigan domicile cost his three sons $8,000 of their inheritance, they remained clients of the firm.[9]

Other business litigation concerned railroad construction debts, the construction of the Newhall House (a luxury hotel), and other matters central to the economic growth of the city. A study of the firm's clients from these pre-Civil War years reveals the essential pattern of Milwaukee's commercial and industrial growth. The business development of tanneries, clothing and textile concerns, breweries, sausage companies, and heavy machinery manufacturers is reflected in the law firm's list of cases.[10]

The first record of a retainer for the firm appears in connection with litigation for Dutcher, Sexton & Company, a lumber company with large interests in Juneau County, Wisconsin. Defending the company in a series of suits, the firm managed the payment of company debts, as ordered by the courts, and worked to keep title to timber lands seized by the U.S. marshal. Keeping the company afloat in the face of this series of reversals required business counsel, as well as the management of cases in court.[11]

Another troubled lumber business that was liquidated to pay the debts of eastern noteholders was the McVickar and Engleman Company. The company had interests in Wisconsin land and lumber, as well as ties in Chicago and St. Louis. Finches, Lynde & Miller managed the payment of the debts incurred when the company did not deliver shingles, boards, and other materials to New York. Later the firm also handled Lawrence McVicar's insolvency proceedings.[12]

The firm's expertise in corporate matters and finance brought the Fifth Ward Gas and Light Company to its doors in 1859. The company served the west side of the city, and the east side was served by the Milwaukee Gas Light Company, which Lynde had incorporated. Single, merged utility companies were not yet granted monopolies to serve an entire urban area. The experience of Asahel Finch and Lynde as stockholders and officers in the east side Milwaukee Gas Light Company helped them to propose appropriate safeguards for the charters of other utilities. Lynde represented the company in an early consumer rights case challenging the rules the utility imposed as a condition of service. Both parties conceded that reasonable rules could be imposed, but the plaintiff—an East Water Street merchant—successfully argued that some of the company's rules were not reasonable. The Supreme Court agreed, holding some of them "capricious, arbitrary, oppressive or unreasonable." Among them was an inspection requirement that made "the dwellings of gas consumers . . . subject to instantaneous visitation at all times without notice."[13]

Clients like the Fifth Ward Gas and Light Company illustrate how the firm's client base broadened in the decade before the Civil War. Businessmen in the predominantly German Fifth Ward had often turned to such German lawyers as Nathan Pereles and Edward Solomon. However, after the successful chartering of the gas company, the firm was asked to assist Solomon in managing several cases for a series of German merchants, most notably the Mack brothers, wholesalers and dry-goods retailers.

Lynde's new home on Vliet Street near the city limits was located in a predominantly German neighborhood. Both Finch and Lynde had invested in west side city lots during the 1840s, and the earliest atlas of the city showed areas named "Finch's subdivision" (later the site of Marquette University) and several Lynde subdivisions. Lynde was a partner of Garret Vliet in several large land ventures that profited from the flood of German immigration and settlement on the west side. Finch had made his home on the far west side, on Watertown Plank Road (now the site of the Milwaukee County Medical Complex), for a short time in the early 1850s and then returned to the city to live. Lynde later built the stately mansion he called Lynden at Twenty-third and Chestnut (now Juneau), a neighborhood of newly wealthy beer barons. His nearest neighbor in the 1870s was Captain Fred Pabst.

The German immigrants brought new capital to Milwaukee and, with it, the need for larger and more sophisticated banks. Finch and Lynde became involved in the Farmers and Millers Bank, directed by their old friend Edward D. Holton. It later became the First Wisconsin National Bank and then Firstar. As legal adviser, Asahel Finch helped to steer the institution through the banking crises of 1857 and the 1860s. He also helped Alexander Mitchell try to control the issuance of inadequately secured notes and to increase the credibility of the city's strong banks. Angered at Mitchell's refusal to accept questionable notes, Milwaukeeans stormed his bank at Water and Michigan in the Bank Riot of June 1861. A mob carried furniture and records into the street and burned them before being dispersed by the authorities.[14]

The Panic of 1857 that closed many banks was equally a disaster for the railroads whose bonds fell in value. Debt service devoured profits while competition reduced revenues. Overextended and underfinanced, Wisconsin's railroads, beginning with Kilbourn's La Crosse and Milwaukee line, began to fail early in 1857. By the beginning of 1858, the state's other major railroad company, the Milwaukee and Mississippi, failed to pay interest to its eastern bondholders. The bubble had burst. Burdened with debt, the farmers of Wisconsin, who had been major investors, were left with only the worthless stock of bankrupt corporations.

Just before the Milwaukee and Mississippi Railroad failed, the farmers who had pledged their farms for shares mounted an attempt to replace the directors of the company with men who might represent their interests. This attempt proved to be futile. The old directors, including Asahel Finch, were reelected. They reorganized the company into the Chicago, Milwaukee, and St. Paul Railroad, more commonly called "The Milwaukee Road." Unlike Kilbourn's La Crosse and Milwaukee, the Milwaukee and Mississippi was never found guilty of intentional fraud. The Milwaukee Road was restored to health by a group of new investors led by Alexander Mitchell. It continued to carry increasing loads of wheat and produce into Milwaukee for reshipment even as issues of railroad debts were being litigated in New York courts.

The tide of political outrage over railroad debt ran high. Wisconsin's attempt to let farmers repudiate their debts gave the state a bad name with eastern creditors for years to come. Despite the farmers' protests and the stay laws passed by the sympathetic Wisconsin legislature, the eastern creditors prevailed. The Wisconsin Supreme Court found the stay laws unconstitutional and declared the farm-mortgage obligations legitimate and enforceable. Wisconsin farmers were forced to honor their mortgages, even at the cost of hundreds of foreclosures.[15]

As work in the area of railroad debt, banking matters, and other commercial and corporate cases continued to multiply, Lynde emerged as the firm's chief litigator before the Wisconsin Supreme Court. He also became one of the Democratic leaders of a new political reform coalition in Milwaukee—the Albany Hall movement, named for the building where the firm's offices were located. In several protest meetings there, Lynde, John Tweedy, Francis Huebschmann, and others called for a new city charter to correct fiscal mismanagement, reduce the city debt, and achieve budget and tax reform.[16]

Success for the reform charter came two years later after a long political struggle. Lynde's prominence in the crusade drew a good deal of public attention. He was nominated by the Democratic party in 1859 to succeed Abram D. Smith as Supreme Court justice. However, the four-year-old Republican party was gaining ground as a result of increased antislavery sentiment. It turned to thirty-two-year-old Byron Paine, the Milwaukee lawyer who had eloquently, albeit unsuccessfully, defended Sherman Booth when he was haled before Judge Andrew G. Miller in 1854, charged with violating the Fugitive Slave Law. Paine had quickly become a symbol of courage to the many in Wisconsin who hated the Fugitive Slave Law of 1850.

The campaign was not as bitter as earlier judicial races. In the political turmoil over the Booth case, the candidates' qualifications were largely overlooked. National issues carried more weight than Lynde's or Paine's stands on local matters like farm mortgages and the fate of the railroads. Voters made up their minds on questions the Wisconsin Supreme Court could do nothing about.

Most injurious to Lynde was the fact that he was a member of the Democratic party, which in 1859 was still equivocating on the issue of slavery in an attempt to keep its southern wing intact. Lynde was accused in many newspapers of being proslavery, disloyal to the North, and a defender of the hated Fugitive Slave Law. Democrats tiptoed around the issue of states rights and abolitionism until the outbreak of the war. As a Democrat loyal to his party, Lynde could express his personal hatred of slavery, but had to defend the national party's cautious position. Foremost among Lynde's outspoken antislavery critics were Rufus King, editor of the *Sentinel;* Horace

Rublee, a leading Republican and editor of the *Wisconsin State Journal;* and Sherman Booth himself. One rising young Republican, the German immigrant Carl Schurz, also entered the campaign on Paine's behalf.

As the April 5 election day approached, Democratic papers cited Byron Paine's youth and legal inexperience as handicaps to his fitness for the high court. His brief term as Milwaukee county judge, they argued, did not compensate for his limited experience in practicing law. As much as Lynde tried in private and in public to shake the label of being proslavery, his allegiance to the Democratic party cost him the election. But in light of the strength of the Republican party and the power of the emotional currents at work, Paine's margin of only 2,145 votes was surprisingly small.[17]

Following Lynde's defeat, the Waukesha *Democrat* called the victorious Republicans "radical abolitionists" who would rip the country apart rather than work for a peaceful solution to the slavery question. Troubled by these charges, many Republicans denied that they advocated the immediate abolition of slavery. Wisconsin voters turned back every Democratic candidate in 1859, placing the state in the vanguard of the movement that elected Lincoln the following year. Emotions on the side of both the North and the South were already so raw that John Brown's invasion of the South to free slaves by armed force merely foreshadowed the greater violence to come.[18]

By the fall of 1860 Lynde's party had split in two and no unified national Democratic party existed to work for further sectional compromise. Lynde and other Northern Democrats were thus free to oppose slavery actively. As an ex-Whig and, after 1854, a stout Republican, Asahel Finch supported Byron Paine in 1859. However, as Lynde's friend and law partner, Finch took no public stand in the judicial race. Their seventeen-year-old friendship and partnership had weathered far more bitter political struggles. Finch was also prominent among the Milwaukee leaders who rallied behind Abraham Lincoln when he campaigned in Wisconsin in 1860.

Following his unsuccessful judicial campaign, Lynde was honored in May 1859 by the newly organized Milwaukee Bar Association and elected as its first vice president. An informal group that called itself the Milwaukee Bar had been in existence since 1841, but many attorneys in the city now believed a more structured professional association was needed. The Milwaukee Bar Association's Law Institute was officially established with a capital stock of $10,000 on October 28, 1858. Finches, Lynde & Miller and the city's other substantial law firm, Butler, Buttrick & Cottrill, each subscribed $2,000 for eighty shares of stock. Charter members included Judge McArthur, Judge Miller, and twenty-eight other lawyers. The Milwaukee Bar Association's goals included improving professional standards, establishing a law library and law institute, and writing court and disbarment rules.

It also wrote a fee schedule for its members. Among the 1858 fees were $40 to litigate a claim of more than $1,000, $40 to foreclose a mortgage of more than $1,000 dollars, and $75 to argue a case in the Supreme Court. Contingency fees for collection cases ranged from ten percent on amounts under $300 to two and one-half percent on amounts over $1,000. "Procuring a petition for divorce" cost $50 and, like the fees for criminal matters, was to be "paid or secured in advance." [19] At about the same time Milwaukee's median household was worth $2,376 in real and personal property. The average annual income for a carpenter in 1860 was $320. Day laborers averaged $150 to $250.[20]

In 1860 Lynde ran as a Democrat for mayor of Milwaukee. Since reform Democrats had gained acceptance, the new city charter drafted by his Albany Hall movement was no longer seen as a threat. Although the Albany Hall movement had disbanded, Lynde's nomination amounted to an endorsement of the reform program. Lynde had worked within the party to thwart Milwaukee's Democratic boss, Jackson Hadley. Hadley became Lynde's most active enemy. He had denied him the mayoral nomination in 1858 and refused to help him in the close Supreme Court race in 1859, but Hadley's influence had waned by 1860 when Lynde was nominated for mayor. Later the firm represented several clients in suits against Hadley, who had fallen upon hard times. Lynde did not involve himself personally in the litigation, but assigned the Hadley matters to Matt Finch, who pursued them successfully.[21]

The Republican candidate was Otis H. Waldo, an attorney who had come to Milwaukee from New York after studying and practicing law for several years in Mississippi. In an effort to court the German vote, the Republicans nominated John H. Tesch for city treasurer. He was their only successful candidate that year. Lynde and other reform Democrats won, but their victory was narrower than Democrats usually enjoyed. The Republican party was successful in converting many Germans to its fold and in gaining momentum for the presidential candidacy of Abraham Lincoln in the fall.

Lynde was sworn in as mayor on April 11 in the gallery of the old Market House, recently converted to city hall. He reminded the crowd that the city was close to financial ruin, and pledged to salvage its failing credit. "We shall find it no light task successfully to administer the public affairs entrusted to us," he warned.[22] During their year in office, Lynde and the Republican treasurer John Tesch worked together to reduce the city debt and became good friends in the process. Tesch later turned to the firm to handle several matters involving land investments and collections. Lynde surprised Democrats and Republicans alike by vetoing many spending measures, including a new market house in the city's Irish Third Ward, a Democratic stronghold. Lynde also forced a reduction in all city salaries and temporarily shut down the high schools, which many considered a luxury in the years before passage in 1875 of Wisconsin's mandatory public-high-school law. He trimmed the fire department and held off on further improvements to the harbor.

Cutting the fire department budget was risky. There were two major fires during Lynde's year in office, one of them in a warehouse that contained all of the city's records. Matt Finch's home was destroyed by fire in February 1861, during Lynde's last months in office. On one occasion, Lynde personally guaranteed payment for a new fire engine. He could afford it: according to the federal census of 1860 (the first to publish citizens' net worths), Lynde's net worth of $200,000 made him one of Milwaukee's wealthiest men. Several clients of the firm were wealthier. Alexander Mitchell was listed at $700,000, Elisha Eldred at $600,000, James H. Rogers at $500,000, and Byron Kilbourn and Daniel Newhall at $300,000 each.[23]

Lynde enjoyed the prestige that accompanied the office of mayor. In September 1860 he and Mary attended a gala social week in Montreal as part of the state visit of the Prince of Wales. While Lynde was in Montreal, Milwaukee was rocked by news of the worst shipping tragedy in its history. On September 8, the *Lady Elgin* sank while returning to Milwaukee from Chicago filled with many Irish citizens and members of the city's military companies. The 400 merrymakers were thrown into panic when a heavily laden lumber schooner crashed into the excursion vessel. About 300 lives were lost. Lynde returned home to make an appeal in behalf of the victims' families. He could identify with the tragedy, for his own two brothers had been killed in the wreck of the steamer *Erie* twenty years earlier.[24]

In the fall of 1860 and early 1861, the city and the country watched national developments with great concern. Lincoln's victory was tinged with feelings of anxiety and trepidation. The nation waited out the waning months of the Buchanan administration during the winter of 1860–1861 and wondered if war would come.

⚹ 6 ⚹

Milwaukee and the War Years
1861–1865

Abraham Lincoln's victory in November 1860 brought to the White House the country's first president from a purely sectional party. Wisconsin had proved itself soundly in the antislavery camp when it elected Byron Paine to the Supreme Court in 1859, and it went for Lincoln in 1860. But not even Lincoln could win Milwaukee, the continuing Democratic stronghold.

The Civil War began in April 1861 with the attack on Fort Sumter. The four-year conflict helped to unify and strengthen the northern industrial economy. In Wisconsin, reorganized railroads, banks, wheat suppliers, and a growing number of new industries supported the war effort and benefited from the new national markets. The wartime turmoil and the industrial and corporate expansion that accompanied it brought great change to Wisconsin's economy and to the country as a whole. To transport men and war materials, the North invested heavily in a national rail system, part of it connecting Milwaukee's railroads to the Pacific Ocean. The war stimulated an unprecedented growth in technology and invention, as well as a more formal organization of banking and currency and the development of the New York stock market. It was ironic that the nation that was being torn asunder was coming of age economically.

By the close of the war, Finches, Lynde & Miller had emerged as the most active business law firm in Milwaukee. The risks and difficulties of carrying on certain kinds of litigation during a civil war were exemplified by the firm's problems in managing two suits for a client trying to collect $10,000 from a family in South Carolina. The Wisconsin circuit court granted favorable judgments, but they were returned "unsatisfied" each time they were sent out. The client gave up in 1865 on the "advice of plaintiff's counsel." Similarly, Lynde himself tried to collect a substantial note due him from a resident of North Carolina. When the debtor could not be located even after the South's surrender in April 1865, the court concluded that he was "possibly a casualty of the war," and the suit was dropped.

Lynde served three wartime terms as president of the Milwaukee Bar Association, in 1861, 1863, and 1865. The Bar Association flourished and its law library grew under the care of a volunteer librarian. Additional books and journals were donated, and money was collected to purchase others. As the collection expanded, more library space was needed. The leadership decided in November 1861 to establish permanent quarters in the Albany Building. A door was to be cut between the two adjacent offices, numbers 5 and 7, behind the suite occupied by Finches, Lynde & Miller at numbers 6 and 8.[1]

But by January 1862 the firm had become increasingly cramped in its Albany Building two-room suite. As the Bar Association moved into the Albany Building, the firm moved to larger quarters in the new Excelsior Building, on the southeast corner of Wisconsin and Water streets, across from where their offices had been twenty years earlier. Nicknamed the "Iron Block," James Martin's new building was the first cast-iron structure in town, a landmark that remains 130 years later. Architects and engineers from around the country came to study its construction, particularly the inverted arches that supported its tremendous weight in marshy soil.[2]

Unfortunately for both the bar and the attorneys who had offices there, the Albany Building was destroyed by fire early in the morning of March 1, 1862. With most of their books and records already moved, Finches, Lynde & Miller suffered only the loss of the volumes they had loaned to the Bar Association. At an emergency meeting, the association decided to follow Finches, Lynde & Miller to the

Iron Block building and to rebuild the collection lost in the fire. The firm and the Bar Association were to be neighbors once again.[3]

Throughout the war Milwaukee and Wisconsin enjoyed a return to prosperity as profits from wheat and manufactured goods soared. Good times brought a renewed emphasis on culture and leisure activities. In 1860 Rufus King helped organize Milwaukee's first baseball team, the Cream City Club. These first Milwaukee Brewers won the state championship in 1868, defeating rivals such as the Cincinnati Red Stockings. (The Milwaukee club joined the National League in 1878.) The beer industry grew and prospered. Two hundred saloons were doing business in town, and breweries were exploring ways of shipping beer to distant markets.[4]

By December 1860 the population of Milwaukee had reached 45,246. There was a rich ethnic mixture, and an estimated 80 percent of the people were foreign-born. The city supported four English-language and five German-language newspapers. Other ethnic groups began to establish their identity as well. In 1863, St. Stanislaus opened as the first Polish Catholic church in the city. Catholics also obtained a charter that year for Marquette University. Classes did not begin until 1881, when the first building was completed on the plat known as "Finch's addition," on present Wisconsin Avenue and Thirteenth Street.[5]

Shortly after Lynde's term as mayor ended in April 1861, the firm took on a series of cases against a failed German merchant, Isadore Hochstadter. On one day, April 22, Matt Finch and B. K. Miller filed twenty-six separate claims in Milwaukee circuit court against him. Although twenty-six separate judgments for collection were handed down by the court two weeks later, they were returned unsatisfied, due to bankruptcy. According to the revised bar rules, the firm charged the standard fee of $12 for filing each of these cases. One of the claimants was the firm's former partner and nemesis, Levi Hubbell, who was similarly unsuccessful in collecting money even after winning a judgment.

In May 1861 Edward P. Allis established a company that produced pumps, piping, and sawmill equipment and later rose to pre-eminence in the machinery business as Allis-Chalmers. The city's leading hardware merchant, and a client of the firm, John Nazro, organized the Milwaukee Merchants' Association in 1861, and in 1863 the Milwaukee Chamber of Commerce moved to new headquarters in Mitchell's building on the site of the old Albany.

The war was joined in earnest with the bloody Confederate victory at Bull Run on July 21, 1861. As war orders began to pour into Milwaukee, commodity agents prospered with products such as wheat, pork, shoes, and clothing. The abundance of wealth in foodstuffs, machinery, and other war materials proved to be the North's major advantage as the war dragged on beyond the hoped-for "quick and glorious victory." Wisconsin's wheat crop, the nation's largest, was a vital part of this decisive supply, and Milwaukee's orderly shipment of grain was of prime importance to the state's economy. By 1862, trade in wheat and flour made the city the largest primary wheat market in the world. Wheat sold for an incredible $2.26 per bushel in 1864, up from 70 cents in 1861.[6]

The wholesale market for wheat shipment and storage inevitably required competent legal counsel. Finches, Lynde & Miller handled a number of cases dealing with the fairness of railroad shipping rates and elevator storage coupons. Daniel Newhall, the Midwest's largest grain wholesaler, asked the firm to handle litigation involving cash and credit sales of wheat and promissory notes for shipment to agents for the federal government in New York. Involved in these cases were thousands of bushels of wheat shipped to Buffalo by lake steamer. Twice Newhall succeeded in collecting the "fair and promised price" from New York agents who had suddenly tried to lower the price, which would have caused Newhall to default on his own warehouse debts in Milwaukee.[7]

Shipping by water led to litigation as well. Lynde was unsuccessful in one case in which Judge Miller held a shipowner blameless, even though the vessel ran aground and water leakage ruined an entire load of sugar in the hold. In another case, the owner was held liable because negligence caused a loading pipe to disconnect from the ship and pour 700 bushels of wheat into the Milwaukee River. Wartime commerce brought many maritime matters to the firm. Even during his term as mayor, Lynde appeared in federal district court several times for clients on admiralty matters.

With the enormous profits to be made by selling foodstuffs to the army, many commodity brokers began the practice of selling on margin at greater risk for greater returns. In 1862 Finches, Lynde & Miller represented one such broker whose margin contracts for 15,000 bushels of wheat and 300 barrels of lard were sold to an agent for the army, but at far less than the contracted price. The case was settled in June, forcing fair payment for the wheat and lard that went to feed the Union army.[8]

As the prosperity of the city grew during the war years, work in behalf of Milwaukee's burgeoning industrial base brought increasing pressures on the firm of Finches, Lynde & Miller. At first the war was sufficiently popular for Lincoln to fill up an army with volunteers. But as the conflict dragged on, Congress had to enact the nation's first draft law in November 1862. None of the firm's four partners served in the Union army. At fifty-two and forty-four, Asahel Finch and Lynde were beyond draft age. Thirty-three-year-old Matt Finch and thirty-two-year-old B. K. Miller no doubt purchased substitutes for the going rate of $300. The custom of "buying out" became more common in Milwaukee as the war grew less popular. The usually reticent Matt Finch supported the Union cause by speaking at several wartime Republican rallies. He urged voters to remain loyal to Lincoln and not to despair of a Union victory.[9]

Draft riots occurred in several Wisconsin cities in 1863. The worst was in Port Washington, where many of the city's Germans could not afford to buy out but spurned the hated enlistment quotas. Many of them had emigrated from Europe to escape conscription. Lynde and Finch, like many men of wealth, both loaned and gave money to families to prevent a father or a brother from being drafted. Lynde served on a citizens committee that met with the governor to protest the fact that the draft fell "most heavily upon our poor citizens who have large families to support." The committee urged the city to raise funds to pay these poor enlistees a $200 bounty and thereby reduce the hardship upon their families. However, Lynde and the others deplored resistance to the draft: "The Government cannot and will not yield to resistance. . . . The only way is to fill our quota."[10]

As a "War Democrat," Lynde supported Lincoln and the war effort. But Milwaukee's Democrats carried the city in 1864 for Lincoln's opponent, General George B. McClellan. Lincoln received less support in Milwaukee in 1864 than he had four years earlier.

In September Lincoln and his able general, William Tecumseh Sherman, announced the surrender of Atlanta, a key Confederate rail center. The victory boosted Lincoln's election chances in November. Just as the South was hampered by its inferior rail system, the North used its railroads to great advantage throughout the war. Nevertheless, many Northerners, including Wisconsin's citizens, continued to oppose the power of the major railroad companies.

Meanwhile the firm continued to handle many railroad cases. Lawyers who represented the railroads in court against farmers faced public animosity that was sometimes life-threatening. One Milwaukee lawyer who was bold enough to go to Prairie du Chien in 1861 to foreclose and collect on thirty farm mortgages found his trip to be both dangerous and futile.[11]

As directors, legal counsel, and stockholders of the Milwaukee and Mississippi Railroad, Finch and Lynde were in the middle of many disputes. They advised the company to seek a settlement of the stock claims through means other than litigation. Efforts to increase the railroad's viability as a profitable enterprise and a sound investment proved to be a better strategy in the long run than simply pursuing foreclosures.

Finch and Lynde also remained actively interested in the financial welfare of the railroad and continued to serve as attorneys on a number of cases. Political considerations may have been important in the firm's reluctance to oppose the farmers. In the early 1860s, while the battle over railroad debts remained snarled in the state courts, few Wisconsin candidates who opposed the farmers' claims were elected to office. Henry Lewis Palmer, who was a friend and onetime assistant to Lynde, became the Democratic candidate for governor in 1863 and faced defeat and bitter repudiation by the farm mortgage lobby. Many men involved in railroad management or ownership kept a low profile.

Most of the firm's clients were white businessmen. But the firm did occasionally represent a woman after an 1857 Wisconsin statute granted married women the right to own and dispose of property in their own names. One client was a woman who was sued by creditors after her clothing store failed.[12] The gradual entry of women into the business world reflected both their changed legal status and the economic necessities of the Civil War.

In two other cases, the firm persuaded the Wisconsin Supreme Court that individual members of Indian tribes had the right to convey land that had been granted by Congress in 1843. Justice Jason Downer noted in language typical of the day that the federal act "was based on the idea that the Stockbridge Indians would drop the customs of savages and assume those of civilized men." Both judgments quieted the title of white land speculators who had bought land from individual members of the Indian tribe.[13] The firm's involvement with Indian affairs dated back to Lynde's term as territorial attorney general, when he enforced rules protecting the northern tribes from encroachments by land-hungry whites.

Judge Miller's clarity of reasoning and cogent prose style were far superior to the written decisions of most of Wisconsin's jurists in this era, even the justices of the state Supreme Court. Although Miller was later accused of favoritism toward his son's firm, his record appears to have been even-handed. In fact, Finches, Lynde & Miller won 80 percent of their appeals to the Wisconsin Supreme Court in the years between 1857 and 1865, but succeeded in a far lower percentage of cases in the federal district court before Judge Miller.

In 1863 Lynde's success before the Supreme Court in these cases and in commercial matters led to the mention of his name once again to fill a vacancy on the bench. However, he chose not to pursue the nomination, preferring instead to concentrate upon the growing business of the firm. Before the end of the war he accepted an appointment to serve as chairman of the Commission of Public Debt for Milwaukee. There he oversaw completion of the task he had begun as mayor to solve the city's budget woes.[14]

More active as a business adviser than Lynde, Asahel Finch argued less often before the Supreme Court. For Finch the war was a national tragedy that echoed several catastrophes that befell him personally. Having lost his first wife in 1855 and his father in 1858, he married again in 1860. His second wife was Mathilda Douglas, also a native New Yorker, and twenty-six years his junior. Within the next four years, the couple lost two children in infancy, and Finch also lost one of his two grown daughters, Delia, age twenty-seven. A month after their second baby died in July 1864, Mathilda Douglas Finch herself died of the complications of childbirth.[15]

Milwaukee County contributed more than 17,000 men to the Union forces, including the heroes who fought under Brigadier General Rufus King in the "Iron Brigade," famous for suffering a higher percentage of casualties in combat than any other in the Union army. Most regiments trained at Fort Scott, on the fairgrounds near the city limits, before heading east to join the Army of the Potomac, or south to fight with Ulysses S. Grant. Wisconsin lost 3,600 men in battle, and twice that number from disease and festering wounds.[16]

A former assistant in the law office of Finch & Lynde, John Starkweather, commanded the Milwaukee Light Guards in the battle of Chickamauga and was promoted before the war's end to the rank of brigadier general. Captain Gabriel Bouck, also a former associate in the firm, entered the war as a captain of the Second Regiment of Wisconsin Volunteers in 1861, and fought at Shiloh in April 1862. Arthur McArthur, Jr., son of the circuit judge, joined a regiment at the age of eighteen and became a hero in 1864 in the battle of Missionary Ridge in Tennessee. "The Boy Colonel" was awarded a Congressional Medal of Honor.

Conditions in field hospitals were so deplorable that even the U.S. Sanitary Commission, forerunner of the Red Cross, could do little to fight the infections and diseases that killed many wounded men. To help stem this loss of life, Milwaukeeans founded the first soldiers' hospitals behind the front. They raised $110,000 to finance this branch of the National Soldiers' Home, today part of the Veterans Administration Center on Milwaukee's near west side. Lynde, B. K. Miller, and both Finches took a leading role in founding the soldiers' home. B. K. Miller's brother, Andrew, Jr., died there of his war wounds in October 1865. The city also founded Milwaukee Passavant Hospital (later the Milwaukee County Medical Complex) on the grounds of the old Finch estate west of the city on Watertown Plank Road.[17]

Young Andrew Miller was the only war casualty among the firm's families. Lynde's three sons were too young to serve, and B. K. Miller's two sons (later partners in the firm) were less than ten years old. Matt Finch had no sons, and Asahel's only surviving daughter had no surviving children.[18]

When the news of Lee's surrender reached Milwaukee on April 10, 1865, "the city was one vast 'lunacy of joy.'" As the newspapers described it, "all the Fourths of July rolled into one were not a comparison. With business suspended, processions filled the streets, and more than one effigy of Jefferson Davis hung from a 'sour apple tree.'" New horsecars were draped in banners, and the rumor circulated that the mayor "had issued a proclamation compelling every citizen to become drunk before three o'clock." Five days later, the banners were exchanged for black crepe, and the city went into mourning with the news of President Lincoln's assassination. Asahel Finch was one of the leading Republicans who headed the parade of mourners down Wisconsin Street on April 19, the day of the martyred president's funeral.[19]

1. *Asahel Finch*

2. *William Pitt Lynde*

3. *The Post Office, foreground, was built on the northwest corner of Wisconsin Avenue and Milwaukee Street in 1856. The firm's offices were in the building to the left of the post office from 1847 to 1857.*

FINCH & LYNDE,

ATTORNEYS AND COUNSELLORS AT LAW,

AND

SOLICITORS IN CHANCERY,

Will attend to Collections in any part of the Territory,

A. FINCH, JR.]　　MILWAUKEE.　　[WM. P. LYNDE.

L*

4. *Announcement in Milwaukee City Directory, 1846–1847*

5. *Judge Andrew Galbraith Miller was appointed by President Polk as Wisconsin's first territorial judge in 1839. His son, Benjamin K. Miller, joined Finch & Lynde in 1857.*

6. *Milwaukee's first courthouse, on what is now Cathedral Square, 1836*

7. *Solomon Juneau,
founder and first mayor of
Milwaukee and an early
client of Finch & Lynde*

8. *Levi Hubbell, partner
in Hubbell, Finch & Lynde,
1844–1845*

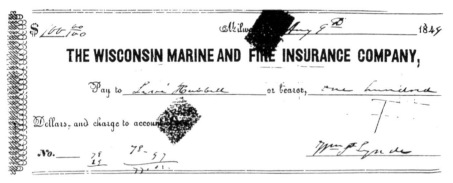

9. *Check, from William Pitt Lynde to Levi Hubbell, 1844, drawn on the Wisconsin
Marine and Fire Insurance Company; although officially chartered only as an
insurance company, the Marine actually functioned as a bank when banking was
prohibited in Wisconsin.*

10. Benjamin Kurtz Miller, Sr.   *11. Henry Matt Finch*

12. The Albany Building, on the southwest corner of Michigan Street and Broadway, was the location of Finches, Lynde & Miller offices from 1857 to 1862.

13. Milwaukee Bar Association Fee Schedule in 1858, when William Pitt Lynde was its president

Procuring a petition for divorce, to be paid or secured in advance..$ 50
Retaining fee in all litigated suits............................. 20
Retaining fee in United States District Court................... 25
Collections, 10 per cent on $300 or under; 5 per cent on excess
    to $1,000; 2½ per cent on excess over $1,000.
Litigated cases for sums over $1,000.......................... 40
Litigated cases in tort when settled before trial................. 25
Litigated cases in tort when tried............................. 50
Argument for new trial...................................... 10
Services of counsel in litigated cases, per day.................. 10
Foreclosure of mortgages over $1,000......................... 50
Arguing case in supreme court................................ 75
Litigated cases before justices................................ 10
Drawing petition for mechanic's lien.......................... 10
Drawing assignment for benefit of creditors................... 30
Supplemental proceedings 10

    Fees in criminal cases (to be paid or secured in advance):

Managing case in police court................................. 10
Habeas corpus cases... 25
Defense in misdemeanor...................................... 25
Defense in felony.. 50
Defense in manslaughter or murder........................... 100

14. The firm moved its offices in 1862 to James Martin's Excelsior Block or Iron Block Building on the southeast corner of Water and Wisconsin Streets.

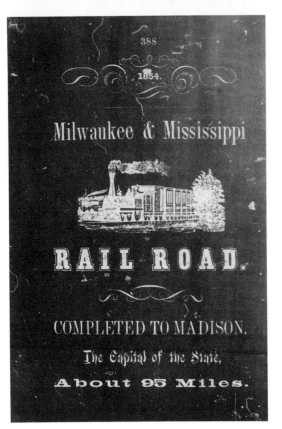

15. *Asahel Finch, attorney for the Milwaukee & Mississippi Railroad, participated in ceremonies celebrating the completion of its tracks to Madison in 1854.*

16. *Alexander Mitchell, Milwaukee's first successful banker and an early client of Finch & Lynde*

17. Milwaukee City Hall, 1860

18. Mitchell's new bank building and Chamber of Commerce was built on the site of the old Albany Building on Michigan Avenue.

⋘ 7 ⋙

Practicing Law in the Gilded Age
1866–1873

As the black crepe of mourning was folded at the end of April, 1865 the city of Milwaukee and the North as a whole looked forward to the fruits of their Civil War victory. The years after 1865 brought unprecedented growth to American business. In Mark Twain's sardonic phrase, it was a "Gilded Age."

Milwaukee emerged from the Civil War a thriving and prosperous city. The volume of wheat that flowed through Milwaukee's railroad terminal, grain elevators, and harbor during the war had brought with it an entirely new level of national and international enterprise and an air of sophistication as well. The 1860 census had listed 558 companies operating in the city. Most were small, with only five employees or so. By the end of the decade, the number of companies in the city had grown to 828, and the number of wage earners increased from 3,406 to 8,433. Many of these businesses grew to become major corporations, and soon more specialized legal services were needed to guide them through the maze of corporate details and challenges that characterized the post-Civil War era.[1]

The war had settled the issue of states' rights, and the power of the federal government had increased accordingly. The war also had brought promises of reform in race relations—promises that went largely unfulfilled, except for the ending of slavery itself.

The postwar years brought one small victory for Wisconsin's few black men. Byron Paine, who had resigned from the Supreme Court in July 1864 to enter the Union army, represented a black Milwaukee citizen, Ezekiel Gillespie, in an 1866 suit to win for black males the right to vote in all state and federal elections. Wisconsin voters had approved black suffrage by a vote of 5,265 to 4,075 in 1849, but because the favorable votes made up less than a majority of those who voted for state officers in that election, the board of canvassers had declared the suffrage proposition defeated. In *Gillespie v. Palmer* a unanimous court reversed the canvassers' seventeen-year-old decision, holding that only a majority of those who voted on the particular subject was needed to approve black male suffrage. Justice Downer wrote that any other statutory construction would be "forced and unnatural." Four years later, the Fifteenth Amendment to the United States Constitution mandated nationwide black suffrage.[2]

The Gilded Age was more apparent in the cityscape and workplace. Soon gaslights graced Milwaukee's streets. At the war's end, Milwaukee was beginning to enjoy better urban transportation, in the form of the River and Lakeshore Railway, the first horsecar line serving the downtown area. Its successor, the electric railway, later became the city's first electric utility company. By 1880 the typewriter and the telephone brought new tools to the fast-changing world of business. The days of mud streets, wandering pigs, and quarrels over the theft of land or horses had come to an end. There was a new economy now, in the city, the state, and the nation.

By 1866 the bluff at the east end of Wisconsin Street, where the old lighthouse had stood, was gone. The earth had been moved inland and used to fill marshy areas of the growing city. In 1868 Milwaukee established its first Board of Public Works to improve dock facilities, sidewalks, streets, and bridges. Its consideration of a sewerage system was long overdue. (As one commentator put it: "The city literally stinks!"[3]) New technology made possible a system of fire-alarm boxes on street corners. The state legislature authorized a city board of health to oversee conditions in the slaughterhouses and monitor the spread of disease. One year later the board closed Milwaukee schools for a time to stem a smallpox epidemic.[4]

Along with urban growth came problems of poverty and homelessness. Mary Lynde's campaign for recognition of the special problems of poor children succeeded in 1866, when the county established the Home of the Friendless to shelter orphans, a number of whom had lost their parents in the *Lady Elgin* disaster. A temporary Milwaukee children's shelter was established. Responding to pressures generated by Mary Lynde and other volunteers, the 1875 legislature forbade placing five- to sixteen-year-olds in county or city poorhouses. The county also built a new house of correction to handle yet another group of urban casualties: the long-term incarcerated.[5] Along with other prominent women in the community, Mary Lynde served on many of the boards of nonprofit agencies that established and supported asylums and orphan homes. Both of the Lyndes worked as volunteers to improve the lot of poor children, the indigent, and the mentally ill. The mental problems exhibited by two of their three sons may have been a compelling reason for their continuing involvement in these causes.[6]

New buildings were needed to care for the hundreds of wounded Civil War veterans. The National Home for Disabled Volunteer Soldiers was one of only three in the nation. Located on the city's west side, the soldiers' home was designed by Milwaukee architect Edward Townsend Mix and completed in 1867.[7]

Under Lynde's leadership in the year after the war the Public Debt Commission succeeded in retiring $890,000 of Milwaukee's railroad debt. The commission ushered in a new reform era in city government, patterned on many of the demands of Lynde's Albany Hall movement eight years earlier. The city created a Board of Street Commissioners to supervise streets, gutters, sewers, and sanitation. In 1867 the city charter was revised to separate the city from Milwaukee County, end the machine control of the ward bosses, and reduce graft by relying on appointed boards rather than the elected commissions, which had proved corrupt.[8]

Milwaukee remained strongly Democratic even in the Republican years after the war. In November 1865 Lynde won a seat in the state assembly with little opposition. In the legislature Lynde sponsored the incorporation of the Milwaukee Building Company in 1870. His partner, B. K. Miller, was one of its five directors. Lynde introduced a bill to allow the Milwaukee Gas Light Company, of which Asahel Finch was a director and president-elect, to issue $800,000 in capital stock. Finch's subsequent presidency of the gas company and his purchase of many shares of its stock composed the foundation of his fortune in the 1870s. It exceeded the value of his share in the law partnership.

As a legislator, Lynde placed the support of social-service institutions and the furthering of education at the top of his list of priorities. He continued the campaign for better legal education that he had favored since the beginning of the Milwaukee Bar Association in the late 1850s. He also proposed a measure to correct existing deficiencies in the law department of the state legislative library and sponsored a bill to authorize the librarian to purchase law books at not more than $1.50 each. In a further effort to bring credibility to the Wisconsin legal system, Lynde asked that all decisions of the Wisconsin Supreme Court be indexed and that a copy be sent to the library of the United States Supreme Court. He also asked that the state library contract for a new index to Wisconsin statutes, a measure that passed in March 1870.[9]

The decade after the war brought many changes to the firm. Asahel Finch began to involve himself less in its daily work as he became more active as a leader in the Milwaukee business community, where he served with distinction as corporate director and legal counselor. Lynde continued to work on cases in the federal district court and before the Wisconsin and United States Supreme Courts. He, too, was away from the office a good deal between 1865 and 1879, serving terms in the Wisconsin Assembly and Senate and in the U.S. Congress.

The law firm's practice reflected the state's changing economic and social climate. Wisconsin retained its position of leadership in wheat and flour production for less than a decade. Wisconsin farmers had to turn to other crops by the mid-1870s, when a national railroad network linked eastern markets to Nebraska and the Dakotas.

Lumber and timber products led all other Wisconsin manufactured goods in value for many decades. The firm found itself on both sides of cases involving lumber companies. In a significant case argued before the Wisconsin Supreme Court in 1869, Finches, Lynde & Miller argued successfully that the sale of lumber in rafts that could not readily be inspected included the implied warranty of merchantability. The court relied on a legal principle described by Justice Story, Lynde's law professor at Harvard, who wrote in his treatise *On Contracts* about the implied warranty that accompanies sales of goods at sea.[10] In another case, the firm successfuly invoked the powerful fellow-servant rule to defend a lumber company whose employee had been injured.[11] Defending the Dunn County treasurer against millionaire lumberman Andrew Tainter in a third case, the firm won relief from an injunction that had barred the county from selling Tainter's land for unpaid property taxes.[12]

Wisconsin's railroads continued to bring immigrant settlers to the northern and western parts of the state. In 1867 the Wisconsin Board of Immigration published a pamphlet describing the state's economic attractions and emphasizing its cultural richness and progressive spirit. A convenient map detailing routes from the East Coast was included, along with information about the cheap Wisconsin land. Printed in English, German, Welsh, French, Norwegian, Dutch, and Swedish, it was designed to be mailed by Wisconsin citizens to friends and relatives back home. Foreign-born immigrants to Wisconsin in the 1870s and 1880s numbered in the hundreds of thousands. In 1890 first- and second-generation immigrants numbered 1.5 million, about two-thirds of the total population.[13]

Spurred by the growth of lumbering in the northern counties, many new railroad companies were established in the late 1860s and early 1870s. Most quickly folded or were merged into the state's two major lines, the Chicago and Northwestern and Alexander Mitchell's Milwaukee and St. Paul (later the Chicago, Milwaukee, and St. Paul, then the Milwaukee Road). Between 1868 and 1873 trackage in the state doubled from 1,030 miles to 2,379, reaching such northern outposts as Marinette, Stevens Point, and Hudson.[14]

In 1867, when the railroads (with Lynde on their side) failed to win state economic assistance, they turned to local units of government once again. Municipalities in southern Wisconsin were still struggling to meet their prewar obligations, but northern counties were ready to take the plunge. Even Ashland County, with a population of only 300, agreed to fund $200,000 in railroad bonds, undeterred by the fact that its total revenue was considerably smaller than the anticipated interest. The city of Milwaukee, only recently solvent once again, contributed $105,000 to the Milwaukee and Northern for its line to Green Bay and $100,000 to the Northwestern for its Fond du Lac line.[15]

Finches, Lynde & Miller unsuccessfully litigated several cases on behalf of parties who asked for injunctions to stop their municipalities from issuing bonds for railroad construction. The federal courts held that the Wisconsin Enabling Act of 1869 authorized city or county officials to issue bonds for railroad construction.[16] On the whole, city councils proceeded with far more caution in incurring municipal debt for railroad construction than had their pre-Civil War counterparts. As railroad profits soared, speculators from Wall Street entered the Wisconsin railroad game to manipulate the market in railroad securities. In 1866 New York investors won control of the old Milwaukee and Prairie du Chien Railway Company, founded by Byron Kilbourn and once boosted by the financial and legal support of both Finch and Lynde.

The power of the railroads remained a major concern for Wisconsin voters, who charged the railroads with fixing unpredictable, sometimes exorbitant, rates for both freight and passengers. As a legislator Lynde remained a friend to the railroads and introduced many measures in their behalf. But he was a reform Democrat and voted in 1866 for regulations that forbade duplicate billing. As agitation grew from farmers who felt gouged by railroad charges, the Grangers began to lobby for more stringent rate controls and better enforcement. In many agricultural areas farmers turned to state legislatures for relief from fraudulent double charges on shipments and exorbitant or unpublished rates. In 1874, after Lynde's term ended, the Wisconsin legislature enacted a far-reaching measure—the Potter Law—that established a schedule of maximum rates that were lower than actual 1873 railroad rates.[17]

In *Ackley v. Chicago, Milwaukee and St. Paul Railway Co.,* Finches, Lynde & Miller represented a client suing to recover two carloads of lumber that the railroad had detained to collect its $18 freight bill. The constitutionality of the railroad rate regulation had been generally upheld in earlier cases. Represented by its first in-house attorney, John Cary, the railroad contended that the regulation unconstitutionally required a receiving railroad in specified circumstances to deliver freight, even though it would receive no compensation from the originating railroad. The Supreme Court was unimpressed. Ruling that the defendant railroad could sue the originating railroad for its share of the freight bill, the court did not reach the constitutional question.[18]

The movement toward regulation came of age in 1887 with the passage of the federal Interstate Commerce Act, establishing the first federal regulatory commission. While not allowed to fix rates, the Interstate Commerce Commission was given the mandate to guard against railroad pools, insist on the posting of rates, and disallow discriminatory rate fixing.

As the most powerful railroad in the state, the Milwaukee and St. Paul required extensive legal services. Cary retained Finches, Lynde & Miller on most of the railroad's tort actions, though not on securities or financial matters. For part of this period Asahel Finch served on the board of directors of the Milwaukee and St. Paul. Both Finch and Lynde were major shareholders in the Milwaukee and Prairie du Chien, also their client.[19]

Throughout this era of railroad building and mergers, the firm also served as counsel to many smaller rail lines. As passenger and freight miles steadily increased, so inevitably did the incidence of loss and injury. State legislatures, including Wisconsin's, began by the 1860s to pass legislation increasing railroad liabilities. As a result of Wisconsin's law of 1860, which called for increased liability for the safety of passengers, many suits came to trial. The firm attempted to minimize the railroads' liability by arguing contributory negligence on the part of passengers. Asahel Finch himself was injured in 1871 in a rail accident between Waukesha and Milwaukee, though he did not bring suit.

In an 1866 case the Wisconsin Supreme Court ruled against the firm by giving a broad construction to a statute that had imposed strict liability on railroads for domestic animals killed by trains on unfenced tracks. Following a New York decision, the court held that the statute was *really* intended to protect humans. It affirmed the railroad's liability to a plaintiff whose leg had been permanently injured when a train on which she was a passanger hit a cow, but reversed the award of $8,000 on an evidence issue.[20]

Finches, Lynde & Miller also lost its appeal of the $1,000 awarded to a woman passenger who had broken her arm in jumping from a Milwaukee and Prairie du Chien Railroad car that had stopped too far from the depot platform. The railroad had relied on the woman's contributory negligence, but the court held a passenger was not negligent when she took a risk that the railroad had created.[21]

The national economy was becoming increasingly dependent on the telegraph, and the Western Union Company was a regular client of the firm. The form for the company's half-price overnight service stated that it was not responsible even for its own employees' negligence. Rejecting the firm's freedom-of-contract defense, the Wisconsin Supreme Court invalidated the form waiver on public policy grounds in 1873. But the court also applied the rule of *Hadley v. Baxendale,* holding that Western Union was liable only for the cost of the telegram, unless it should have foreseen greater damages from its failure to transmit a message. In another case handled by the firm nine years later the Supreme Court upheld the twenty-day time bar contained on the company's form.[22]

By 1871 Milwaukee had become the fourth largest slaughterhouse and meat-packing city in the country. The mainstay was pork, not the beef that was filling the stockyards of Kansas City, St. Louis, and Chicago. John Plankinton and Frederick Layton, who had begun as local butchers with a small retail meat market, operated one of the largest packinghouses in the country. After Layton left in late 1863 to set up his own company, Plankinton took in a new partner, Philip Armour, who developed the national marketing side of the business and specialized in orders of pork for the Union Army. To cater to the growing business in meat exports, the Milwaukee and St. Paul Railway Company established Milwaukee's Union Stock Yards in 1869.

During the war, even preserved and salted meat had occasionally arrived at Union army depots unfit for consumption. In 1871 Michael Cudahy, an employee of the Plankinton-Armour firm, introduced an ice-storage process that revolutionized the industry and enabled packers to ship across the country. Eventually, however, he began his own meat-packing company, and Armour moved to Chicago in 1875, also to launch his own company.[23]

Directly related to the growth of the meat-packing and meat-processing industry in Milwaukee was the development of tanneries. With hides and hemlock bark abundant, Milwaukee was the largest tanning center in the West by 1872. Guido Pfister began his leather business in 1847 and brought in his friend Fred Vogel. In 1858 Albert O. Trostel and A. F. Gallun opened the Blue Star Harness Company. Before the Civil War Milwaukee had nine tanneries, mostly German-owned, with sales of $218,000. By 1870, thirty tanneries produced $2.5 million worth of leather goods. Several were clients of Finches, Lynde & Miller.[24]

In managing cases before the Wisconsin Supreme Court that tested the legalities of markets that were increasingly regional or national, the firm worked with the central economic issues of the Gilded Age economy. It had changed from handling hundreds of cases for many diverse clients to serving as counsel for a few businesses on key questions of trade. No longer was it as active in collecting business and personal debts. Litigation began to decline as the mainstay of the practice. By the late 1860s only Matt Finch remained active in the Milwaukee circuit court.

By the middle of the 1870s Asahel Finch began to devote himself increasingly to serving as president of the Milwaukee Gas Company. Although active in the state and federal governments, Lynde involved himself only in important trials, appeals to the Wisconsin Supreme Court, and federal court matters. Matt Finch assumed the role of backup man, a partner who did supplementary research and handled the bulk of routine litigation. He also argued some cases in the state Supreme Court. B. K. Miller assisted Lynde on several key cases, but began to follow more directly in Asahel Finch's footsteps, withdrawing from the courtroom itself and serving as counselor to several corporations, including the gas company and, later, the telephone company. Asahel Finch's writing appears only infrequently on a few legal documents of this period. He no longer practiced in the Milwaukee circuit or federal district courts, but he remained a presence and a force in the firm's office until his final illness in 1883.[25]

The firm outgrew its offices in the Iron Block Building and moved in 1872 to the newly refurbished Library Building on the northeast corner of Wisconsin Street and Broadway, where the Milwaukee Public Library was also housed for a time. The suites in the Library Building provided sufficient space for more law clerks and for the firm's growing library. This building was later purchased by B. K. Miller, Sr., and became known as the Miller Building.[26]

The continuity provided by B. K. Miller during the 1870s was vital to the partnership. A contemporary described his special role:

Rarely in court, still more rarely personally engaged in the trial of a cause, Mr. Miller's energies . . . realized their most brilliant successes in the unraveling of tangled estates, in the solution of complicated questions concerning trusts, in the promotion of far reaching business interests, in rescuing tottering firms from their greedy creditors, in negotiating peace among quarreling kinsfolk, in all the varied diplomacy which would have made a large modern law office the delight of a Talleyrand or a Metternich.[27]

The development of B. K. Miller's role as a corporate attorney epitomizes the changes that were taking place in the practice of law in the closing decades of the century. As clients sought a different kind of legal assistance, they developed a distaste for litigation, regarding it as a costly luxury, and sought counsel on ways to avoid it.[28]

Besides serving as managing partner, Miller practiced in the area of estate planning and probate. As large fortunes were amassed, an orderly system for protecting and devising them became a major focus of the firm's practice. While Miller continued to advise clients in the office about probate matters, Matt Finch and Lynde argued many probate cases in the Wisconsin Supreme Court. For example, they were there three times between 1872 and 1875 in the *Meadows* cases. Each time the court held for the firm's client, ruling that a widow and her heirs had waited too long when she tried to challenge the five-year-old probate of her husband's will.[29]

Of all the trust and probate work that the firm undertook in this post-Civil War period, the biggest piece of litigation involved the estate of Cadwallader Washburn, handled by Lynde. Once the congressman from La Crosse, Washburn was governor of Wisconsin from 1872 to 1874. A good friend of Asahel Finch, Washburn was one of the Reform Republicans who opposed the corrupt political machine in the state, known as the Madison Regency. He also knew Lynde from their years together in Congress. His enormous estate was based on lumbering as well as on Minnesota flour mills, that used the revolutionary steel rollers developed by the Edward P. Allis Company of Milwaukee. Washburn's holdings became the nucleus of General Mills.

When the firm drafted his will in 1881, Washburn's wife had been insane, "without a lucid interval," for twenty years. He left her no bequest, but authorized unlimited sums for her care. After Washburn died in 1882, her guardian asked the probate court to renounce the will in the widow's behalf. If she had been competent to do it herself, she would have taken real estate worth as much as $700,000 instead of custodial care valued at $5,000 per year. The probate court in La Crosse ruled for the guardian and Finches, Lynde & Miller appealed on behalf of the executors. The Wisconsin Supreme Court held that the probate court had discretion to reject the will for the widow, but that it would best exercise its discretion by following Washburn's intentions. It directed the lower court to enter judgment accordingly.[30]

As trust and corporate work expanded, Finches, Lynde & Miller brought in additional assistants to help with the paperwork, to draft documents, and to do supplementary research. By 1879 a surviving letter from Asahel Finch described the staff: "We now have four clerks *under pay*," he wrote, emphasizing that he was not referring to the two apprentices who worked for the firm in return for legal training.[31] Finch was responding to Wisconsin Supreme Court Chief Justice Edward G. Ryan's request that Finches, Lynde & Miller take in his son as a new associate and get him away from the "evil climate" in Madison.[32] Finch declined, pleading his own age and the fact that the firm already had as many clerks as it could manage.

The clerks' $1,100 salary was a fairly substantial sum in the 1870s. A circuit-court judge received $4,000 then, the governor $5,000, and the lieutenant governor $1,000. The average wage in 1874 for a male schoolteacher was $47 per month. A common laborer earned 12 to 15 cents an hour.

The salary paid to a law clerk in the 1870s can also be compared with what we can infer about the income of the firm's four partners. The firm collected $5,000 to $15,000 retainers from a number of companies. While legal fees varied from state to state and from small town to large city, they were traditionally established according to bar guidelines or by agreement with the client. An article in the *Albany Law Journal* in 1872 estimated that leading lawyers in the nation's big cities earned $36,000 to $100,000 annually. The average for a prosperous sole practitioner was estimated at $3,000 to $10,000.[33]

In addition to partnership income, numerous investment opportunities were available to attorneys. Finch owned many shares in the gas company, as well as in various railroads. Lynde had heavily invested in Milwaukee land in the 1840s and sold lots profitably as late as the 1870s. He also invested in street railway companies, the railroads, and various lumber and utility stocks. Matt Finch and B. K. Miller, too, had sizable investments in the telephone and electric companies as well as in many other corporate ventures. In 1874 B. K. Miller purchased a large number of town lots in Grand Rapids, Wisconsin, after foreclosing on them for the firm's clients.[34]

Even after the University of Wisconsin Law School opened in 1868, it was customary for the son of a lawyer to seek a clerkship in his father's office or in that of a family friend. In the office of Finches, Lynde & Miller, three sons of partners became clerks. Two of them, Benjamin Kurtz Miller, Jr., and George Miller, later became full partners. The third, William Pitt Lynde, Jr., was admitted to the bar in 1877 after a stormy and unstable early life. He had run afoul of the law several times. As a recent graduate of the scientific program at Yale, his father's alma mater, "Will" hoped to follow in his father's footsteps with a career in law. Although the cause of his growing mental problems is unclear, his tenure as a clerk at Finches, Lynde & Miller ended with the death of his father in 1885. He then tried to pursue various business interests, but illness and what the nineteenth century labeled an "unsound mind" confined him to his home. He received a small maintenance allowance of $150 a month from his father's estate and died less than two years later at the age of thirty-four.[35]

Although he was less active in the courtroom after the Civil War, Asahel Finch continued to pursue political aspirations for almost a decade. In 1867, he became the leader of Milwaukee's Greenback Club, a splinter of the national movement that wanted federal paper money to be solidly backed by gold and silver. In the same year Finch ran again for mayor of Milwaukee, only to be defeated easily by Democrat Edward O'Neill, who ran on what the *Sentinel* labeled "the Corruption-Copperhead-Shillelagh-Kneeland" ticket. Finch's last campaign for mayor came three years later in 1870, when he once again agreed to carry the Republican banner under the new title of reform, the People's party. But Finch was not beloved among Milwaukee's Irish, and he was defeated once again.

Democrats were successful in the municipal campaign of 1870, but it was the last election in which the party's dominance was undisputed. Ironically, one reason for Finch's defeat was the fact that

Lynde's Commission on the Public Debt had succeeded so well by 1869 that the outgoing Democratic mayor could boast that "not a city in the U.S. could show so encouraging a financial exhibit." In the fall, following Finch's narrow mayoral defeat, a petition was circulated in favor of his appointment to succeed Andrew G. Miller as federal judge. However, Miller's decision to stay on the bench for another two years and Finch's railroad injury temporarily ended his campaign for the bench.[36]

By the fall of 1872 a fully recovered Finch became one of the Republican sponsors of Ulysses S. Grant's reelection campaign by donating one hundred uniforms to the party's guard that marched in the election parades. That same November he became the Republican candidate for State Assembly from the Third Ward. Defeated once more, Finch never again sought public office. However, he remained active in Wisconsin's Republican party behind the scenes, criticizing Republican "boss" Elisha Keyes of the Madison Regency, and serving as a powerful delegate to state conventions.

Finch's long and distinguished record in legal practice kept his name at the forefront of the Wisconsin bar as a prime candidate for a judicial appointment. Judge Miller announced his retirement in November 1873 after thirty-four years on the bench and died on September 30, 1874. Even though the sixty-five-year-old Finch was one of the oldest lawyers in Milwaukee, he still hoped to succeed Miller. Although Finch had many powerful friends among Wisconsin Republicans, Attorney General Leander Smith won the appointment.[37]

Finch was greatly disappointed and blamed Republican Senator Matthew Hale Carpenter for blocking his nomination in favor of a crony. Two years later, Finch and several political allies fought the Madison political machine of "Boss Keyes" and successfully blocked Carpenter's reelection to the United States Senate. Lynde also did his part to break the power of the machine by sponsoring a congressional investigation of the political fraud that surrounded the "Madison Regency."[38]

Finch had sought public office many times, but with little success. The marriage of law and politics, for which his natural bent and talents had prepared him well, had eluded him again and again. The climate was never quite right. Forces over which he had no control continually defeated him. Now at last he resolved to devote the remaining years of his life to his work at Finches, Lynde & Miller.

⨳ 8 ⨳

The End of an Era
1874–1885

In the fall of 1874, when Asahel Finch was suffering the final disappointment of his hope of becoming a judge, William Pitt Lynde was once again elected to Congress. The Wisconsin Democratic Committee had nominated Lynde only two weeks before the November election, after Samuel Rindskopf had suddenly withdrawn as the nominee, explaining that he did not meet the seven-year citizenship requirement. The Republican candidate for the Fourth District seat was Harrison Ludington, a wealthy lumberman and a former Milwaukee mayor, who would later be elected Wisconsin's governor. Ludington was also a client of Finches, Lynde & Miller.

The *Sentinel* had been harsh to Rindskopf, and it now turned its invective on Lynde. The paper accused him of fraud as Milwaukee mayor and as debt commissioner in the 1860s, claiming he had sold out the city in favor of the railroad cartel headed by his friend Alexander Mitchell. Because Mitchell was a candidate for United States senator in 1874 and John Cary, Mitchell's railroad attorney, was running for the state assembly, the *Sentinel* charged that all three made up a "cartel of money, owned by the 'money king' Alexander Mitchell." It called all three Democrats "swindlers."[1]

Lynde won. But Ludington's 7,025 votes (to Lynde's 8,418) showed that Republicans were gaining ground in Milwaukee's German community.[2] The *Sentinel's* charges did not stop with the election. A week afterward it accused Lynde of paying Rindskopf $4,000 to pull out of the race. Lynde sued for libel. The trial opened on November 26, just three weeks after the election. Republican U.S. Senator Matt Carpenter, part owner of the *Sentinel* and Mitchell's opponent, repeated his belief that Lynde had bribed Rindskopf but testified that he couldn't remember who had told him about it. Lynde settled for no cash and a weak retraction, published on November 28. The *Sentinel* wrote that it had believed the bribery charge, but "as it is not our purpose to publish untruth in regard to any gentleman, [Lynde was] entitled to this retraction at our hand."[3]

Early the next year, Lynde and his family entertained an exotic visitor. Daughter Clara had met King Kalakaua of Hawaii while on a trip around the world with her Uncle Martius Lynde in 1872. Now he came to Milwaukee to seek Clara's hand in marriage. She and a group of distinguished guests greeted the king at the Lynde mansion on Chestnut Street, but she refused the king's proposal and he soon left to continue his state visit around the country. Shortly afterward she became engaged to Harry C. Bradley. Their sons later founded the Allen-Bradley Company.[4]

Lynde was sworn in as a member of the 44th Congress in December 1875 and took his seat with other freshmen in the back row of the chamber. He was assigned to the Judiciary Committee, a very active post during the next four years, and to the Committee on the Pacific Railroads. The latter oversaw and encouraged the construction of railroads to the West Coast. The first had been completed in 1869, when the Union Pacific and the Central Pacific lines were joined at Promontory Point, Utah. The committee was to supervise future federal land grants to other lines such as Jay Cooke's Northern Pacific, James J. Hill's Great Northern Railroad, and Jay Gould's Southern Pacific, which linked Texas to the West Coast in 1882.[5]

Active on the floor of Congress from the beginning, Lynde joined with Republicans in the protectionism that characterized federal trade policy in the Gilded Age. He introduced a bill to restore the import duty on hams and prepared meats, a measure that helped to protect Milwaukee's meat industry from foreign competition. As a probusiness Democrat, Lynde was also active on the House Judiciary Committee as the author of a series of bills on patent protection. He viewed the nation's upcoming Centennial Exposition in Philadelphia as an opportunity to encourage scientific inventions. At the exposition, Milwaukee brewer Valentin Blatz won the blue ribbon for the first bottled beer, an award that became the company's trademark.

In support of trade Lynde also introduced bills to improve the harbors at Milwaukee and Port Washington and to allocate federal funds for the greatly needed ship canal connecting Green Bay to Lake Michigan. The new Sturgeon Bay Canal helped the lumber trade and increased the access of northern Wisconsin and the Fox River Valley to interstate shipping.

A pressing concern of the House Judiciary Committee during the 1870s was supervising and reordering the federal court system. As an active member of the committee, Lynde joined in the debate over the reimbursement of federal district judges who assisted in neighboring districts. He proposed an extra $10 per day for these traveling judges to encourage them to help out in busier courts.

Lynde also supported an 1876 proposal to enlarge the intermediate appellate level of the three-tiered federal court system. Federal courts then lacked jurisdiction for appeals of criminal convictions and for civil matters involving less than $5,000. Lynde and others argued that the $5,000 limitation was not fair and that basic equity demanded a right to appeal in criminal cases. The proposal passed the House of Representatives in February 1876 but failed in the Senate. It finally became law in the Circuit Court of Appeals Act of 1891.

In 1875, during Lynde's first congressional term, the Milwaukee Chamber of Commerce and the Merchants' Association of Milwaukee appealed to him to introduce legislation that would make it easier to collect debts on the frontier. Lynde introduced a measure that called for a uniform bankruptcy law for all federal territories, repealing the 1841 and 1867 bankruptcy statutes. At Finches, Lynde & Miller such bankruptcy reform assisted the collections work being carried out by partner Matt Finch, who traveled to the territory of Colorado to press claims on behalf of Wisconsin and eastern creditors.

While Lynde heard petitions from constituents ranging from calls for relief of Civil War veterans to the need for expanded mail service in outstate Wisconsin, he found his greatest legal challenge in the Belknap trial during his first term. President Grant's secretary of war, William W. Belknap, was accused of taking bribes from men who sought appointments as Indian agents in the West. Though Belknap resigned to avoid prosecution, the Judiciary Committee proceeded against him in June 1876 and the full House impeached him.

As the Senate trial began in the hot centennial summer of 1876, Lynde was chosen as one of four managers. However, the Senate decided it had no jurisdiction over an official who had already resigned. The partisan nature of the acquittal gave Democrats like Lynde a campaign issue in the 1876 elections.[6] He beat Republican William E. Smith, a good friend of Asahel Finch's, for reelection to Congress. Democratic presidential nominee Samuel Tilden won more popular votes than Rutherford B. Hayes, but they tied in the electoral college, leaving the choice of a president to the House of Representatives. The Judiciary Committee faced the task of certifying disputed election returns from southern states that had newly rejoined the Union. Lynde's subcommittee worked on the Louisiana returns. Since Republicans controlled the House, Hayes became the next president over the objections of Lynde and other Democrats.

Lynde's final term in Congress found him pressing for several reform measures. In February 1877, when hostility toward American Indians was at a peak following Custer's defeat in June 1876, Lynde submitted a proposal to give Indians the right to bring suit in federal courts, even though they were not United States citizens. He also sponsored a woman's-suffrage amendment to the federal constitution. Several Wisconsin women, including Lavinia Goodell of Janesville, the first women to be admitted to the Wisconsin bar, and Mathilde F. Anneke, a radical German-American leader, had asked for Lynde's support. The suffrage amendment did not succeed for another twenty-three years. Lynde's wife Mary was involved in the women's movement, as well as in charitable causes, and was one of the founders of the Milwaukee Woman's Club in 1876 and later its president.[7]

In his final session in Congress in 1878 Lynde pressed for further trade and navigation measures, among them a lighthouse for Racine and a new breakwater for Milwaukee. Following the close of the summer session in June 1878, Lynde declined to seek a third term, and the family returned to Wisconsin for good.

During his first term in Congress Lynde made two appearances before the United States Supreme Court and lost both. One client was the owner of a steam tug that had towed the brig *Margaret* to its destruction in the Racine harbor. The lower court found the tug had been operated negligently. The Supreme Court reviewed the evidence of negligence at length and affirmed. Ten years later, after Lynde's death, the *Sentinel* reported that the *Margaret* case marked the beginning of Lynde's reputation as an expert on maritime law.[8]

In the other case that term he represented a New York bank whose suit against a creditor in Wisconsin had been dismissed as beyond Wisconsin's statute of limitations. Lynde argued unsuccessfully that the statute discriminated against out-of-state plaintiffs and thus violated the rights and immunities clause of the United States Constitution. Justice Bradley thought Lynde's argument was "at first view, somewhat plausible," but ultimately unsound.[9]

The next year Lynde brought a patent appeal to the court, again for an appellant. This time Lynde won reversal of the lower court injunction, persuading the justices that his client's wrench for screwing bung bushings into beer barrels was a patentable improvement on the plaintiff's device.[10] Lynde's Supreme Court cases in the next two years related to municipalities that refused to redeem bonds they had issued to build railroads. In the first, Lynde represented the town of Weyauwega, which had lost in the lower courts. He argued unsuccessfully that Weyauwega's $40,000 bond issue was invalid because the town clerk had signed the bonds after he had resigned from office. The Supreme Court affirmed, holding that the town had received the proceeds of the bonds and was therefore estopped from arguing that its bonds were invalid.[11] In the other case Lynde represented a creditor who had won a $43,000 judgment on bonds the town of Racine had issued in 1853. By the time the creditor sued, town boundaries had been changed and part of the town had been incorporated into Racine City. Two of the surviving towns appealed their portions of the judgment, but Lynde prevailed.[12]

Lynde won his second Supreme Court reversal in an 1884 case. He represented Gibbs & Sterrett Manufacturing Co., a Pennsylvania manufacturer of reapers, which had delivered $7,400 worth of machinery to a trio of new Wisconsin dealers on credit. When they paid for less than half of the machinery, Gibbs and Sterrett sued a guarantor for the $4,664.49 deficit. The guarantor won in the lower court because he had signed on a Sunday, in violation of the Wisconsin statute that made it a misdemeanor to do business on the Lord's Day. The Supreme Court reversed because only Gibbs & Sterrett's independent agent (and not the company itself) had participated in the illegal Sunday transaction.[13]

Lynde's seventh and last case before the United States Supreme Court was argued in October 1885, just two months before he died. His name was on the brief, but associate George P. Miller argued the case on behalf of a New York iron broker who had sold 500 tons of pig iron to Edward P. Allis, founder of the Allis-Chalmers Co. Allis had paid in advance, but refused to accept the iron when it turned out to be of poor quality. Allis sued for a refund and won a $16,500 judgment in the lower court. Lynde and Miller appealed, arguing principally that Allis was entitled only to the difference between the sale price and the value of the iron as delivered. The Supreme Court affirmed, holding that the rule Lynde relied on did not apply where the goods were to be manufactured after the contract was signed.[14]

When Lynde returned from Congress in 1878, Milwaukee was flowering in an economic recovery. The Schlitz Brewery opened its first large beer garden, complete with a zoo, theater, fountains, and refreshment center. Milwaukee also boasted its own orchestra, a world-championship Turnverein Club (for gymnastics), and evening schools for adults. The public flocked to exhibits of paintings and sculpture. The first German panorama paintings, the "motion pictures of the day," made Milwaukee a "sort of Hollywood." Marquette University opened on September 5, 1881.[15]

Technology also brought dramatic changes to American city life during the 1870s. In 1877 Milwaukee inventor Charles Haskins opened the first telephone switchboard. It had fifteen subscribers. The unified Milwaukee Telephone Exchange, which B. K. Miller helped to organize, was placed in service in May 1879. By 1881 there were 600 subscribers in the city, and a new era in communications had begun. Finches, Lynde & Miller played an active role in the orderly growth of the Milwaukee Telephone Company. As service expanded beyond the city, B. K. Miller helped to incorporate the company in 1882, and served as its general counsel. He was also a major stockholder.[16]

In 1884 the firm successfully challenged Oskhosh's attempt to impose an annual $300 fee in the guise of regulating the location of telephone poles and wire. The Wisconsin Supreme Court first had to decide whether a telephone company (which the statutes did not mention) was enough like a telegraph company to be validly incorporated. *"Noscitur a sociis,"* wrote Justice Cassoday; it was close enough. The court then rejected Oshkosh's transparent attempt to disguise a tax as a valid exercise of the power to bar obstructions of city streets and alleys.[17]

Haskins had inaugurated Milwaukee's first electric streetlighting system several years before, in 1880. Connected with the city's electric street-railway companies, the electric-light firms and the several competing trolley companies did not merge into a centralized utility until the 1890s.[18]

The industrial revolution changed everyday life dramatically during the 1870s. Hot-air furnaces replaced coalburning stoves in many homes. Washing machines came on the market. Canned goods and readymade clothing appeared on store shelves. Ten cents would buy a three-pound can of peaches, a two-pound can of corn, or two pounds of rolled oats or wheat. Large department stores allowed shoppers to select among many different products under one roof. T. A. Chapman and Company expanded its operations in the early 1870s, and numerous other retail establishments, such as the Atlantic and Pacific Tea Company, opened their doors about the same time.

In 1879 Milwaukee instituted a regular schedule of garbage collection and began the inspection of elevators in several six-story buildings. The city started the first municipal kindergarten. The public library was founded in 1878 by the Young Men's Association, of which B. K. Miller was a leader. The library moved its collection of 15,000 volumes in May 1880 from quarters in the Music Building, owned by Matt Finch and B. K. Miller, to the Library Building, where the offices of the firm were then located.[19]

Ethnic issues continued to play an important role in Milwaukee politics in the Gilded Age. Immigrants from Poland, the Serbian and Slavic countries, and Italy came to work in Milwaukee's factories and breweries, tempting politicians to protect their political bases by manipulating ward boundaries. Lynde served as a consultant for the city government in 1881 on the legal ramifications of redistricting and reapportionment.

Leading bankers, manufacturers, brewers, and attorneys worked to promote the city. In 1879 the Milwaukee Merchants' Association joined the Chamber of Commerce in sponsoring an industrial exposition patterned after the Centennial Exposition in Philadelphia three years earlier. An elegant Exposition Center was erected, and annual expositions were held until it was destroyed by fire in 1905. It was replaced by the Civic Auditorium, which now stands at Kilbourn and Sixth streets.[20]

Civic pride was further boosted in the summer of 1880 when the National Encampment of the Grand Army of the Republic brought 140,000 Civil War veterans to Milwaukee. The event received wide publicity because ex-president and Civil War hero Ulysses S. Grant attended. When President James Garfield was assassinated the next summer, a committee led by Lynde and officers of the Chamber of Commerce called a mass meeting of mourning in the newly completed Exposition Building. Lynde had known and worked with Garfield during their four years together as congressmen. Once again black crepe draped Milwaukee buildings as it had when Lincoln was assassinated sixteen years earlier. Milwaukee Republicans staged a memorial parade that rivaled what they had done nine months earlier to mark the death of Senator Carpenter.[21]

One of the greatest disasters in Milwaukee history occurred on January 10, 1883 when the Newhall House burned to the ground, killing eighty people. The once-elegant hotel stood on the northwest corner of Broadway and Michigan, one block from the offices of Finches, Lynde & Miller. As an investigation of the fire began, the new *Milwaukee Journal* provided vigorous coverage of the building violations that had caused the deaths. Firemen had arrived promptly at the scene, but they faced too many handicaps as they tried to rescue victims. Bitter cold froze their hoses, and the poorly planned exit system forced many sixth-floor residents to jump to their deaths. Fire and insurance inspectors had frequently warned the hotel's owners, but no safety measures had been taken.

Lucius W. Nieman, who had bought into the *Milwaukee Journal* several weeks before the fire, later credited the rapid rise of his paper to its coverage of the criminal negligence that cost so many lives. Within a short time Nieman and the *Milwaukee Journal* became clients of Finches, Lynde & Miller. Although the firm did not represent claimants in the Newhall House disaster, B. K. Miller took an active role in aiding the victims of the fire and helped select a plot in Forest Home Cemetery for many of the unidentified dead.[22]

Safer and more sophisticated than the fire protection in Milwaukee were the city's growing transportation facilities. Along with the electric streetcars, the horse-drawn omnibuses carried hundreds of passengers daily. A team of four to six horses pulled cars sixteen feet long with a capacity of thirty people. Finch helped to incorporate a very profitable city rail line, the Cream City Railroad, and served as a major stockholder and director for many years. Lynde also invested in urban transit, and was instrumental in the development of the West Side Street Railway Company. The West Side Railway purchased part of his large estate for its western terminus along Chestnut Street (now Juneau). It carried passengers all the way into the city, but Lynde himself used his own livery to travel from his west-side mansion to his law office.

The 1880s marked the end of the forty-year association of Asahel Finch and William Pitt Lynde. Troubled by rheumatism, Finch had visited the office less frequently after 1878, the fortieth anniversary of his admission to the Michigan bar. He had boarded with his only surviving daughter, Mary Finch Papendiek, at the Newhall House for several years, but spent his last years in his "Mayberry Homestead" on the corner of Milwaukee and Division (now Juneau) streets. Finch died at home on April 4, 1883. He was seventy-four and very wealthy. Finch's funeral was a simple one, with members of the Milwaukee bar joining the Lynde and Miller families, Matt Finch, and Mary Finch Papendiek in mourning. Finch's obituary noted that his greatest public disappointment was not the numerous political elections he had lost, but his failure to achieve the much-hoped-for federal judgeship on Judge Andrew Miller's retirement.[23]

Beyond his success in the practice of law, Asahel Finch's most notable achievement had been his selection of William P. Lynde as a partner forty-one years before. Despite political and professional differences, Finch and Lynde had maintained a relationship that brought them great stature in the bar as well as financial rewards. The two men complemented one another in their legal and personal styles. While Lynde was always the more affable and popular, Finch retained a common touch that reflected his more humble background. Noted for both his close friends and his inveterate enemies, Finch remained devoted to his profession and his church. In his name Finch's daughter donated the rose window still to be found in the tower of St. Paul's Episcopal Church, and the firm donated his portrait to the State Historical Society of Wisconsin.[24]

Less than a year later, his nephew Matt Finch died at age fifty-four on March 27, 1884, while arguing a case before the Wisconsin Supreme Court. Although he was often overshadowed by the forceful personalities of his three partners, Matt had brought a quiet strength to the firm. Like his uncle, he made both strong friends and bitter enemies, some of whom had christened him "Deacon Jr." Miller and Lynde and other members of the bar met to eulogize him, calling him "all lawyer, thorough in preparation, forcible in utterance, always strong even when in the wrong, and almost irresistible when in the right."[25]

The absolute determination with which Matt Finch devoted himself to litigation was also his undoing; his fellows at the bar believed that he had died of overwork. Matt Finch's death left the sixty-seven-year-old Lynde and forty-four-year-old B. K. Miller to shift the weight of his enormous workload onto other shoulders, including their own. In the summer of 1884 they brought B. K. Miller's two sons, B. K., Jr., and George, into an increasing number of cases. Their third associate, William Pitt Lynde, Jr., proved unable to take on the additional work.

William Pitt Lynde, Sr., continued to handle most of the firm's major appeals in 1884 and 1885, appearing before the Wisconsin and the United States supreme courts a number of times before his health failed in November 1885. He died of a heart ailment on December 18, 1885, at the age of sixty-eight. The courts of Milwaukee closed in his honor, and the members of the Milwaukee bar, which he had led for many years, met in special session to memorialize him. Lynde's eulogy at the Wisconsin Supreme Court was presented in May 1886 by Justice Harlow Orton, who had known Lynde from his boyhood in New York. B. K. Miller later presented memorial gifts of $5,000 to the Milwaukee Law Library to honor Lynde and the two Finches.

As charter subscribers to Forest Home Cemetery in the 1850s, Finch and Lynde had chosen burial sites on the opposite sides of the same rising ground. The Lynde family plot was on the north slope, whereas Finch chose the south side for himself, his father, brother, infant daughters, both wives, and his grandson.[26] In death, as often in their personal and professional lives, the partners chose the same hill, but faced in opposite directions. The partnership of Finch and Lynde had survived forty-one years of legal changes, strong personal differences, and political turmoil. Now only B. K. Miller remained to carry on the tradition his two senior partners had begun.

❦ 9 ❧

The Miller Years
1886–1890

In 1886, when Benjamin K. Miller, Sr., took the helm of Finches, Lynde & Miller, the city of Milwaukee was changing. As more and more immigrants poured in, they settled into neighborhoods defined by both economics and ethnic heritage. The newcomers were not Anglo-Saxon, nor were they Protestant; they were largely Catholic or Jewish. By 1888 the few Polish settlers who had founded St. Stanislaus parish in 1863 had grown to 30,000, with several new churches, a newspaper, and parochial schools that followed a curriculum based on the Polish language.[1] The Polish population dominated the Democratic party that had once been the province of Irish, Germans, and liberal Yankees. The Republican party bemoaned its lack of a Polish candidate. The old Yankees in town felt threatened. It seemed doubtful that the new immigrants, determined to preserve their heritage at all costs, would be readily assimilated into the American melting pot.

Miller, the sole remaining partner, held the reins tightly, increasingly centering the firm's business around estates, trusts, and corporate work. His associates included his two sons, Benjamin Kurtz Miller, Jr. ("Ben"), and George Peckham Miller, aged twenty-eight and twenty-seven. Moving quickly, he made them partners on January 1, 1886, only two weeks after Lynde's death. To maintain continuity, the name of the firm was left unchanged for four more years.

Ben Miller was born in Milwaukee on June 6, 1857. The eldest of three sons, he was educated in Milwaukee at Markham's Academy (later called the Milwaukee Academy), the private preparatory school for boys that his father had helped to charter in 1864. He graduated from Pennsylvania College in Gettysburg at age nineteen. Like his father and Asahel Finch, Ben prepared for his legal career not in a law school but by reading the law. Having served a three-year apprenticeship in his father's firm, he was admitted to the Wisconsin bar in 1880.[2]

George was born on October 12, 1858. He was named for his mother's family, the Peckhams, who were prominent bankers in town. George attended private schools, first Markham's Academy and later Sellicks's School in Norwalk, Connecticut. He completed the classical course at Pennsylvania College at age eighteen, graduating with his brother in 1877.[3] Alexander Mitchell, president of the Milwaukee Marine and Fire Insurance Company and an old friend of both Finch and Lynde, had promised George a place after college, and George planned on a career as a banker.

But B. K. Miller encouraged George to pursue a career in law and to embark on professional studies at a German university. George took his father's advice. He journeyed to Göttingen to study civil law at the university there, and later went on to Breslau. In 1880 he received his Juris Doctor with honors from Göttingen and joined the offices of Finches, Lynde & Miller on November 14, 1881, less than a year and a half before the death of Asahel Finch. In 1882 he was admitted to the bar. Until his death in 1885, Matt Finch took a special interest in George's training and served as his mentor.

Lynde assigned George Miller to argue a case in the United States Supreme Court in October 1885.[4] When Lynde died two months later, George Miller had to shoulder the burden of the firm's litigation alone. But despite dire predictions that the firm would fail and that the two brothers were too young and inexperienced to handle the sophisticated matters before them, they seemed to rise to the challenge.

Under the leadership of B. K. Sr., the firm's roster of clients grew during the next five years. Ben handled some litigation, but preferred to assist his father in the area of trusts and probate and served as a counselor to several Milwaukee corporations. George became the firm's chief litigator. Later, after his father's death, he took over some in-house corporate work as well.

The differences in interests and in temperament between Finch and Lynde had proven valuable to the vitality of their partnership and had added strength to the firm. The sons of B. K. Miller, too, were very different in their personal styles and abilities. By far the more aggressive of the two, George enjoyed courtroom battles and the exhilaration of litigation. Ben did not enjoy the courtroom, although he assisted his younger brother when the trial work became too heavy. Much quieter than George, Ben was described by his contemporaries as a "philosopher of law," a young man who enjoyed quiet debates about ideas and whose intellectual interests embraced a wide variety of subjects, from history to political economy and from science to wildlife.[5]

Ben enjoyed the quiet forum of the firm's offices in the old Library Building at Wisconsin and Broadway, where he made time each day for reading on a variety of subjects. He appeared before the Wisconsin Supreme Court on several occasions before Lynde's death, but gradually took on fewer large appeals and limited his litigation practice. Ben Miller's name appears on many small collection cases and garnishments in local courts in these years, but perhaps he only supervised associates in this drudgery.

After the deaths of both of the Finches and of Lynde within two years, there was concern whether the firm could maintain its standard of excellence after losing three of its four partners. Despite all such apprehensions, B. K. Miller was able to sustain the work of the firm and, with the increasing competence of George and Ben as litigators and counselors, continued to serve the clients well. The firm's resilience stemmed from the elder Miller's stature and reputation in the Wisconsin legal and business community. A "complacent looking gentleman in Gladstone whiskers and a Prince Albert coat," he had already been in effective charge of the law office for several years. He was a well-known businessman, investor, and community leader.

In addition to offering legal counsel, the elder Miller became a financial leader in the Milwaukee community. He served as the incorporator and a charter stockholder of the Milwaukee Telephone Company (later Wisconsin Bell) and bought stock in the American

Telephone and Telegraph Company, with which it was affiliated. He was also one of the founders of the Milwaukee Trust Company in the 1890s, which, several decades later, became the First Wisconsin Trust Company, an affiliate of First Wisconsin Corporation (now Firstar Corporation), the state's largest banking institution. Like Finch and Lynde before him, B. K. Miller invested wisely in the securities of many of the companies he advised or helped to create.[6]

Miller was a trustee of the Milwaukee Chamber of Commerce and was an elected delegate to the Fourth District nominating convention of the Democratic party in 1890. But he was more interested in cultural and community affairs than in politics. In 1890 he served as secretary to the Milwaukee Theatre Association, which tried to offer high-quality dramatic productions. The popular entertainments in the nineties ranged from the music and comedy of the beer halls to the traveling stock shows and performances of visiting artists who came either to the Academy of Music on Broadway (which Miller had owned for a time with Matt Finch) or Nunnemacher's Grand Opera House on Wells Street. One critic labeled Milwaukee the "poorest theatrical city in the United States." Even performers such as Edwin Booth, the greatest Shakespearean actor of his day, and Sarah Bernhardt, in *Tosca* and *Cleopatra,* found small and unreceptive audiences until the Theatre Association's efforts boosted their following in Milwaukee.[7]

Miller was also active in the Young Men's Association, which sponsored the Milwaukee Public Library, housed for several years in the building that Finches, Lynde & Miller occupied at 102 East Wisconsin Street. He helped plan the library's new neoclassical home on West Grand (Wisconsin) Avenue, begun in the early 1890s and completed in 1899 at a cost of $630,000.[8] As a leader of the Milwaukee Art Society and attorney to Frederick Layton, the wealthy meatpacker, Miller was involved in founding the Layton Art Gallery in 1888, forerunner of today's Milwaukee Art Museum. It was Layton's gift to the city, along with his collection of thirty-eight paintings valued at $50,000 and an endowment of $100,000.[9]

In 1884 Miller became a director of the Milwaukee Club, an association of prominent businessmen, attorneys, and civic leaders that had been founded two years earlier. Alexander Mitchell was its first president. Miller led the building committee that in 1883 erected the red brick and sandstone edifice, designed by architect

Edward Townsend Mix, that still stands on the northeast corner of Jefferson and Wisconsin.[10]

Milwaukee's first social register, the "Blue Book," listed the Alexander Mitchells, the William P. Lyndes, and the B. K. Millers among the leaders of Milwaukee society in 1884. The Millers hosted the social event of the 1885 season, a "November Ball," at their home at 559 Marshall Street. Among their guests were such leaders of the business and legal community as John Van Dyke, a prominent lawyer; Grant Fitch and Charles Ilsley, leaders in Milwaukee banking; Henry Lewis Palmer, officer at Northwestern Mutual Life Insurance Company; and Elisha Eldred, financier and longtime client of the firm. Also invited were such elite sons and daughters as Harry C. Bradley, Lynde's son-in-law, and Laura Chapman (soon to be the fiancée of George Miller), the daughter of department-store tycoon Thomas A. Chapman.[11]

Just before his death in 1898, B. K. Miller, Sr., purchased two lots overlooking Lake Michigan on Terrace Avenue, where he planned to build homes for his son William and his only daughter Madeleine, engaged to financier Clement C. Smith. These lots bordered prestigious Lake Park on the bluff, landscaped and designed by planner Frederick Law Olmsted.[12] Miller and his wife lived an elegant life-style, resplendent as only a few could afford at the turn of the century. A connoisseur of wine and gourmet food, Miller ordered specialties for his cellar and table from the finest suppliers in New York and Chicago, never hesitating to return any substandard item. The Millers ordered silver spoons during a trip to St. Petersburg and other household furnishings and fine art from around the world. They traveled abroad frequently, often visiting the Carlsbad health spa in Austria. On returning from the spa in 1897, in ill health, Miller wrote to its owner complaining about inferior service: "Americans are not accustomed to this kind of treatment." In his rigid standards and his strict adherence to style and form, B. K. Miller typified the new breed of exacting businessmen and professional leaders who were at the pinnacle of American society in this Gilded Age.[13]

From 1886 to 1890 the success and survival of the oldest law firm in the city rested on the shoulders of the three Millers. Several of the cases that George and Ben handled during the first year after they became partners involved the issue of libel. Once again Finches, Lynde & Miller represented controversial newspaperman William E. Cramer. In one case the firm won reversal of a $5,000 award to the widow of a suicide because the Rock County trial judge had made a mistake in jury instructions. The Wisconsin Supreme Court concluded that the jury had probably included punitive damages in its award even though it had found Cramer's *Evening Wisconsin* innocent of malice. The Supreme Court chided the trial judge for delivering instructions so prolix as to make error inevitable:

> An opportunity for elegant discourse is always tempting to genius and ability. But while some circumstances invite, others repel, the indulgence. To be apt, the expression must not only be accurate, but appropriate. A strict adherence to the case in hand is one of the highest qualities of juridical discussion. Such discussion is necessarily concise, direct, and restricted, rather than ornate. It is, moreover, cold, logical, pointed, and without superfluity.[14]

In another successful appeal from a libel judgment against Cramer, B. K. Miller persuaded the Supreme Court that the jury should have been told expressly that "a woman whose reputation for chastity is bad cannot suffer the same damages as a woman of good reputation would." The $1,200 judgment was reversed and the case remanded for a new trial.[15]

Lynde had handled several libel cases, but after his death, the firm did little work for Milwaukee's major newspapers, the *Sentinel* and Lucius Nieman's *Milwaukee Journal,* until the twentieth century, when the firm again began to handle libel cases for the *Journal.*

In the late 1880s the firm handled the estates of several of Milwaukee's wealthiest men, including that of Alexander Mitchell, the city's foremost banker, who died in 1887. It also successfully defended a lower court decision denying a $5,000 bequest by Judge Jason Downer's widow to the Wisconsin Female College. Judge Downer had been generous to the school, and Mrs. Downer's will bequeathed another $5,000, but only if its name had been changed to Downer College before she died. The school's name was changed, but not before Mrs. Downer died. The college trustees argued in the Wisconsin Supreme Court that they hadn't known about the condition (which was true) and that they had started the name-changing process in good faith before she died. The court was unimpressed, for the condition in Mrs. Downer's will was clear and absolute.[16]

In the years after 1886 the firm handled a steadily increasing number of wills and estates. The letter book of B. K. Miller, Sr., included his frequent correspondence with a number of heirs to Milwaukee fortunes for whom he served as guardian and trustee. Of the many estates he administered, the most difficult, in fact, was that of his brother John, whose widow, Margaret Miller, wrote him numerous complaints about his stinginess with the assets and his management style. Miller dealt with her complaints curtly, without giving in to her repeated pleas for an increase in her allowance from the trust funds.[17]

Several probate cases that brought the firm to the Wisconsin Supreme Court had unusual twists. One father, for example, had conditioned his son's inheritance on reforming into a "sober and respectable citizen of good moral character" within five years. The son died within five years without reforming. The local court decided the son's failure to reform absolutely deprived his own heirs of the inheritance. The firm appealed successfully to the Supreme Court on behalf of the young children. The court held that the father had intended "to preserve the inheritance for his grandchildren, not to deprive them of it."[18]

The firm handled a child custody case on behalf of a New York widower. His first wife's relatives, who lived in Milwaukee, refused to give up the child to live with her father and his new wife in New York. They defended against the father's suit by claiming the father had solemnly promised them custody in the presence of his first wife's coffin. The trial court held for the Milwaukeeans, but the state Supreme Court reversed because there was no evidence the father was unfit.[19]

In addition to its work in probate and trusts, the firm tried a number of cases growing out of the increasing complexity of city life, cases dealing with traffic accidents, mass-transit liability, and rate controls. These negligence cases were routine, and the Supreme Court usually deferred to jury findings. In one example George Miller argued that the North Chicago Rolling Mill Company and its subsidiary railroad had no duty to keep a flagman at a street crossing, and therefore it could not have been negligent to run a train after the flagman had gone off duty. The Supreme Court agreed as a general rule, but held that negligence was a jury question in this case because the company usually kept a flagman at the crossing.[20]

During the 1890s a quiet revolution was brewing in American politics that soon had a significant impact on American law as well. At the dawn of this period of progressive reform, attorney Louis D. Brandeis (later a justice of the United States Supreme Court) pioneered in this reform effort when he worked on behalf of a Boston utility to establish safety precautions, an equitable rate system, and insurance protections that would serve both corporate interests and the public good. George Miller became acquainted with Brandeis as they worked together on the restructuring of the bankrupt Wisconsin Central Railroad and the receivership matters of its parent company, the Northern Pacific Railroad. However, Brandeis's call for social responsibility from American corporations did not become a successful rallying cry for many American businesses and the attorneys who served them. In Wisconsin, most reforms were achieved not by corporate initiative, but by the regulatory legislation of the progressive period after 1890.[21]

Although George Miller became involved in railroad receiverships during the 1890s, most of the firm's corporate clients during the eighties and nineties were banks, utilities, commercial corporations, and financially solvent railroads. From 1893 through 1895 the firm handled a great many collection cases for the major banks, including the Wisconsin Marine and Fire Insurance Bank, the National City Bank, the Importers and Traders Bank of New York, the National Park Bank of New York, and the First National Bank of Milwaukee, of which Miller was a director. Bank collection matters had been streamlined by the introduction of simplified garnishment proceedings that could be handled by a clerk. Injunctions and receiverships were developed for use in larger matters. In serving large corporations B. K. Miller and his sons, like other corporate attorneys, became adept at using these new legal tools to protect their clients from strikes and other economic pressures.

The firm had a wide roster of major clients. They included the Northern Pacific Railroad (which was also represented by Sullivan & Cromwell of New York), the Wisconsin Central Railroad, the First National Bank and the Wisconsin Marine and Fire Insurance

Bank, Western Union, the American Express Company, and the transit and telephone companies. There were numerous other small business and individual clients as well. The Chicago Board of Trade, Marshall Field and Company, and the Continental Bank of Illinois used the firm for their Wisconsin work, as did a number of other out-of-state concerns.

Among the Wisconsin corporations that were the firm's clients were the Allis Company (soon to be Allis-Chalmers), the Milwaukee Cement Company (of which B. K. Miller, Sr. was a director), the Harnischfeger Company, the Schlitz Brewery and a number of other breweries, the Kurz and Huttenlocher Ice Company, the Badger State Lumber Company and other lumber concerns, the Herman Zoehrlaut Leather Company and several shoe companies, tanneries, the Pottsville Iron and Steel Company and several other iron and steel companies (including the North Chicago Rolling Mill Company that later merged with Carnegie to become part of United States Steel), the White Rock Mineral Spring Company of Waukesha, the New York Bottlers Supplies Manufacturing Company, the Peim Refining Company (a Pennsylvania oil refinery), the Crane Elevator Company, the Sheboygan Chair Company, the Illinois Can Company, the Paragon Cigar Manufacturing Company, the Agawann Paper Company, the Rockford Mitten and Hosiery Company, the Falls City Jeans and Woolen Company, and several clothing retailers.

Before 1906 the client list can only be glimpsed in records of litigation, since no ledger books remain from that period. Yet the many matters litigated represent only a part of the story of the flexibility and vision needed to keep abreast of the ever-changing business conditions, tax laws, and government regulations of the Gilded Age. The new, urbanized society of the 1880s and 1890s brought important changes in the practice of law. The stylized and formal procedures that reflected the culture of the Yankee elite gave way little by little to less traditional, more improvised approaches.

As early as the 1850s legal reformers had called for procedural changes to streamline the state and federal court systems and to make law less cumbersome. David Dudley Field played an important role in the development of a code in New York State to "simplify and abridge the practice, pleadings, and procedures of the courts."[22] Reforms such as the Field Code, partially adopted in 1851, attempted to simplify pleadings in civil actions.

By the late 1800s both businessmen and lawyers began to demand further improvements in the legal process. The Milwaukee Bar Association, at one of its six yearly meetings, finally voted in 1879 to amend the rules of practice to conform more closely to Field's ideas. Two other reforms followed in 1887, when Wisconsin passed legislation allowing women to serve as witnesses in court and circuit-court-judge Dyer undertook the formal publication of new rules of practice for lawyers in his courtroom.

The legal profession came under fire increasingly during the 1890s and after 1900, as many middle-class Americans faulted corporations for all of the country's social and economic ills. One critic believed that law firms with corporate clients had ceased to be honorable and independent practitioners and had instead become "employer and employee." Elihu Root, a leader in the American bar, vehemently denied the charge, maintaining that he and his legal brethren were not "corporation lawyers, but lawyers who happened to have corporations among their clients."[23]

The senior Miller kept the law firm on course through the 1880s and 1890s, serving a largely Yankee and elite German clientele who commanded the economic establishment, if not the political power, of the city and the state. The office staff included an office manager, Mr. Harper, and a chief law clerk, William Morris, who worked under Miller to oversee the clerks, the associates, and several secretaries.

In the 1890s the offices at 102 East Wisconsin Street consisted of a suite of rooms (one for each partner), a corridor for the growing library, several large rooms for the support staff with their modern typewriters, a telephone switchboard, and the vault for legal documents and wills. A photograph of the senior B. K. Miller taken about this time shows his office furnishings, rolltop desk, top hat, and well-organized work space.

While some firms were small and flexible enough to adopt new office systems and new technologies easily, others resisted them. At the New York firm of Sullivan & Cromwell, which was already doing correspondent work with the firm in the 1890s, for example, the new clerk, John Foster Dulles, reported that "neither telephones nor stenographers were fully accepted. Some of the older partners felt that the only dignified way of communicating between members of the legal profession was for them to write each other in . . . script and have the message delivered by hand."[24]

By contrast, the telephone became an early tool at Finches, Lynde & Miller, whose leader, B. K. Miller was a major stockholder of the Wisconsin Telephone Company. Miller's style of management allowed for a sufficient number of office clerks and stenographers, supplied by the second-floor tenant of the firm's building, the Spencerian Business College. Most of the students at the college in the Miller Block (as it became known) were young men who sought training in the new technology and business practices that were changing the marketplace.

The firm's first female employee, Daisy E. Wright, appeared on the records in 1899 when she was empowered by George Miller to sign letters in his absence. In New York, the law firm begun by former Finch & Lynde associate Walter Carter moved slowly into the era of modern office organization. In 1899, when Paul Cravath joined the firm, he was reportedly dismayed at its "lack of system and organization . . . it employed no filing clerk and did not have the semblance of a filing system. Though it did employ stenographers and copyists, it did not yet use typewriters."[25]

Bringing a law office into the "modern age" in the 1890s demanded the leadership of a powerful partner such as B. K. Miller, Sr. Office rule by management committee was many decades in the future. Cravath worked to upgrade his firm's systems and to bring in new machines to upgrade billing and other back-office procedures. Calculating machines, electric lighting, and other devices made law offices more businesslike. Miller's "letter book," with its alphabetical and chronological index and exact copies of all letters written, was an efficient method of record keeping. Copies were made by wetting the original and placing the thin book page over the wet letter in a "letter press" that forced the ink to transfer under pressure.

There was never any doubt within the firm that B. K. Miller was the man in charge. He supervised, scolded, and encouraged everyone, including his two sons and office manager Harper. In an 1891 letter to associate Morris, Miller wrote that he was "very much troubled at the mass of letters and papers on your table . . . and other matters . . . which have not received your attention."

Miller proposed intense supervision: "I have directed Mr. Harper to stay in your room and take charge of the outside business and for you to remain in the offices until your table is entirely cleared." The rule of the office was promptness in all matters, Miller reminded him. "Letters received should be answered the same day. I must insist upon a change in this regard." While his stern rebuke was clear, Miller closed the letter on a note of fatherly concern, reminding the clerk that "none of us have any but the very kindest feelings in regard to you, but we are very anxious that you should improve and not deteriorate."[26]

Mary Blanchard Lynde, widow of William Lynde, also experienced both the sternness and the exacting business management of her husband's successor. Just before her husband's death she wrote to B. K. Miller inquiring about a matter of office policy. Miller's brusque response revealed that he did not wish to deal directly with her.[27] Nine years later Mary Lynde wrote to Miller once again, this time in reference to her growing financial troubles, requesting that he investigate whether her portion of income from her husband's estate had been paid. Once again Miller was all business:

> I regret exceedingly your financial difficulties, but your husband received his full share of the income of the office. His interest in the firm assets was settled by paying to you . . . $15,000.00. You were aware of this adjustment, which was made nearly nine years ago, and which was made in accordance with the firm contract.[28]

Miller sent a copy of this letter to Lynde's daughter, Mrs. Harry Bradley, with only a cursory note attached. In reality, it is doubtful that Mary Lynde was without financial resources. However, Lynde's fortune had, no doubt, been severely strained by the numerous difficulties of his three sons, and his widow may have felt that the firm owed her more from his contributions to its success. Though he was unwilling to give her any direct financial assistance, Miller did represent her and her only surviving son Tilly when creditors pressed for payment of rent and other unmet obligations.[29]

In dealing with his own two sons Miller was also an exacting and stern taskmaster. Ben remained a bachelor and lived with his parents on Marshall Street during these early years. He escaped the pressures of the office through travel to faraway and exotic places, ranging from the jungles of South America to a voyage around the world. Over the years Ben collected stamps and read widely of world history and philosophy. In 1906, less than a decade after his father's death, Ben left the firm at the age of only forty-eight to travel and pursue his hobbies. In doing so he became the first partner in the firm's sixty-four-year history (with the exception of Hubbell) to leave the firm before his death.

George, who had initially resisted pursuing law as a career, had by 1890 become the mainstay of the firm's litigation practice. But even his stalwart nature and great social success did not bring immunity from the pressures of the business and of working for his father. Early in the 1890s, under severe stress, he wrote his father from New York that he desperately needed to get away for an extended sabbatical.

B. K. Sr.'s response was immediate and unrelenting. Brushing aside George's complaint of nervous prostration, he noted, "Ben is nervous, but you are not. You have no disease or natural physical weakness, but in the reverse have a most excellent constitution." Without much apparent sympathy, he continued, "Neither does your present condition come from over study, over work, or too great responsibility." Posing a rhetorical question, he asked, "Now what is your trouble?"

He answered the question himself. George had wasted away his excellent constitution by not eating correctly and not getting sufficient exercise. The father went on to prescribe the exact remedy: "Come home, simply a man who understands his business to train your times of day regularly, commencing with moderation. Buy a horse and ride it every day, rain or shine. Dress warmly. Eat reasonably good food, *stand and sit erect* and . . . I will guarantee your health, appetite, and increase of weight commencing after thirty days trial."[30]

George acceded to his father's wishes and returned to Milwaukee. There is no evidence that his health either markedly improved or suffered noticeably under his father's regimen. However, he did thrive in the practice of law and succeeded even beyond the achievements of his father during his fifty years with the firm. Like his father, who died in 1898 while still active in the firm, George practiced law until his death, without substantially forgoing the challenge of daily trips to the office. He died in 1931 at the age of seventy-two, a highly skilled and respected legal counselor.

George Miller served his clients well and pursued his career with distinction. To what extent his father's advice on health and horseback riding played a role in his success we will never know.

10

Expanding the Partnership
1890–1905

In 1890, B. K. Miller, Sr., decided that he and his two sons needed the help of an experienced partner. He had just passed his fifty-ninth birthday, and he looked forward to more travel with his second wife and their daughter Madeleine. He found the man he wanted in George H. Noyes, the superior-court judge of Milwaukee County, who became a partner in what came to be called Miller, Noyes & Miller.

A native of New York, Noyes was raised in Delafield, Wisconsin, where his parents had settled in 1855, when he was six years old. At sixteen he became an elementary-school teacher in Waukesha County so he could save money for college. He studied first at Lawrence University in Appleton, and then transferred to the University of Wisconsin. He graduated with honors from the classical course in 1873 after working his way through school for six years. Determined to study law, Noyes worked as an assistant to Professor O. M. Conover at the state law library while he took courses at the university. Through his work at the library he met several justices of the Wisconsin Supreme Court, most notably Luther Dixon, the chief justice. Dixon took Noyes under his wing, and when Dixon retired from the court in 1874, he brought Noyes to Milwaukee. Noyes clerked for the new firm of Dixon, Hooker, & Palmer, later becoming a partner in the successor firm of Dixon & Noyes when Henry Palmer left to become president of Northwestern Mutual Life Insurance Company. Dixon & Noyes disbanded when Noyes was elected to the Superior Court bench in 1888 as the "citizens" candidate and Dixon moved west for his health.

Noyes left the bench and joined Finches, Lynde & Miller in 1890 when he learned that a judge's salary did not permit him to provide as well as he wanted for the education of his five children. He was the first judge to affiliate with the firm, and he remained in the partnership for sixteen years. In that time he also served terms as a member of the Board of Regents of the University of Wisconsin and a commissioner of the State Historical Society.[1]

Noyes immediately began to assist George Miller in his litigation practice. He brought with him the account of the Northwestern Mutual Life Insurance Company, headed by his former partner, Henry Palmer. Northwestern Mutual Life used the firm of Miller, Noyes & Miller in the areas of employee relations and insurance settlements.

Four years later, in 1894, B. K. Miller decided to expand the firm, again by bringing in a new partner from the outside. He turned to thirty-three-year-old George H. Wahl, son of a teacher who had come to Milwaukee from Germany in 1848. Like Noyes, Wahl had taught school at the age of eighteen to save money for college. He graduated from the University of Wisconsin in 1883, and from its law school in 1885. Following graduation, Wahl clerked for John M. Olin of Madison, who was also a professor at the law school. Wahl later entered into partnership with Emil Walber, a Milwaukee lawyer who became the city's mayor and a judge of the municipal court. In 1891 and 1892 Wahl served as assistant district attorney of Milwaukee County, before joining the firm of Walker, Brown & Wahl. From that partnership, B. K. Miller brought him into Miller, Noyes & Miller in March 1894. The firm was then styled Miller, Noyes, Miller & Wahl.[2]

The new partnership agreement signed by the three Millers, Noyes, and George Wahl on March 1, 1894, listed Wahl's pay as $4,000 per year, with the other four partners each receiving one-fourth of the remaining profits. The firm listed $35,000 in assets, with its extensive law library making up a substantial portion of the whole.[3]

During the 1890s, as the power of the utility companies grew, the conflict between private capital and public welfare required concessions from both corporations and city governments. The courts functioned as referees. As the gas companies had done before, the newly merged transit companies and electric-power utilities sought monopoly privileges in return for favors. The need for regulation was recognized. The new city hall with its 393-foot bell tower that dominated the Milwaukee skyline was a powerful symbol of the new spirit of enlightened politics. Yet city government remained tainted by corruption. Franchises were bought with gifts to aldermen, and mayors repaid favors by making untoward concessions. Amid the smoke were reports that the transit company and the firm had bribed Milwaukee aldermen and Mayor Rose to win a favorable vote on the charter ordinance of 1900. The charges were never proved; indeed, no formal charges were ever brought against either the transit company or the firm. In 1895 Wisconsin passed the first civil-service bill for Milwaukee, an echo of the Pendleton Act of 1883, which had established the federal system.[4]

The catalyst for this reform movement among the city's elite was the Municipal League, which worked in 1893 and 1894 to elect Republican John Koch, a native of Hanover, Germany, as mayor. It was hoped that Koch could provide a sensible balance between the socialists' demands for municipal ownership, the public call for regulation, and the demands of the private utilities for franchises. Koch had a further mandate to root out corrupt officials who stood in the way of reform and regulation. He had to deal with constituencies varying from Yankees who opposed many of labor's demands to socialists who called for economic as well as political changes.

The public also joined in the socialists' call for the abolition of child labor, factory inspection and safeguards for workers, uniform street lighting and street cleaning in poor as well as wealthy districts of the city, better public education, and, later, the eight-hour workday.[5]

New political movements came into being. In 1886, as Milwaukee celebrated its fortieth anniversary as a city, a socialist labor organization was founded that would later emerge as a powerhouse of urban reform. A progressive movement was stirring in Milwaukee as elsewhere in Wisconsin. Although the progressives defended private corporate ownership, they called for rate control, fair taxation, and an end to corruption in all levels of government.

In this atmosphere of public discontent, courts and juries were often hostile to the Milwaukee City Railway Company, the firm's client. In one case a passenger insisted on a transfer so he could ride from Fourth and Mitchell to the baseball ground at Twelfth and Wright without paying a second five-cent fare. When the conductor of the second horsecar put him off "by no great display of force" and without injury, the man paid the second nickel under protest and proceeded to the ball game. He sued for his injuries and the jury awarded him $150. The firm's appeal was successful.[6] But the city later changed the rules: By 1889 a passenger from anywhere along Milwaukee's eighty miles of street railway could travel within the city boundaries for a single fare.

In the 1890s the firm was called on to deal with a variety of issues involving mergers of the city's transit lines. Milwaukee had been served in the 1880s by five separate street railway companies. One of the five was chartered and partly owned by Finch and one by Lynde. With rapid urban growth, the public demanded more efficient mass transportation. It was achieved by merging several horsecar companies into a unified network that was later replaced by the electric trolley system. Capital was needed for the new technology, and New York and Boston investors came to the bargaining table in Milwaukee. With eastern backing, Henry Villard and Henry Payne created the Milwaukee Street Railway Company. By 1894 it owned all of the city's transit lines. A writer to the *Milwaukee Journal* praised the new electric trolleys because one could "slide through the city like a greased pig through a lasso."[7] B. K. Miller served as legal and financial consultant to Payne and Villard.

Milwaukee's population had quadrupled between 1870 and 1900, growing to 280,000. Wishing to escape the new congestion, many moved farther away from the city center along the mass-transit lines. B. K. Miller and other investors appreciated the real-estate potential offered by a unified and expanding mass transit system. Before the Panic of 1893 the rapid growth of streetcar suburbs brought a real-estate boom to the greater Milwaukee area. Real-estate sales jumped fivefold to $15 million between 1880 and 1892, the year before the crash.

The suburbs of Shorewood and Wauwatosa developed during the last decades of the nineteenth century as the city began to spread out along the trolley lines. Patrick Cudahy urged Payne to build a line out to the new suburb of Cudahy near his meat-packing plant. In 1880 one-third of Milwaukee's population had lived within one mile of downtown. Ten years later only 17 percent lived that close. Eighty percent of the city's population depended on mass transportation during these decades before the automobile. The only exceptions were those wealthy residents who owned or hired a livery service.[8]

The firm successfully challenged the city's attempt in 1894 to increase its tax assessment on the street railway company by two-thirds, to $2.9 million. The city defended the increase in part by contending that it could tax the value of the firm's intangible franchise. The Supreme Court set the increase aside. The company needed the relief in 1895 when its profits were virtually zero.[9]

The merger of smaller companies into ever larger corporations during the Gilded Age stimulated a parallel move among workers to unify into labor unions. American labor had made short-lived attempts to organize before the Civil War, but met with little success until the emergence of more powerful national coalitions, such as Samuel Gompers's American Federation of Labor, founded in the 1880s. Midwestern cities, which were then well on their way to industrialization, were also the target of numerous strikes, as workers demanded better safety conditions, an eight-hour day, and higher wages.

During May 1886 strikes around the country signaled serious labor unrest and future labor problems for American industry. Haymarket Square in Chicago was bloodied when an anarchist's bomb brought police reprisals that resulted in seven fatalities and more than seventy casualties. Simultaneously Milwaukee was torn by a series of forty strikes. Twelve thousand workers struck on May 1 to demand an eight-hour workday. When their brethren in the railroad union walked out in sympathy two days later, Wisconsin Governor Jeremiah Rusk called out the militia to restore order. Before the strike ended, violence erupted at the Reliance Iron Works in Bay View, owned by the North Chicago Rolling Mill Company, a client of the firm. Five strikers were killed and four were seriously wounded when the militia fired into the crowd. The strike ended on May 13, with the defeated workers returning to their jobs and the Milwaukee labor movement vowed to use the ballot box in November to continue its protests. Organized labor met with great success, gaining a majority of seats on the County Board and electing the first labor candidate to Congress.

Across the country the national trade-union movement provoked a fierce response from both business and government. Presidents Grover Cleveland (1884–1888 and 1892–1896), a Democrat, and Benjamin Harrison (1888–1892), a Republican, sent federal troops to control strikes on several occasions, including the violent uprisings at the Carnegie Steel Mill in Homestead, Pennsylvania, in 1892 and the Pullman railway workers' strike in Illinois in 1894.[10]

In 1893 the firm represented the receivers of Villard's Northern Pacific Railroad and longtime client Henry C. Payne in obtaining a federal court injunction barring a strike by railroad workers. The controversy over the right to strike was a continuing battle during the Gilded Age and the early twentieth century. Employers were often able to persuade courts that a strike, even a threatened strike, would jeopardize the public welfare or public safety. The Sherman Antitrust Act of 1890 was intended to restrain large business combinations or monopolies. But corporate lawyers quickly learned that the Sherman Act could be used effectively against labor unions as well. District Judge Jenkins's decision granting an injunction in the Northern Pacific case was resoundingly antilabor. The court issued an injunction on December 19, 1893, and a second on December 22, 1893, that prohibited officers of the union from ordering or advising others to quit the service of the receivers of the Northern Pacific Railroad Company.[11] On appeal by the union the Seventh Circuit modified the injunction to allow workers to quit work in an orderly manner, but affirmed the injunction to the extent that it prevented all interference with railroad operations.[12]

The successful outcome for the receivers of the Northern Pacific mirrored a strategy established by employers in the post-Civil War years. A year later the United States Supreme Court approved of using injunctions in labor disputes by its unanimous decision in *In re Debs,* which resulted from the Pullman strike of 1894.

In May 1896 the Amalgamated Street Railway Employees demanded recognition of their union by the Milwaukee Electric Railway and Light Company, commonly known as TMER&L. When it refused, transit workers struck, halting city rail service for several weeks in May and June. Management moved swiftly to break the strike, barricading its property with armed guards and bringing in hundreds of strikebreakers. The strike grew violent following inflammatory speeches by labor leaders at the beginning of the second week. Mobs of workers stoned police and nonstrikers and hanged Payne in effigy. The strike ended in mid-June, and Payne punished the union by refusing to rehire strike leaders.[13]

When Milwaukee enacted an 1896 ordinance reducing trolley fares from five cents to four, the firm sought a federal court injunction to prohibit the decrease. Conceding that the city had the power to regulate rates, the firm argued that the new rate was unreasonable and confiscatory, and therefore a violation of the Due Process clause of the Fourteenth Amendment. The litigation was watched closely by city governments and transit companies across the country. Testimony by the company and its bondholders filled 1,445 pages, but was "so well classified and indexed, with such fair summaries in the briefs, that the [court's] task of examination [was] materially lightened." Finding that the transit company was earning only 3.3 to 4.5 percent yearly, when 6 percent was the current rate of interest on real estate first mortgages, the court made the injunction permanent in May 1898.[14]

In a colorful case for the transit company, the firm confronted several Wauwatosa citizens who challenged the company's right to collect a second nickel fare when its trolleys crossed Hawley Road. Riders had refused to pay the surcharge, contending that it was prohibited by an earlier Wauwatosa ordinance. To vex and annoy the company, riders repeatedly sued in Wauwatosa's justice court for damages from being put off the cars. They often won, and the company appealed each judgment to the superior court in Milwaukee. The new suburb's intensely loyal citizens called the protest over the surcharge a new "Boston Tea Party." Finally, the company obtained a temporary injunction prohibiting the insistent Wauwatosans from attempting to ride without paying the surcharge and from bringing additional damage suits in justice court. The firm appealed when the lower court dissolved its injunction, holding that it had to do so when the plaintiffs answered with a denial. Remanding the case on jurisdictional grounds, the Wisconsin Supreme Court nevertheless told the trial court that there was no merit in the Wauwatosans' refusal to pay the second fare.[15]

George Miller, who had replaced his ailing father as the attorney for Payne and the TMER&L, lobbied state legislators for limitations on the city's power to regulate utilities. As government regulations became more complex, lobbying came to be seen as an important and legitimate function of the corporate lawyer. The conflicting designs of the city and company were finally resolved on January 2, 1900, when the city abandoned its attempt to take over ownership of the trolley system and granted a franchise through 1934. For its part, TMER&L agreed to sell six trolley tickets for a quarter and twenty-five for a dollar, the very rates it had opposed so vigorously in federal court from 1896 to 1899.

Although it had given in on rates, the transit company won the war against the reformers's plan to establish public ownership of the city's utilities. The successful outcome of this long battle meant that the profits and monopoly privileges of the transit company were secured for many years to come. Miller, Noyes, Miller & Wahl had orchestrated the four-year contest with the city, using injunctions, litigation, argument, lobbying, and adroit political pressure.

The Wisconsin Telephone Company was also a stable client. In 1890 it was sued by a man who was injured when his runaway team crashed into a telephone pole located on the right-of-way. The local court ruled that he had pleaded a good claim, but the state Supreme Court reversed, holding that he had been injured by his horses, not by any fault of the telephone company. The court thought he would have been hurt when the team crashed into the roadside fence if the telephone pole hadn't gotten in the way.[16] The firm also prevailed in another case when Milwaukee tried to put a $1 annual franchise fee on every telephone pole.[17]

By 1898, when B. K. Miller died, the partnership had served as counsel to one or more of Milwaukee's utilities for almost five decades. The firm had worked for the Milwaukee Gas Company since the 1850s, when Lynde had written its charter and Finch had begun his lengthy service on its board and as its president. However, after Finch's death, the gas company had turned to other law firms for a time, as the Millers became more closely involved with the competing electric utilities. The firm's association with Payne's transit monopoly led directly to its entry into the era of electric lighting franchises. As attorneys for Payne and on retainer for the Milwaukee Street Railway Company, the firm's wide experience in the area of electrified mass transit became tied in with the emerging electrical monopoly owned by the transit company.

As electric lighting began to replace the old gaslights, B. K. Miller joined other investors in establishing several similar electric utility companies. In 1897, along with financiers F. G. Bigelow, Henry Payne, and Charles Pfister, Miller arranged for the purchase of the Neenah and Menasha Electric Railway Company (later the Fox River Valley Electric Railway Company), which brought electric lighting to several cities in the prosperous central Wisconsin valley. With the firm's help the company managed to steer a path through the regulatory network that produced increased profits by 1906, without the increased burden of either taxation or strangulation by public control. The firm's work on behalf of its utility clients to preserve their existence as privately-owned companies within the provisions of public regulation was the most notable hallmark of the Miller era.

The first municipal service to be publicly owned was Milwaukee's garbage-treatment facility, which was begun in 1898 with an $80,000 bond issue. The facility was designed to replace the earlier methods of using garbage as animal feed and fertilizer. Suing on behalf of taxpayers, the firm won a temporary injunction halting construction because the bonds took the city beyond its legally allowable debt limit.[18] When subcontractors got leave to proceed with construction despite the injunction against the city and the prime contractor, the firm intervened and persuaded the Wisconsin Supreme Court that it was absurd to allow agents to do what a principal was enjoined from doing.[19]

The call for municipal ownership became a harbinger of the socialist movement that was developing in Milwaukee. As a city that had grown to 275,000 inhabitants by 1890, Milwaukee was forced to cope with crucial issues of health and safety. In 1895, with the completion of the North Point water-intake facility, the city finally achieved the ability to draw an abundant supply of clean water from Lake Michigan.

Both B. K. Miller and George Miller remained active not only in utility franchise work but also in the area of urban health and sanitation as promoters of improvements to the Milwaukee water and sewer system. George Miller was one of the leaders who fought for a halt to the practice of dumping the city's sewage into Lake Michigan not far from the newly built water-intake facility.

In 1891 the firm began an attempt to collect about $100,000 owed to its client, National Foundry and Pipe Works, Ltd., for pipe it had supplied for construction of a water utility in Oconto. After

the original owner of the utility lost its stake in a mortgage foreclosure, the pipe works tried to get a lien on the water plant. The Wisconsin Supreme Court held there could be no mechanic's lien that
might cut off a public water supply. For a time federal courts declined to follow Wisconsin's interpretation of its own mechanic's
lien law. Eventually the federal courts yielded. The pipe works's pro-
tracted and tenacious attempts to collect its judgment involved trials
in both state and federal courts and multiple appeals to both the
Wisconsin Supreme Court and the Seventh Circuit Court of Appeals.
In 1902 the United States Supreme Court held that the principal
issues were *res judicata,* and that the pipe works had neither a lien
on the water plant nor a right to collect from successors to the original owners of the plant.[20] In its ruling on another action the next
month, the Seventh Circuit rebuked Judge Noyes for continuing to
press his case: "Almost any person or party less heroic in contested
and stubborn litigation, and not so skilled in shifting attitudes and
raising new points, would have been reasonably satisfied."[21]

Noyes was also involved in a United States Supreme Court case
on behalf of an Illinois corporation that had contracted to supervise
the building of, and then to operate, a glue factory near Milwaukee.
When the contract was repudiated, the Illinois company sued for
breach. The Wisconsin defendant contended that the contract had
been nullified by the plaintiff's failure to register its corporate charter
in Wisconsin and to pay the $25 filing fee, as an 1898 Wisconsin
statute required. When the lower federal courts ruled for the defendant, the firm took the case to the United States Supreme Court, but
lost. Its principal argument was that the statute's retroactive effect
violated the contract clause of the United States Constitution. In a
decision written by Oliver Wendell Holmes, the court distinguished
a rule regulating the conduct of business from a rule affecting a contract. "A prohibition of the doing of business after a statute goes into
effect is not retroactive with regard to that business, even though the
business be done in pursuance of an earlier contract."[22]

As the century drew to a close the city's population grew
to 285,315, almost three-quarters of them first- or second-generation
Germans. The bonds that had developed between prosperous
Germans and Yankee leaders became fruitful for the firm of Miller,
Noyes, Miller & Wahl. Although of English and Yankee ancestry him-

self, Benjamin K. Miller, Sr., serendipitously shared the name of the prominent brewery family. Like Lynde, the elder Miller developed strong social and business ties to Milwaukee's German community. Under Lynde's leadership the firm had reached out to German businesses in tanning, brewing, and other enterprises. Intermarriage between elite Yankees and elite German families was not uncommon during the 1880s and 1890s. Lynde's eldest son married into the German community, and George Miller also added a special dimension to the firm's appeal to German businessmen with his training in both the German language and German civil law.

Similarly, the Wahl family, which had emigrated from Germany in the late 1840s, became prominent residents of Milwaukee's elite east side and leaders in the community. During the 1890s George H. Wahl, as the firm's first partner of German ancestry, further solidified this ethnic tie, bringing to the firm the growing business of the Uihlein family and their Schlitz Brewery. In 1894, soon after Wahl became a partner, the firm handled a series of collection cases for the Schlitz Brewery in circuit court against beer distributors or tavern owners who were hard-pressed by the money squeeze of the 1893 depression. Other German clients, such as George Brumder and the Germania National Bank (which later became part of the First Wisconsin Corporation), occasionally used the firm's services in collection matters in the lower courts, but took other business to firms such as Winkler, Flanders, Bottum, Smith & Vilas (now Michael, Best & Friedrich) or the new partnership of Churchill & von Briesen (now von Briesen & Purtell).[23]

The elder Miller died on September 12, 1898, at the age of sixty-eight. B. K. Miller, Sr., was hailed in one obituary as a leader in the law of public utilities, as well as the trusted counselor and trustee of many of Milwaukee's leading families. To honor his many contributions, the Milwaukee Bar Association placed his bust in the Milwaukee Law Library. He was eulogized by associates at the bar as a "trustee, guardian, executor and administrator . . . [of such] consummate skill that he never lost a dollar of the funds committed to his keeping." Among his colleagues, the elder Miller was hailed as "a brilliant example of that increasing body of lawyers who find their highest success in the quiet diplomacy of the office, rather than in the uproar of litigation."[24]

During his forty-year tenure at the firm, B. K. Miller had witnessed tremendous changes in the law and in American life. He had come to Wisconsin in 1839 when the area was a crude frontier. He had witnessed the attainment of statehood, the development of the first railroads, the growth and electrification of cities, even the invention of the automobile. Joining the partnership before the Civil War, he lived to see two presidents assassinated, cities transformed by immigration and technology, and America made into a world power after the Spanish-American War. At the close of the nineteenth century Miller shared the general optimism about America's military might and economic prosperity and all they portended for the century soon to begin.

On his death his two sons, with their partners Noyes and Wahl, were in the midst of the turbulent transit battle of 1898. Not surprisingly, George Miller emerged immediately as the heir to his father's one-man rule, and Ben kept a lower profile within the firm and the community.[25]

Only two years after Miller's death, George Wahl died unexpectedly on August 26, 1900, at the age of only thirty-eight. His death reduced the partnership to three, and the firm again called itself Miller, Noyes & Miller. The three partners began to search for new associates of high caliber, so that they could begin to promote from within instead of inviting new men to join the partnership from outside the office.

Also in 1906, both Ben Miller and George Noyes withdrew from the firm. George Noyes left at the invitation of Henry L. Palmer, his old friend and former colleague, to lead the legal department of the Northwestern Mutual Life Insurance Company in Milwaukee, a position he filled until just before his death in 1916. Ben Miller had long wanted to retire from active practice and had often been unreachable for key partnership decisions even before his nominal retirement. Once, unable to contact Ben in Siberia, George Miller had written a client that he would handle the matter instead. At the age of forty-eight, with a sizable inheritance from his father's estate, Ben left to travel around the world, to collect stamps, and to write and do research from his retreat at Wild Rose in central Wisconsin. He was able to live the last two decades of his life in the scholarly retreat he had always sought, away from the pressures of the daily practice of law. Miller family legend recalls Ben's telling his brother George that he retired and George did not because of one major difference between them: "I have all the money I want or need, and you want to make more."[26]

With Ben Miller and George Noyes departing in 1906, George Miller decided to rename the partnership Miller, Mack & Fairchild. Arthur Fairchild had become a partner in 1905 and Edwin Mack in 1906. Significantly, he also began to stress the firm's beginnings by including the firm's historic name on its door and on its stationery. The name of Miller, Mack & Fairchild would carry the firm to the middle of the twentieth century. But below it, not to be forgotten, was the name the firm had taken in 1857: "Formerly Finches, Lynde & Miller."

1. *B. K. Miller, Sr., in his law office, circa 1890*

2. *Milwaukee's second courthouse, on what is now Cathedral Square, 1872*

3. B. K. Miller, Jr., in his law office, circa 1890

4. View from top of Mackie Building looking north across Wisconsin Avenue to new courthouse, circa 1890

5. *Lynden, the Lynde family home, located on Chestnut (now Juneau) and 23rd Streets*

6. *Wisconsin Avenue, circa 1890*

7. *Chicago and Northwestern Railroad Station at the east end of Wisconsin Avenue, built in 1896*

8. *Early horse-drawn street car or omnibus*

9. B. K. Miller, Jr.

10. G. H. Noyes

11. George P. Miller

12. G. H. Wahl

13. Home of B. K. Miller, Sr., 733 Marshall Street

14. Miller Block Building on Wisconsin Avenue at Broadway, location of the firm's offices from 1870s to 1914

MILLER, NOYES,
MILLER & WAHL,

(Finches, Lynde & Miller)

Attorneys and Counselors at Law,

102 WISCONSIN STREET.

BENJAMIN K. MILLER,   GEORGE H. NOYES,
    BENJAMIN K. MILLER, Jr., GEORGE P. MILLER,
        GEORGE H. WAHL.
    WILLIAM H. MORRIS,   P. B. MYERS,
EDWIN S. MACK.   LOYAL DURAND.

15. Firm notice in Milwaukee City Directory, 1896

16. *"Made in Milwaukee:" Automobiles manufactured by the Milwaukee Motor and Manufacturing Company, a client of the firm, circa 1910*

17. *Public Service Building at Third and Michigan Streets, home of TMER&L, built in 1905*

18. *First T. A. Chapman Store on East Wisconsin Avenue*

19. *Wisconsin Telephone Company operators, circa 1890*

⋘ 11 ⋙

Miller, Mack & Fairchild
1906–1917

The three men who set out in 1906 to practice law together as Miller, Mack & Fairchild continued the traditions Asahel
Finch and William Pitt Lynde had begun sixty-four years before.
However, the world had changed dramatically from the laissez-faire
economic climate in which the clients of Finch, Lynde and even
B. K. Miller, Sr., had flourished. The first two decades of the twentieth century challenged practitioners of corporate and tax law as
never before. The reform spirit of progressivism and the resulting creation of a new network of government regulations and taxes called
for adroit legal work. Steering corporate clients through the growing
maze of laws and regulations was a challenging task, demanding new
legal knowledge. The rapid pace of this change called on all the
scholarly and diplomatic abilities of the new partnership of Miller,
Mack & Fairchild.

Theirs was still the most active law firm in Milwaukee. Their
clients included banks, utilities, railroads, trolley companies, breweries, and all manner of heavy industries. Like the founders, George
P. Miller, Edwin S. Mack, and Arthur W. Fairchild made law and the
firm their lifelong careers. The name they gave the partnership in
1906 survived for forty-five years.

Mack brought to the partnership almost fifteen years of experience as both a lawyer and a teacher. George Miller considered his to be "one of the best legal minds of the era." Born in Cincinnati and educated in Milwaukee at the public high school from 1883 to 1887, Mack came from an old and distinguished German-Jewish family. The imposing Mack family mansion at 945 North Marshall Street stood only a few blocks from George Miller's boyhood home. Mack was elected to Phi Beta Kappa at Harvard in 1891, and finished first in his Harvard Law School class in 1893. His law-school valedictory address on bankruptcy legislation was published by the *Harvard Law Review* and the *American Law Review,* and later was reprinted in law journals in both Scotland and Ireland.[1]

Despite many opportunities at eastern law firms, Mack was encouraged to return to Milwaukee by Walter Carter, a New York lawyer who had once worked as an associate at Finches, Lynde & Miller. On Carter's strong recommendation, B. K. Miller, Sr., welcomed his old friend's protégé into the firm on September 13, 1893, just as financial panic deepened throughout the country. Mack stayed with the firm only two years, leaving to go into practice alone in the adjacent Wells Building on Wisconsin Avenue just after George Wahl became a partner. Suddenly junior to George Wahl as well as to B. K. Miller, Ben Miller, George Miller, and George Noyes, Mack had misgivings about his own opportunities for partnership.

However, he continued as a sole practitioner to work on several estate cases for the firm and did a great deal of collections work for George Miller. Occasionally he served the firm as a consultant on legal issues. Mack joined the faculty of the University of Wisconsin Law School in 1903. Although teaching suited his scholarly nature, Mack decided to return to private practice to help his father, whose clothing business had failed in the depression of the 1890s. When George Miller invited him to become a partner in 1906, Mack accepted.

George Miller's decision to make Mack a partner was both unusual and courageous. Few Yankee law firms in the early twentieth century had Jewish partners. Prejudice excluded Jews from establishment firms and social clubs for many decades. Like their counterparts elsewhere, Milwaukee's elite clubs had restrictive membership policies in those days. Nevertheless, Mack's quiet brilliance won him respect and acceptance among Milwaukee's business leaders, even though the Yankee and Jewish communities remained socially separate until after World War I. By the time of his death in 1942, Mack was not only a leader in the Milwaukee and Wisconsin bar, but a social leader as well. He was a member of the Masonic Order, a trustee of the Milwaukee University School and of the Layton Art Institute, and a director of the University Club of Milwaukee.[2]

Miller's invitation to Mack was strongly endorsed by Fairchild who, as an alumnus of the law school, knew of Mack's growing reputation there. Fairchild had become an associate at the firm in July 1901 and a partner on January 1, 1905. Descended from Yankee pioneers who settled in the Marinette area on Green Bay in the mid-nineteenth century, the Fairchilds were well known in the state. Arthur's father, Hiram O. Fairchild, had practiced law in Marinette for many years before joining the prominent Green Bay firm of Greene, Vroman & Fairchild. Active in politics, the elder Fairchild was elected speaker of the assembly in 1884 and 1885. He urged Arthur to take a position as page at the 1900 Republican convention, which nominated William McKinley for a second term and placed Theodore Roosevelt on the ballot as vice president.[3]

Arthur Fairchild spent a year in his father's law office before entering the law school, from which he graduated in 1901 with honors. Like Mack, Fairchild was a scholar in the law, but his true gifts were more like those of William Lynde and George Miller. Socially outgoing and adept in personal relationships, Fairchild entered the parlors of Milwaukee society and the board rooms of Milwaukee corporations with a confidence and business savvy that pleased old clients and brought in many new ones.

With the addition of Fairchild and Mack and the departures of his brother Ben and Judge Noyes, George Miller forged a strong new triumvirate of legal talent, a partnership balanced in interest and ability. Miller at age forty-eight was the senior member. The seasoned Mack was thirty-seven. Fairchild, aged twenty-nine, was the junior partner. Each man remained in the partnership until his death: Miller in 1931 at age seventy-two, Mack in 1942 at seventy-two, and Fairchild in 1956 at seventy-nine.

In Milwaukee, the early years of the twentieth century—the years before World War I—were marked by great economic optimism, as well as by tremendous social and political change. The city's population had increased 40 percent during the 1890s. New buildings, including the city hall, a new post office on Wisconsin

Street, and a new library, as well as several new parks, stood as vivid symbols of growth and prosperity. In 1901 the Edward P. Allis Company, a firm client, merged with three other manufacturers to form the Allis-Chalmers Company. The new company employed 5,000 workers at five plants, and had a large complex under construction in the suburb of West Allis. The following year, the Schlitz brewery, another client, surpassed Pabst in becoming Milwaukee's (and America's) largest producer of beer.[4]

There were new facilities for education and training as well. The Milwaukee School of Engineering opened in 1903. Milwaukee became one of the first American cities to offer a four-year commercial-high-school diploma. The Milwaukee Medical College opened as part of Marquette University in 1907. Progressives endorsed educational growth; the early years of the twentieth century witnessed the birth of the "Wisconsin Idea," whereby scholars at the University of Wisconsin worked closely with state government for social, economic, and political reforms.

The excitement of the era resulted from many new inventions as well as from a new spirit in government. New technology brought the first automobiles to the city. The first motion-picture theater opened in July 1906. Two years later, the first dirigible flight gave passengers a panoramic view of Milwaukee. In 1907 the first interurban electric train connected Milwaukee with Cedarburg, making commuting possible from yet farther away. On July 4, 1909, the Milwaukee Road inaugurated through freight traffic to the West Coast. As well as a port, Milwaukee was now an industrial center with rail links to both coasts. Milwaukee experienced its greatest decade of industrial growth, with total manufactures valued at $208 million by 1910. Ole Evinrude's invention of an outboard motor was a further boost to the economy, and soon the manufacture of engines and machinery began to surpass all other Milwaukee industries.

Technology also affected the practice of law and streamlined office procedures. The automobile made it easier for a lawyer to appear in courts outside Milwaukee. The well-established telephone network made possible long-distance conferences, without the delay of mailed communications and consultations.

In its work for many of Milwaukee's businesses, the firm's role as legal adviser and corporate planner took precedence over litigation. The sons and grandsons of many of the Milwaukee pioneer businessmen, who had been clients of Finch & Lynde, turned for legal advice to George Miller, Arthur Fairchild, and Edwin Mack. Some clients, like the Milwaukee Gas Company, Wells Fargo, the New York Life Insurance Company, and American Express, had used the firm for many decades. Families with prominent names like Cudahy, Plankinton, Kieckhefer, Allis, Merrill, Vogel, Pfister, Beggs, Abbott, and Payne maintained relationships with the firm.

There were new clients, too. The 1906–1925 firm ledger reveals the names of the corporations that were changing the industrial climate of the city. Pabst and Schlitz and other breweries retained the firm in the early twentieth century. The firm also represented the Horlick and the Froedtert Malting companies (which were tied to the brewing industry), Briggs and Stratton, Federal Rubber, Link Belt Company, West Bend Aluminum, Johnson Service, Oscar Mayer and Company, Flambeau Paper Company, and the Wehr Corporation.[5]

Retail concerns were thriving, too. Miller, Mack & Fairchild handled matters for the Pranges, who operated a large retail store in Sheboygan. The firm also represented the Boston Store and, of course, T. A. Chapman and Company, whose board president was George Miller. Besides the locally owned department stores, the Kresge Store, which opened early in 1900 on Grand Avenue, became a client. J. Gilbert Hardgrove (then an associate) appeared in the Wisconsin Supreme Court for Kresge, which had settled with a woman shopper who had hurt herself when she tripped over a tool box in the store. Kresge sued its liability insurer, which had denied coverage. Hardgrove prevailed both in the trial court and on appeal.[6]

Growing along with the national retail chain store business were customer-incentive plans, such as trading stamps. Wisconsin viewed trading stamps as "pernicious and evil" and outlawed their "use, issuance, or delivery" in 1917. On behalf of Sperry and Hutchinson Co., promotor of Green Stamps, George Miller made a then-rare appearance before the Wisconsin Supreme Court to challenge the statute on several constitutional grounds, but lost.[7]

Cars changed the practice of law after 1900 as the railroads had fifty years before. Automobile ads became common in newspapers by 1906, when a Buick sold for as much as $2,500 and a Rambler for $1,700. George Miller drove a more luxurious car, a Pierce Arrow, which he ordered from a distributor in California, sending his chauffeur west to pick it up. Wisconsin owners registered 26,000 cars in 1912. In 1914 Henry Ford began to mass-produce the Model T and could sell it for $500, a price within reach of a factory worker. The firm had a number of clients in the automobile industry, including the Four Wheel Drive Auto Company, based near Clintonville; the Crosby Transportation Company of Kenosha, which became Crosby-Nash and, still later, American Motors; the Cruiser Motor Car Company; and the Globe Transportation Company. Auto parts manufacturers also were clients of the firm, such as the A. O. Smith Company, which built car chassis, the National Brake and Electric Company, the Auto Parts Manufacturing Company, and the Pressed Steel Tank Company.[8]

In the years between 1900 and World War I, progressive reforms brought many changes to the practice of estate and probate law. Public policy toward inheritance changed as governments sought new forms of revenue. Wisconsin and Michigan enacted five percent inheritance taxes, known to many as death taxes. The first several thousand dollars of an estate were exempted and relatives were taxed at only one percent. The federal government, envisioning inheritance taxes as a way to pay for the Spanish-American War, used the idea in 1898. It fixed a top rate of 15 percent on estates of $1 million or more. Although this was repealed in 1902, the concept of a federal, as well as a state, tax on inheritance was later accepted by reformers and upheld by the courts. "The idea of death taxes fed and grew fat on fear of dynasties and the money power," wrote one legal historian. Economists like Wisconsin's Richard Ely offered statistical support for the new taxing policies. Some businessmen, including Andrew Carnegie, endorsed the concept.[9]

Thus, with taxes threatening the vast estates accumulated during the Gilded Age, lawyers pioneered in creating and maintaining trusts. The demand for lawyers' services in the area of wills and probate mushroomed by 1910. Firms renowned for managing the estates of the wealthy were now asked to plan and manage smaller holdings for the growing middle class. Working in the rapidly changing area of estate planning, the firm managed a large number of trust funds established in the wills of wealthy Milwaukeeans. An early twentieth-century ledger lists the accounts of many prominent Wisconsin leaders of government and business, as well as the names of dozens of other, less well-known citizens who were charged an average of $30 to $60 for the drafting of a will. Clients with larger estates were billed from $90 to $160 for the original estate-planning session, and an ongoing management fee if the firm served as trustee. Names such as Plankinton, Usinger, Pabst, Uihlein, Mitchell, Allis, and even Elisha W. Keyes (the Republican boss of Wisconsin) were listed as clients in trust work. For one estate, where probate rulings were challenged in the Supreme Court, the bill was $1,937.20.[10]

George Miller worked for several years on the New York estate of Robert Graham Dun, one of the namesakes of Dun & Bradstreet. Asset values were disputed, claims were challenged, and paintings were donated to and then refused by the Metropolitan Museum of Art. Real estate holdings, including the Bradstreet Building, created difficulties. George Miller's longtime friend and adviser, Clarence Dillon, also worked on the Dun estate. With William A. Read of Chicago, he would later found the investment house of Dillon-Read.[11]

All three of the Millers had served as directors of the First National Bank of Milwaukee and its trust company, founded in the 1890s. Many of the estates handled by the firm were deposited with the trust company, and the law firm served as attorney for both the trust company and the bank. In 1919 the trust company and the bank were merged with the Wisconsin National Bank to create the First Wisconsin National Bank, the largest financial institution in the state. This merger was handled by the firm, as were the later acquisitions of the American National Bank and the Second Ward Savings Bank of Milwaukee.

As estate work reached to wealthy clients across the Midwest and on both coasts, the firm continued to grow in numbers of associates and support staff. A nonlawyer, C. M. Rothe, became the office manager and a vital part of day-to-day operations. He handled correspondence with heirs to estates managed by the firm and helped train new associates in office procedures.

Only one year after the addition of Mack and Fairchild, Miller began to recruit associates from the leaders of law-school classes. James B. Blake joined the firm on November 1, 1907, and worked under the tutelage of Miller and Mack until he became a partner on January 1, 1915. He was born in Winona, Minnesota, in 1882, and graduated from the state normal school in Winona and the University of Chicago Law School. J. Gilbert Hardgrove was hired as an associate in 1909 and became a partner on January 1, 1916. He had known Arthur Fairchild in the Wisconsin law class of 1901, had practiced for a time in Fond du Lac in the firm of Edward Bragg, the Civil War hero, and had served there as court commissioner. As its practice continued to grow, the firm hired William F. Adams, Claude J. Hendricks, and Bert Vandervelde as associates in 1915; Walter S. Bartlett and Frederick R. Wahl in 1916; and Paul R. Newcomb in 1917. Newcomb became a partner in 1923 and Vandervelde in 1933.

One secretary, Mildred Roehr, who later served as the firm's business manager, was hired by James Blake in 1925. He scrutinized her transcript from the commercial high school, as well as her previous job record. Finding both to be outstanding, Blake inquired of her references, "Is she a lady?" The firm's clientele, as well as its attorneys, required a high standard of conduct from everyone in the office.[12]

With more lawyers and a larger support staff, the suite in the Guaranty, or Miller, Building at 102 East Wisconsin Avenue became inadequate. In 1914 the firm moved to the newly constructed First National Bank Building at 735 North Water Street, designed by Daniel Burnham of Chicago. Located just north of where Solomon Juneau had first established his trading post in the 1830s on Wisconsin and Water streets, the fifteen-story granite and buff brick structure was built around an interior courtyard that provided the inside offices with natural light and a view.

At first the firm occupied half of the fifteenth floor. Behind swinging leather-covered doors, a long corridor lined with shelves served as the firm's library, although the one bare swinging light bulb made research a challenge. At the end of the hall, past the secretaries' room and several small offices for associates, were the large private offices of Edwin Mack and George Miller. Each had its own adjoining secretarial space and was furnished elegantly with a desk (Miller kept his father's antique rolltop desk), a work table, a leather-covered couch, and a private wash basin just behind the coat rack. A key piece of equipment in the large secretarial room was a buzzer on the wall, which sounded a distinctive signal for each secretary. The firm gradually expanded to fill the entire fourteenth and fifteenth floors of the building and later moved into part of the thirteenth as well.

Visitors to the firm's reception room during this era were struck by the very large Western Union wall clock, which was always kept to an absolutely precise time. Each morning, as Edwin Mack arrived at the office, he glanced at the clock, walked down the corridor to his own private office, and telephoned the receptionist to double-check on the clock's accuracy. Such precision was typical of Mack's approach to all facets of the practice of law and office procedure. Mack refused to substitute carbon copies for the letter-press system because, he said, carbon copies could be altered. In 1900 the support staff included a telephone operator/receptionist, a messenger/file clerk, four secretaries, and a bookkeeper. Twenty years later, there were six more secretaries, two bookkeepers, and a number of messenger boys.[13]

The firm's new location enhanced its ability to work on trusts and estates in cooperation with the First National Bank downstairs. As matters involving estate planning and management began to assume more and more of its time, questions concerning the operation of the stock market, the taxing of securities, and broker liability over stock purchases or transfers took the firm into litigation.

The Western Union Telegraph Company, long a client, was sometimes sued when it failed to deliver messages. Despite the firm's appeal to the Wisconsin Supreme Court, one man won $800 in damages when he lost a chance for a job in Venezuela because Western Union had not delivered the job offer to him. In another case, the firm won a directed verdict in a Waukesha County court against a plaintiff who claimed he lost $1,500 when his telegram incorrectly directed his broker to buy 1,000 shares of a stock instead of 100. The Supreme Court remanded to give a jury a chance to decide whether Western Union was liable. Another case reflected the political problems of the age. The firm defended American Express against a claim that it had not delivered $1,000 the plaintiff had tried to wire to his mother in Russia. American Express sought excuse in the wartime chaos that existed in Russia in mid-1917, but neither the jury nor the Supreme Court was impressed.[14]

The election of Emil Seidel as the first Socialist mayor of an American city in 1910 resulted from the continuing frustration of Milwaukee's citizens with earlier unfulfilled promises of reform. The Milwaukee brand of socialism, which restored honesty and efficiency to government, was palatable even to many middle-class voters. Observers across the country wondered how the Socialists would run a city and deal with private corporations. Socialists achieved much during their four decades in control of Milwaukee city government. They began in 1911 by cleaning up the city's legendary red-light district near the river and continued with a general crackdown on gambling and prostitution. They also established an effective public-works department and provided free textbooks for the city's schools, an eight-hour day for city workers, a municipal ice plant, more parks, free medical care for the poor, and public sale of wood and coal for fuel.[15]

The city's utility companies and large corporations watched and waited, as did the attorneys who served them. Socialists had once demanded public ownership of utilities and had fought the granting of private franchises, but by 1910 they had moderated their views to attract a wider constituency. Milwaukee socialism came to be called "sewer socialism" or "streetcar socialism." The city's Socialist mayors promoted regulation as well as ownership and encouraged corporations to express their public conscience within the confines of social control.

Many of the actions brought by Miller, Mack & Fairchild for various utilities and business interests sought a standard of equity and precision from the regulators and were not necessarily in opposition to regulation itself. George Miller's leadership on behalf of the telephone company represented this search for order. In a series of public hearings in 1906, Miller told a surprised crowd that the Wisconsin Telephone Company favored creating a Public Service Commission, which would enfranchise only one telephone company in a given area. The company believed that subscribers would get better service, and telephone companies would make larger profits, if there were no competition within local calling areas.

The utilities, including street railways, became the primary focus of twentieth-century reformers, just as railroads had been their main target in the nineteenth century. In their effort to regulate utilities the Socialists in Milwaukee relied heavily on the state regulatory machinery that had been established by the Progressive reformers. The most controversial was the Wisconsin Railroad Commission, established in 1905.

Mack appeared before the Railroad Commission thirty times in its first fifteen years of existence. He won a national reputation as a highly skilled utilities lawyer and a technician who could provide the regulators with a fresh and lucid interpretation of the most complex corporate balance sheets. The powers of the Railroad Commission were enlarged in 1907 to include the supervision and regulation of telephone, electric, and gas companies, as George Miller had advocated. But its name was not changed to the Public Service Commission until 1931. Wisconsin's was the first even moderately effective commission in the country. The New York commission, described as "venal and impotent," provided an example to be avoided: the New York commissioners had been quickly bought off by the railroads and had voted to abolish their board after only two years of existence. Witnessing similar patterns in his own state of Massachusetts, the great jurist Louis Brandeis cautioned, "Do not pin too much faith in legislation. Remedial institutions are apt to fall under the control of the enemy and to become instruments of oppression."[16] Mindful of these weak precedents, the Wisconsin commission took direct action in the area of rate control within its first year. Its right to make these decisions was promptly tested in the courts, both state and federal. Thus, representing a client before the Railroad Commission was often only a first step toward litigation.

Mack, assisted by Blake, Hardgrove, and occasionally Fairchild, represented such leading utilities as the Milwaukee Electric Railway and Light Company, the Milwaukee Gas Light Company, and the Wisconsin Telephone Company, as well as many smaller utility companies across the state. Under Mack's leadership the firm became the major legal force appearing before the new Railroad Commission on questions that included routes and pickup points, street-paving ordinances, rates and fares, safety and public comfort, competition, long-distance telephoning, and the underlying issues regarding valuation and fair profits. The firm and its clients had the resources with which to test new regulations and statutes in court.

As it challenged government regulation, the firm often appeared against both the state attorney general and the attorneys for Milwaukee and other municipalities. In particular, Mack faced the young Milwaukee city attorney, Socialist Daniel Hoan, both in court and before the Railroad Commission, dozens of times, establishing, if not a personal animosity, certainly a strong ideological rivalry. During his twenty-four years as mayor (starting in 1916), Hoan continued to take an active interest in the city's legal challenges to the utilities, signing his name as mayor on briefs below that of the city attorneys.

By the time the Wisconsin Railroad Commission was established in 1906, many citizens of Milwaukee wanted the transit monopoly in their midst to be tightly controlled for the public good. The reformers took on TMER&L with a zeal and a vengeance that were characteristic of the muckrakers of the period, viewing the new Railroad Commission as an appropriate forum for its long list of grievances. Although the rate issue was the most bitter battle, the city also raised questions of passenger safety, warmth, and comfort. In 1907 the city attorney filed a complaint with the commission alleging that the use of hand brakes, instead of air brakes, was unsafe; that the trolley cars were full of bacteria; and that the heaters were not sufficiently stoked in winter for passenger comfort.

Appearing for TMER&L, Mack agreed that the transit company would make the extra effort to add additional cars in rush hours, to clean every car at the beginning (and possibly in the middle) of each day, and to stoke the heaters adequately. Streetcar routes were vitally important to merchants and citizens before the automobile came into widespread use. Whole neighborhoods organized—usually successfully—to seek the Railroad Commission's approval of new streetcar lines in their areas.[17]

But while the commissioners were considering questions of routing and safety, there was litigation over the thirty-four-year franchise the city had granted in 1900. In 1913 the Railroad Commission ordered the trolley company to sell thirteen tickets for fifty cents, a reduction from the six-for-a-quarter and twenty-five-for-a-dollar ticket prices fixed by the franchise. (The cash fare of a nickel was unchanged.) The firm appealed to the Wisconsin Supreme Court, characterizing its city franchise as a contract that the commission could not constitutionally impair. When it lost on a four-to-two vote in Madison, it appealed to the United States Supreme Court, also unsuccessfully.[18] Sullivan & Cromwell attorney William J. Curtis of New York joined Mack in the long battle over trolley fares and other issues. He was sent by Henry Villard, whose North American Trust owned TMER&L and thus had an interest in the fare battles. Mack finally succeeded in winning fare increases for the company in 1919, 1922, and 1923.

Fares were not the only issue. In 1911 TMER&L successfully resisted the city's effort to collect a $15-per-car franchise fee retroactively for the years 1896 through 1910. Ruling on the city's appeal, the Wisconsin Supreme Court declared the fee to be only a disguised tax, which was forbidden by statute. Seven years later, the firm won a refund of $8,805 for TMER&L after it had paid the $15 tax under protest for 1911.[19] In 1915 the city ordered TMER&L to use asphalt over a concrete foundation in paving the street between its tracks. That was more expensive than the macadam the city had used the last time it had paved between the rails. Under the ordinance of 1900 the railway had agreed to maintain and repair the between-track areas with the same materials the city had last used for paving them. The company challenged the new ordinance before the Railroad Commission and in the Wisconsin Supreme Court on the ground that the city remained bound by the terms of the 1900 compromise. The city won when the Supreme Court held that the 1900 franchise had not limited the city's authority to provide for the city's health and welfare.[20]

Mack's reputation as an expert in the field of utilities and regulation brought many new clients to the firm in the early twentieth century, including electric, gas, and telephone companies from Rhinelander, La Crosse, Madison, Green Bay, Janesville, Racine, and the Fox River Valley. As small telephone companies developed across the state, the Railroad Commission ordered a long-distance system to link the local exchanges. The Wisconsin Telephone Company, a client of the firm since it was chartered by B. K. Miller, Sr., built it. Mack handled several rate cases for both the Milwaukee Gas Light Company and the Wisconsin Electric Power Company, which was created out of TMER&L in 1919. The following year the firm won the commission's approval for the new electric company to build a $5 million Lakeside Power Plant to meet Milwaukee's growing electric needs.

Underlying the matter of rate assessment and equitable taxation of utilities was the question of the fair valuation of the property on which an allowable profit could be determined. Members of the state's Railroad Commission became accustomed to the financial wizardry of Edwin Mack as he presented arguments based on extensive balance-sheet data and statistical analysis, skills at which he excelled.

Miller, Mack & Fairchild had consolidated its new partnership and served its clients through a period in which corporate expansion had to come to terms with concerns for the public good. The firm's home in Wisconsin—a cradle of progressivism—brought not only exciting opportunities but special challenges as well. Under the strong and expert leadership of Edwin Mack the firm advised and guided its clients and tested a welter of complex regulations at each governmental level. The precedents that were established—sometimes favorably, sometimes not—set the early parameters for government regulation of twentieth-century corporate development.

⫷ 12 ⫸

World War I
and the
Decade of Prosperity
1917–1931

When the United States entered World War I on April 12, 1917, the conflict was already three years old. Milwaukee had been sharply divided about the war since its beginning. Led by Victor Berger, Socialists opposed America's entry and were accused of disloyalty. Many Milwaukeeans of German heritage were sending money, bandages, and other forms of aid to their relatives in the homeland—actions that were completely legal, of course, before the United States was at war.

Milwaukee's German community was badly torn by the world conflict. The German-American League raised $150,000 for the relief of German and Austrian war refugees. Newly elected Socialist mayor Daniel Hoan led a parade of 70,000 marchers for neutrality. The *Milwaukee Journal* launched bitter editorial attacks against pro-German elements, editorials that later earned a Pulitzer Prize. In an atmosphere of growing pro-British feeling, Milwaukee's Germans paid a high price for their ethnic ties.

Progressives and others who opposed the war were vilified. Senator Robert La Follette was hung in effigy on the campus at the university in Madison as enthusiasm for the war became more acceptable than protestations of neutrality. Government censorship and public pressure exacted a terrible toll on the city. Musical groups refused to play the works of Brahms and Beethoven and other German masters. Schools and streets lost their familiar German names. Enrollment in German-language classes in the public schools dropped from 30,000 to 400. The very Germanic flavor of the city was jeopardized, as sauerkraut became liberty cabbage, the Deutscher Club became the Wisconsin Club, the German-American Academy became University School, and the Pabst Theatre suspended the production of all German plays.

Corporations and financial institutions were also affected. The Germania Bank became the Commercial Bank and the Germania Building was rechristened the Brumder Building. After 124 American lives were lost on the *Lusitania* in 1915, and after the resumption of unrestricted submarine warfare, those who continued to oppose American involvement were quickly labeled unpatriotic or even traitors.

War fever reached a frenzy. Milwaukee became the first large American city to fill its draft quota. Milwaukee citizens oversubscribed to the Liberty Loan drive despite Mayor Hoan's veto of a city-council resolution to purchase $500,000 in war bonds. George Miller, Edwin Mack, and Arthur Fairchild bought war bonds themselves and circulated a memo urging all office personnel to do the same. Miller later donated $50,000 of his bonds to Milwaukee Downer Seminary, which his two daughters had attended. The Wilson government enlisted the full support of the private sector by mandating a government-managed effort through such agencies as the War Industries Board and the War Labor Board, and by placing the nation's railways under government control.[1]

As President Wilson moved to regulate industries and railroads for the war effort, the firm appeared for several clients in suits against William McAdoo and the Railroad Administration Agency on railroad securities matters. The firm also returned to the Railroad Commission for TMER&L, which complied with the wartime orders to save fuel by limiting the number of its streetcar stops and reducing the heat on its cars—an ironic reversal of earlier orders to do exactly the opposite.[2]

Arthur Fairchild played an active role as special attorney for war activities for the Federal Trade Commission from August to October 1917. Later he was appointed a major in the ordnance department of the United States army, and later still he became a lieutenant colonel, first with supervisory duties over the procurement of various war materials and then serving on a special mission to Europe for the secretary of war in 1918. While on official trips to France, Fairchild looked up several firm clients who had remained in Europe. He wrote George Miller to reassure him about the safety of his daughter, Alice Miller Chester, who worked with the Red Cross in Paris as an ambulance driver.[3]

Future partners Frederic Sammond and Leon Foley also served in the war, Sammond in the 120th field artillery and Foley in the navy from 1917 until 1919.[4] Although too old for active duty in the military, Mack assisted the state attorney general's office in supporting the constitutionality of Wisconsin's food rationing program, which preceded the federal rationing plan.[5]

The end of the war to end all wars on November 11, 1918, was heralded by joyous celebrations in Milwaukee and around the country. The fifteenth-floor windows of the Miller, Mack & Fairchild offices at 735 North Water Street provided a bird's-eye view of the festivities on the streets below. Festering at war's end was the legacy of bitterness and hatred toward Germans and Socialists that the conflict had aroused. Socialist leader Victor Berger had been refused his seat in Congress and jailed under Wilson's Sedition Law for publishing antiwar material. Berger and former Milwaukee mayor Emil Seidel sued Lucius Nieman and the *Milwaukee Journal* for libel and "vilification" in its descriptions of their wartime activities. The firm represented the paper. The case was settled.[6]

One of the most significant events of the postwar period was the passage in 1919 of the Eighteenth Amendment to the Constitution and its accompanying enforcement legislation, the Volstead Act. Prohibition began officially on July 1, 1919. Taverns and breweries were forced to close, notwithstanding Mayor Hoan's prediction that "the whole United States army couldn't dry up Milwaukee." The mayor was right: illegal liquor flowed freely. In December 1924 the police reported a 2,500 percent increase in drunken-driving arrests in the five-year period since Prohibition began. Milwaukee breweries and taverns employed 7,900 workers, many of whom lost their jobs despite the breweries' efforts to diversify. The Miller brewery began to make a cereal-based beverage and a malt syrup, while Schlitz tried to sell its newly created candy bars. At Pabst, malted powder became a supplement to dairying as the firm's focus shifted to the company-owned dairy farms forty miles west.[7]

Gilbert Hardgrove was an outspoken opponent of Prohibition from 1919 onward, promoting the argument that the Eighteenth Amendment applied only to private enterprise. The argument noted that the Eighteenth Amendment gave concurrent enforcement authority to states as well as to the federal government. Since the states were sovereign, it followed that they must have the right to produce and distribute alcoholic beverages themselves, Hardgrove argued in the 1930 *Marquette Law Review*.[8]

The 1920 census disclosed for the first time that more Americans lived in cities than on farms. With acceptance of the eight-hour workday in factories and stores, the 1920s brought a great increase in leisure time for American workers. In 1922 WAAK, Milwaukee's first radio station, began its regular broadcasts from Gimbel's Department Store. The jazz age was celebrated at the new Hotel Wisconsin Roof Club with the big band sound of Vaughn Monroe. From baseball and Babe Ruth to radio coverage of professional tennis, golf, and Man o' War's victories in horse racing, organized sports became more popular. TMER&L started bus service across the city and out into the growing suburban ring.[9]

Yet the 1920s also brought social and legal challenges as labor violence rocked many American cities. The firm litigated fine points of the Wisconsin Workmen's Compensation Act and the Federal Employers' Liability Act on behalf of industrial employers. These new statutes resulted from compromises between working men and their employers. Their no-fault provisions enabled workers to recover for on-the-job injuries and made the common-law fellow-servant rule irrelevant. They also kept employer costs at reasonable levels through an employers' insurance program and limitations on recoveries.

In the long run, worker's compensation legislation reduced the firm's involvement in personal injury litigation, once a staple of Finch & Lynde's work for the railroads. The new system succeeded in reducing the costs of compensating injured workers, as their claims were usually handled without litigation by administrative commissions and boards.[10]

The 1920s brought several new skyscrapers to Milwaukee. The firm resolved building code problems so the Wisconsin Telephone Company and the Wisconsin Gas Light Company could build the downtown towers that still bear their names. Construction of the 225-foot, sixteen-story telephone company building on Broadway had begun before the effective date of a 1923 statute that limited new buildings to 125 feet. Affirming a lower court decision, the Supreme Court decided the legislature had not intended its new law to apply to buildings that were under construction. Mack represented the Milwaukee Gas Light Company in 1928 when it wanted to raze a speakeasy on the site of its new Wisconsin Avenue building. Prohibition was still the law, and the tavern rooms of the old frame hotel building had been padlocked by order of the federal court, whose permission was needed to demolish it. To avoid delay, contractors excavated under and around the padlocked portion of the old hotel, which they jacked up until the padlocks could be removed.[11]

Edwin Mack headed the Wisconsin State Bar Committee to create an innovative Children's Code. Adopted in 1928, it called for treatment of juvenile offenders, outlined protections for neglected children, authorized probation officers and court-appointed social workers, and established adoption proceedings and child-custody regulations. The far-reaching reform also mandated licensed child-welfare agencies and included supervision of foster homes, as well as a county system of aid to dependent children. Following its passage, the state created a ninth circuit court for Milwaukee County so that juvenile cases could be served by a full-time judge. Mack's efforts, and those of the social workers he consulted, resulted in what was then considered an enlightened breakthrough in which Wisconsin led the nation.[12]

Reform was afoot in the legal community, too, in these years of the progressive movement. Standards for admission to state bars had varied widely before 1900. Professional associations controlled admissions in some states. In others, courts or statutes governed standards. An effort to upgrade the licensing of lawyers came in 1921 when the American Bar Association proposed requiring more than a high school diploma for admission to the bar. A written examination was suggested, a procedure which had been adopted in several states (including Wisconsin) as early as 1885.

Mack took the lead in the Wisconsin bar in 1924 to push for further reforms. A committee he chaired recommended that the state bar stand behind the bar examiners to exclude men without "fundamental training and without ideals." Mack and others felt that many lawyers viewed the profession "merely as a trade [with] no real interest in professional standards." Tighter admission standards and more severe disbarment procedures were the answer. Lawyers would need at least two years of college. The Supreme Court alone, and not all state courts, would control admission and disbarment under the proposal. Working as a vice president of the state bar, Mack lobbied for the reform legislation, which passed in 1927.[13]

Like the increasingly sophisticated profession of which it was a part, the firm of Miller, Mack & Fairchild had changed dramatically during the first quarter of the century. Now much of its corporate practice involved appearances before state commissions, and tax questions became increasingly important in estate planning and management.

The firm had matured in the number of its partners and associates as well as in the size and diversity of its support staff. From three partners in 1906, Miller, Mack & Fairchild grew by 1933 to eight partners and a support staff of twenty. All of the secretaries at the firm were now women, while the office manager, the delivery boys, and the accountant were men. Delivery boys, or "office boys," mostly students at the commercial high school, carried documents and messages to law offices, banks, and courthouses throughout the city.

The practice of business law became more profitable during the 1920s. George Miller received $20,000 from the firm in 1928, when he was semiretired. Like their father, George and Ben Miller were shrewd investors in the stocks of local corporations and utilities. Mack, too, built his fortune by purchasing bonds issued by the utilities whose balance sheets he so meticulously analyzed. Firm records for the year 1917 show Mack's monthly draws were $1,300, with a year-end distribution of $4,970. Newer partners Hardgrove and Blake drew about half as much as Mack. The firm's four partners shared profits of $69,000 in 1915. Partner distributions were $60,000 and $67,500 in 1916 and 1917. With Hardgrove a fifth partner in 1918, the firm distributed $69,533.[14]

During his many appearances before the Railroad Commission, Mack became acquainted with a young accountant, Fred Sammond, whose command of the intricacies of financial statements impressed him greatly. He encouraged Sammond to read law and in 1928 invited him to become an associate in the firm. Sammond was the last partner to serve such an apprenticeship. Mack and others worked to raise the educational requirements for the legal profession in the decade that followed. Sammond later testified about the drawbacks, as well as the few advantages, of entering a law office without a degree. Although he considered training as an auditor a great asset in the corporate and tax work of the firm, he admitted that his lack of formal courses in the law had been a drawback in understanding legal concepts.

Leon Foley, who also joined the firm as an associate in 1921, had served in the navy during the war and returned to the University of Wisconsin to attend law school in 1919. Graduating first in his class in 1921, Foley was the first editor of the *Wisconsin Law Review* and was elected to the honorary legal society, Order of the Coif. He joined Miller, Mack & Fairchild in July following his graduation and followed in George Miller's footsteps as an adviser to many leading Wisconsin corporations. Both Sammond and Foley became partners in 1933, following Miller's death.[15]

In 1928 Ben Miller died at his home in Wild Rose, Wisconsin, at the age of seventy. He had stayed in close touch with the firm during his twenty-two years of retirement, even when he was traveling around the world. C. M. Rothe, the firm's bookkeeper, and Elizabeth Kittredge, George Miller's secretary, corresponded with him regularly, reporting on business and sending dividends from his father's estate, which they managed. By 1931 Edwin Mack, Arthur Fairchild, and Leon Foley dominated the firm's practice. George Miller gradually reduced the time he spent in the office. Gilbert Hardgrove and Fred Sammond, who would together carry the firm well into the 1950s, were also assuming prominent roles.

Milwaukee, too, had entered the modern age. Car ferry service began across Lake Michigan and down to Chicago in 1929. Airmail became regularly available, and what is now Mitchell Field opened on the south end of town. On the eve of the Great Depression, in 1930, Milwaukee ranked second in the nation as an industrial city, and its population reached 500,000 with only 18 percent foreign-born.

On June 24, 1931, George Miller died of a heart attack at his lake home in Oconomowoc at the age of seventy-two. With his death, the firm lost its last link to the era of Finch & Lynde and Miller, Noyes & Miller. Miller's fifty years in the practice of law had spanned the decades from the assassination of Garfield in 1881 at the dawn of the Gilded Age to the catastrophic collapse of the American economy. He had witnessed the aftermath of the Civil War, the heyday of laissez-faire capitalism in the 1880s and 1890s, the imperialism of the Spanish-American War, and the crusade embodied in the war to end all wars. His grasp of corporate and trust law had made him a much-valued adviser to Milwaukee's banks and industries. And he had followed his father in working to clean up the city. Appointed to the Metropolitan Sewerage Commission in 1913, he served as its leader until his death, supervising the creation of the Jones Island sewage treatment plant in 1925. One year later, sales of the fertilizer "Milorganite" brought $500,000 in revenue to help offset the cost of the new plant.[16]

Miller's wife, Laura Chapman Miller, and two daughters, Isabelle Miller and Alice Miller Chester, survived him. His honorary pallbearers included many of the city's leading businessmen and lawyers: George and W. D. Van Dyke, Walter Kasten, Fred Vogel, Jr., Grant Fitch, L. J. Petit, Judge F. Geiger, William Horlick, Julius Heil, Lucius Nieman, Herman Falk, Gustave Pabst, Joseph Uihlein, Harry Grant, Frank Hoyt, Clement Smith, Edwin Mack, Arthur Fairchild, Clarence Dillon, and Howard Greene.

Edwin Mack and Arthur Fairchild assumed leadership of the firm on George Miller's death. Having worked together for twenty-five years, they were well prepared to continue the traditions passed to George Miller by Asahel and Matt Finch, William Pitt Lynde, and by George's father, B. K. Miller, Sr.

≈≪ 13 ≫≈

Legal Changes in the
Depression Era
1932–1940

The year 1932 was a watershed in American history and a turning point in the Miller, Mack & Fairchild partnership. George Miller's death in the previous year had left a void that Edwin Mack and Arthur Fairchild only gradually succeeded in filling. Nationally, with 14 million Americans unemployed and relief money running out, the blame fell on President Hoover and the Republicans. Government efforts to stem the tide of joblessness, hunger, and general despair proved to be too little, too late; in November voters elected Franklin D. Roosevelt.

Many business leaders and business lawyers opposed Roosevelt's election and the supposedly "radical" programs of his New Deal. The network of laws and regulatory agencies that emanated from FDR and his "brain trust" surpassed the reforms of the Progressive years in scope and number and vastly increased the work of attorneys, both in government and in the private sector. The number of commissions and regulatory boards increased dramatically at both state and federal levels. Once the executor of legislative will, the administrative branch of government became a mammoth pseudolegislature, establishing new guidelines for virtually every segment of American life, including taxation, commerce, home loans, labor and employment practices, banking, and securities. New regulations required interpretation; many invited legal tests. It was ironic that, although most of the partners at Miller, Mack & Fairchild were conservative and Republican, the firm flourished under the administrations of Democrats and progressive Republicans.

The catastrophe on Wall Street in October 1929 precipitated a chain of events that affected the entire financial structure of the nation. Caught in the maelstrom of financial insecurity, many clients of the firm sought counsel on questions related to securities investments or bank solvency. In spring 1933, Miller, Mack & Fairchild was involved in the appeal of litigation to force an investor to make good on his stock subscription. Another appeal involved the validity of a contract to buy securities.[1]

In 1931 the Wisconsin Public Service Commission (formerly the Railroad Commission) had been granted full authority to regulate railroads, public utilities, urban transportation systems, motor buses and motor vehicles, and all water power and dams. The regulation of stock and bond sales, bond ratings, and other matters relevant to the orderly and ethical buying and selling of securities within the state was separated from the commission's domain and delegated first to the Banking Commission and, in 1939, to the newly created Wisconsin Securities Commission.[2]

As stock prices continued to fall following the October 1929 crash, many banks and trust companies faced suits by beneficiaries of some of the estates in their care. Miller, Mack & Fairchild defended the First Wisconsin Trust Company in a number of suits in the circuit courts over the loss of trust monies due to devalued or worthless stocks and bonds. In one of these suits the defendant company had not seen a notice that certain bonds would be redeemed. The beneficiary lost about $2,000 and sued. The case turned on a trustee's duty to find the notice, even though it was not published in the usual places. The firm appeared as *amicus* in another case that turned on certain trustees' obligations to invest only in securities approved by state statute.[3]

With passage of the Glass-Steagall Act in 1933, the federal government established new regulations that prohibited banks from investing the money of their depositors in the stock market, separated investment from banking functions, and established the Federal Deposit Insurance Corporation, which at that time insured deposits up to $5,000.[4]

Banks had proliferated in small towns across the state during the 1920s, when banking laws were lenient and farm credit was readily available. Many failed between 1929 and 1933, especially in agricultural areas, where the farm debt had proved disastrous. Half of Wisconsin's banks closed following the market crash and the credit contraction of 1929, resulting in enormous work for the Banking Commission and for the law firms that represented banking interests. A number of banks that survived the financial debacle, such as the First Wisconsin, sought counsel from the firm on issues of interbank debt and government taxation policies, matters crucial to their fiscal well-being in the 1930s.[5]

The firm helped thwart Wisconsin's attempts to levy an *ad valorem* tax on bank stock. In 1927 Arthur W. Fairchild had successfully argued in the United States Supreme Court that the state tax on national bank stock discriminated against banks in favor of competing investments, in violation of a federal statute. Five years later, the Wisconsin Supreme Court ruled in a case brought by the firm that the tax on state bank stock violated the Equal Protection clause.[6]

One massive piece of litigation involved the First Wisconsin Bank, which had made secured loans to the Liberty State Bank. After Liberty failed, the Wisconsin Banking Commission accused First Wisconsin of having conspired with Liberty's officers to defraud its creditors. Paul Newcomb represented the bank in a court trial that lasted seventy-three days and involved eighty witnesses, 1,000 exhibits, and 10,000 pages of testimony. The trial court found for First Wisconsin, and the Supreme Court examined the evidence at length, then affirmed.[7]

Leon Foley and Paul Newcomb became the firm's preeminent banking specialists, advising the First Wisconsin and other clients about state and federal banking regulations. Litigation was relatively rare, and most banking matters were handled by negotiation. What occupied many of the firm's associates, under the direction of partners Newcomb or Foley, were the myriad collection cases against individual noteholders and the large number of businesses that could not repay loans made during the prosperous years before the market crash. Collections for gas and electric companies and other utilities also occupied associates's attention. To give them a diversity of experience, however, the firm set up a rotation system, whereby no associate had to work on collections for more than six months.

Mack and Fairchild relied increasingly on the legal talent and leadership ability of Leon Foley, who had joined the firm in 1921 and was made a partner in 1933. With partners Gilbert Hardgrove, Bert Vandervelde, Paul Newcomb, and Frederick Sammond (several of whom were much older than he), Foley followed the path taken by George Miller in his work with banking, corporate, and utility clients during the years of economic crisis and world war. Foley did not enjoy the courtroom, preferring instead to practice law as a business counsel in the style of B. K. Miller, Sr. His skills in this area made him a highly valued and trusted adviser to banks and corporate clients during his five decades in the practice of law.[8]

Two other young associates joined the firm when Miller's death in 1931 and the demands of the Depression workload made a staff increase necessary. Vernon Swanson, a graduate of the University of Wisconsin Law School, became an associate in July 1931, just after Miller's death; Theodore ("Pete") Bolliger, also a Wisconsin graduate, joined the firm in September 1934. Bolliger enjoyed the luxury of a regular paycheck at Miller, Mack & Fairchild; the $75 monthly stipend at his previous firm had been "paid in some months and not in others."[9]

Three more associates came to the firm before the war. Steven E. Keane was hired right after he graduated from Marquette Law School in 1937. The firm hired Paul M. Barnes and Lynford Lardner, Jr., in 1940. A native of Oconomowoc, Wisconsin, Lardner joined Miller, Mack & Fairchild following his graduation from Harvard Law School. None of these men became partners until after the war. Swanson and Bolliger waited a full twelve years, while Barnes and Keane, whose tenures were interrupted by military service, achieved partnership after approximately seven years of work at the firm. Lardner, too, achieved partnership after almost seven years, and the seven-year pattern became a standard. Miller, Mack & Fairchild and other firms like it shortened the partnership track to attract and hold top recruits in the postwar era. The firm also modified the Cravath system of encouraging many associates to compete against each other for a small number of partner positions. Instead, associates at Miller, Mack & Fairchild competed only against themselves for advancement to partnership.[10]

Vernon Swanson and Steven Keane had worked their way through both college and law school, unable to rely on family resources for professional training, in the tradition of William Lynde and George Miller. Swanson played in a dance band and worked in restaurants, and Keane held down as many as three jobs at once. Swanson, editor-in-chief of the *Wisconsin Law Review* and a member of the Order of the Coif, had worked as a research assistant for Professor William H. Page, author of *Page on the Law of Wills*. Page had recommended Swanson to Mack and Fairchild after George Miller died in June 1931. Swanson was offered $1,500 a year at a time when New York law firms were paying about $2,500.[11]

Pete Bolliger was just completing his course work at the University of Wisconsin Law School in August 1934 when he was recruited by Leon Foley, one month after the sudden death of James Blake. Before entering law school, Bolliger had worked briefly as an electrical engineer and, during law school, at a New York patent law firm. He had special expertise that would be valuable to Miller, Mack & Fairchild. His first assignments were to work with Mack on telephone rate cases.

Steven Keane never lost the determination to become a lawyer that he had nurtured from boyhood. Keane's father died soon after the Depression bankrupted his warehouse business in 1933, and the family moved from their home in Aberdeen, South Dakota, to Milwaukee to live with relatives. Keane entered law school at the age of eighteen; only two years of undergraduate college work were required at that time.

Even though Keane had completed three years of law school and ranked first in his class, he had no immediate prospects for a job. There were no on-campus interviews with law firms, no jobs posted on bulletin boards. Keane's mentor, E. Harold Hallows of the Marquette law faculty (and later chief justice of the Wisconsin Supreme Court), offered to set up appointments with the city's three largest firms. At Miller, Mack & Fairchild, Keane interviewed with Leon Foley. Foley scrutinized Keane's record carefully; the firm had not yet hired a lawyer directly upon his graduation from Marquette. Keane's interviews with all seven of the partners were successful. He began work on Friday, June 18, 1937, at a salary of $100 a month.

The firm's twentieth-century associates came from a variety of backgrounds and were largely self-made men. Keane was from Aberdeen, South Dakota, and Blake from Winona, Minnesota. Hard-

grove was from Fond du Lac, Wisconsin, and Lardner from Oconomowoc, Wisconsin. Leon Foley was the son of a policeman from
Wisconsin Rapids. Paul Newcomb's father had been a riverboat pilot
on the Mississippi, and Newcomb also had worked on the river and
taught school to afford a legal education. Bert Vandervelde and Fred
Sammond also were men of middle-class origin who rose in the
ranks of the legal profession through their associations with George
Miller and Edwin Mack.

As a heavily industrialized city, Milwaukee withstood the
early years of the Depression better than many. But by 1932 hard
times began to take a severe toll on both manufacturers and workers.
Public relief rolls escalated from 1,000 families in 1930 to 32,000
individuals and 6,000 families in late 1932—one-fifth of the city's
residents. Local charities couldn't cope with the pressing needs of
the homeless, the hungry, and the jobless, and there was a cry for
federal assistance.[12]

Across Wisconsin, the problems multiplied. Manufacturing sales
dropped from $960 million in 1929 to $375 million in early 1933.
The total number of wage earners fell from 264,000 to 116,000
during the same period, and the average wage fell 60 percent. Farm-
commodity prices also reached a disastrous level, falling from a base
of $100 in 1929 to $43 three years later.[13]

Milwaukee mayor Daniel Hoan, well-known to the law firm for
his fight against the transit company, called on state government
to help in the city's crisis. As president of the United States Conference of Mayors, Hoan led the call for federal and state relief. In
answer to these appeals from cities and citizens, both the state of
Wisconsin and the federal government established agencies to provide economic relief, work programs, and new regulations to meet
the economic crisis. Milwaukee benefited directly from the Reconstruction Finance Corporation's infusion of badly needed cash following the 1933 report that less than half of its outstanding property
taxes could be collected and that almost half its wage earners were
on relief.

The firm's revenues also fell during the Depression as a
number of clients found legal fees difficult to pay. Partner distributions of $171,000 in 1932 plummeted to $67,000 in 1933 and
remained at that level until 1935. The need to cope with New Deal

taxes and regulatory agencies brought increased profits by 1937, when the distribution pool rose to $307,000. Even during the lean years, however, the incomes of the two leading partners, Mack and Fairchild, remained substantial, ranging from $77,000 in 1933 to a low of $40,000 in 1934, rebounding by 1936 to $74,000. Other partners' incomes ranged from $17,000 in 1933 to $12,000 a year later and back up to $20,000 by 1937. According to one study of lawyers' incomes during 1930 (when the American Bar Association first began to keep such statistics), the mean net income for the top 50 percent of lawyers was $12,000.[14]

Billing procedures in the 1930s differed little from those that B. K. Miller, Sr., had established four decades earlier. Lawyers kept a day book with a record of each matter. When Steven Keane first joined the firm, he billed at $25 per day. The day was divided into fifths, and each client was billed proportionately.

Costs increased for both personnel and technological reasons. By the end of the 1930s the firm included seven partners, ten associates, one telephone operator (who handled an intercom system as well), one receptionist (who also took charge of the library), three messengers, one file clerk, fifteen to twenty secretaries, and two bookkeepers. Innovations like the telephone and typewriter may have tripled lawyers' efficiency, but they also increased law firm expenses and capital needs. The result was a "revolution in the cost of legal services."[15]

Keeping track of the firm's 10,000-volume library and its growing number of government and bar publications became a full-time job within the next decade. In 1935, the partners voted to transfer ownership of the library to the firm itself, in perpetuity, rather than keeping the books within the partners' personal collections. As a result of this agreement, Mack's collection of nineteenth-century law books, several of which were inscribed by William Pitt Lynde or even by his father, Tilly Lynde, became part of the firm library. Files had grown, too: in 1942 the system of logging client files for warehouse storage (the "morgue") required a full-time file clerk.

The leading partners were active in the state bar association, as well as in Milwaukee social and business circles. Fairchild, Mack, Sammond, Vandervelde, and Newcomb sat on many corporate and civic boards. Following in the footsteps of B. K. Miller, Sr., and George Miller, they served as directors of many of Milwaukee's leading companies and were trustees of the Layton Art Center, the Milwaukee Symphony, the Milwaukee Sanitarium, the University School, Downer School and College, Country Day School, and various other charitable or arts associations. In addition, they were active members of the University Club and the Milwaukee Club, once led by B. K. Miller, Sr.

Gilbert Hardgrove became president of the Wisconsin Bar Association and Paul Newcomb of the Milwaukee Bar Association. Mack and Sammond presented scholarly papers at bar meetings, Mack on utilities matters and Sammond on tax law. In addition, Mack and Hardgrove—and later Foley, Keane, and Sammond, among others—became members of the prestigious American Law Institute, organized in 1923 as a scholarly association centered in Philadelphia.[16]

The expansion of powers of the federal government brought dramatic changes to legal practice. A knowledge of federal law and administrative procedures became essential, particularly in matters such as taxation, interstate commerce, environmental issues, public utilities, labor, and banking.[17] Studies by the American Law Institute and by the American Bar Association helped bring about a long-awaited revision of the federal judicial code in 1938. In 1943 Wisconsin adopted its own administrative code in response to a demand for further refinement of procedures before state and federal regulatory commissions. The federal government followed suit with its Administrative Procedures Act in 1946. The goal of these reforms was fairness, efficiency, clarity, and uniformity in legal procedure.[18]

Antitrust work became increasingly important during the New Deal. The firm defended the Paramount Corporation against charges of unfair trade practices in distributing its films solely to its own movie theaters in Wisconsin. The successful defense of Paramount brought in business from other film distributors as well. Goldwyn and Fox faced similar questions regarding their relationship with theater owners and movie-distribution rights.[19]

Corporations needed guidance through the maze of new government taxation laws and regulations that developed during the 1930s. The firm began to handle an increasing number of tax cases, relying on the expertise of Fred Sammond. Sammond's reputation as a tax expert was well established during the early years of the

Depression. His 1932 article on misconceptions about income-tax law was a skilled review not only of tax law itself but also of the disposition of cases by the tax commission and the courts.[20] Corporations that sought the firm's counsel and representation on tax issues before the federal courts and state Supreme Court included several of Wisconsin's largest corporations, such as the Rahr Malting Company, the Froedtert Malting Company, the Trane Company, the Burroughs Adding Machine Company, and the Aluminum Goods Manufacturing Company.[21]

Tax questions also became paramount in the probate and estate matters handled by Miller, Mack & Fairchild after 1929. The firm continued to represent numerous beneficiaries of many of Milwaukee's largest fortunes. New Deal tax codes and state inheritance-tax reforms under Governor Philip La Follette had resulted in the need for extensive revisions of many estate plans for which the firm was responsible. The implementation of new taxes also resulted in litigation on behalf of several large estates to test the parameters of inheritance taxes and their enforcement by state and federal tax commissions. In litigation for such clients as John and Michael Cudahy, millionaire lumberman William Hatten, and the Wehr, Allis, and Prange family estates, Sammond spearheaded challenges in the federal courts involving the federal tax on trust income, the charitable-deduction exemption, the federal estate tax on life-insurance benefits, and the effect of the federal tax on the computation of state inheritance taxes.[22]

One matter that proved to be extraordinarily complex and particularly troublesome to Mack was the estate of Lucius Nieman, owner of the *Milwaukee Journal*. Mack advised Nieman's widow Agnes, who wanted to endow fellowships in journalism in the name of her husband. Having ruled out the University of Wisconsin because she felt it was dominated by the La Follettes and Marquette on religious grounds, she chose Harvard as the site for what became the prestigious Nieman Fellowships. After her death several heirs challenged the will on the ground that she was incompetent to make it and that Mack had unduly influenced her in favor of Harvard. The trial court held in favor of the will and the Supreme Court affirmed in a remarkably brief opinion. But Mack suffered a heart attack after the *Nieman* litigation, perhaps linked to the stress of the case and the accusations against him.[23]

Fairchild continued to serve as watchdog and legal defender for the state's largest utility companies. But the reforms of the 1930s triggered new challenges in the state and federal courts, often mounted by the firm of Miller, Mack & Fairchild. On the federal level, passage of the 1935 Public Utility Holding Company Act came as a direct result of the disastrous collapse of the Samuel Insull empire, a financial pyramid of utility companies glued together by fraudulent securities deals in Chicago. With Insull's disgrace and the resultant decline in utility stocks, several Wisconsin companies were hard hit, as were stock and bond holders who had trusted Insull and his financial manipulations.

The Wisconsin Power and Light Company had become part of the Insull empire during the 1920s and fell with it into receivership in the debacle of 1932. Recovery came slowly with help from federal and state subsidies under the Rural Electrification Act, which funded the extension of electrical service to many farmers across the state. Through the 1935 legislation, the Federal Power Commission gained control over the interstate transmission of electrical power. The new act also established the famous Section 11, or "death sentence," which mandated that within five years "any utility holding company which could not demonstrate its localized, useful and efficient character" would be dissolved.[24]

Representing the Wisconsin Gas Company of Milwaukee (formerly the Milwaukee Gas Light Company), Vernon Swanson spent many months in Washington, appearing before the Federal Power Commission. Other law firms with large utility clients also found that the presence of an attorney in the national capital was necessary after passage of the Rural Electrification Act.

During the 1930s the firm represented the Wisconsin Telephone Company in fighting off the Public Service Commission's attempt to reduce telephone rates. Led by David Lilienthal, the state commission had issued a temporary order in 1932 to cut rates by 12.5 percent. Similar "temporary" reductions were ordered in each of the next several years. Mack and Sammond won a preliminary injunction from a three-judge federal panel barring enforcement of the order, but the United States Supreme Court remanded because the district court had not explained its decision. The company's challenge was vindicated in a state court judgment in February 1938, and the Wisconsin Supreme Court affirmed. The court faulted the Public

Service Commission for its failure to provide due process and "full public hearings," as mandated by law.[25]

The decision made clear that courts would require the commission to follow its own procedures in setting rates, even in times of economic hardship. Mack and Bolliger later served as consultants to a number of telephone companies in similar rate battles in New England, New York, and several midwestern states.

One of the major administrative changes brought about by Roosevelt's New Deal was the enhanced power of the federal government to regulate labor and employment, particularly through the National Labor Relations Board. Labor violence escalated during the 1930s as unions flexed their muscles and employees struck to protest wage reductions, long hours, or unsafe working conditions. The federal government enacted the Wagner Act in 1935 and Wisconsin followed suit with the "Little Wagner Act" of 1937, outlawing interference with the right to organize, discrimination against union members, refusal to bargain with union representatives, blacklists, and spying on employees.

As one of the nation's leading industrial centers, Milwaukee felt the full force of the labor movement during the 1930s. In 1934 there were 107 strikes in the city, involving 27,000 workers. Like many other business law firms, Miller, Mack & Fairchild developed an expertise in labor law. In 1935 the Wagner Act established the federal National Labor Relations Board to oversee labor organization. At the same time the American Federation of Labor grew stronger, and unskilled workers created their own national union, the Congress of Industrial Organizations (CIO). As part of La Follette's "mini-New Deal," Wisconsin created the state Fair Labor Board in 1937. These two new regulatory agencies and the growing power of unions made labor work a necessity for firms serving corporate clients.

Vernon Swanson, the youngest associate, was asked to begin work in labor negotiations and found his first case an "ordeal by fire" when a bloody fistfight erupted at the first negotiating session he attended.[26] Swanson, Keane, and new associate James Poole continued to represent such clients as Nordberg Manufacturing, the Wisconsin Gas Company, Burlington Mills, the Wisconsin Telephone Company, the A. O. Smith Company, Froedtert Malting Company, and National Rivet Company in labor matters.

In 1940 public attention turned to Hitler's conquest of Norway, Belgium, Holland, and France and to Roosevelt's unprecedented campaign for a third term. The Depression appeared to be over, but the peril of world war was at hand. The political legacy of the New Deal and the state reform movement of the 1930s left in their wake a changed American society, one regulated by bureaucratic agencies and administrative codes, and one that made private interests more dependent than ever on legal expertise.

❈ 14 ❈

Partners in Wartime
1941–1945

Immediately after the bombing of Pearl Harbor and Roose-velt's request for a declaration of war, patriotic citizens of Wisconsin rallied to enlist. On December 8, 1941, Wisconsin residents volunteered in record numbers to fight against the Axis powers. Patriotism swept the city. By January 71,000 young men had signed up at the Milwaukee draft board. Milwaukee was no longer the bitterly divided ethnic enclave it had been at the onset of World War I. Even Milwaukee mayor Carl Zeidler, Daniel Hoan's successor, won an officer's commission in the navy. He was killed in action in the Pacific in 1942.

The legislature had appropriated $50,000 in 1939 to subsidize Milwaukee's attempt to win the 1941 American Legion Convention. The state treasurer refused to issue a check for the $27,500 needed as a deposit on the application, arguing that the legislation served no statewide public purpose and was therefore unconstitutional. The firm sued on behalf of the convention organizers, but the Wisconsin Supreme Court agreed with the treasurer. It did, however, offer a patriotic acknowledgment that

> The holding of the national convention in this state with the use of funds appropriated will serve to inspire, inculcate, and promote the highest type of patriotic sentiments and principles of American

patriotism, and thus aid in the preservation of our American ideals and the perpetuation of our state and national democratic systems of government under our constitutions.[1]

The American Legion chose Milwaukee despite the high court's rather reluctant denial of its subsidy, and legionnaires convened in the fall of 1941. Beer flowed like patriotism as the city's breweries distributed it free. Movie stars came to town for the Legion parade. Street vendors sold lapel buttons reading "To Hell with Hitler." The onset of the war itself two months later brought more sobering reflections, as the casualty lists from Pearl Harbor arrived before Christmas and the city's Council of Defense demanded blackouts in case Milwaukee became a target for enemy bombers.

In January 1942 the federal government established a new network of administrative boards and a multitude of wartime regulations. Many businesses opposed the new price and rent controls, deeming them assaults on free enterprise. In one case Miller, Mack & Fairchild represented a Milwaukee sausage maker who complained to the special Emergency Court of Price Appeals that price ceilings on sausage in carload lots arbitrarily and capriciously discriminated in favor of its competitors. But the complaint was dismissed, the court holding that the ceilings were "generally fair and equitable and reasonably essential to the maintenance of price control" and the avoidance of black marketeering.[2]

The wartime shortage of working men affected law firms as well as factories. In his history of Cravath, Swaine & Moore, Robert T. Swaine noted that fifty of the firm's eighty-one associates left for military service or work in government during the first two years of the conflict.[3] There were few "Rosie the Riveters" in law firms to take the place of partners and associates who went to war. In those days few women enrolled in law schools; opportunities for women in the legal profession were still more than three decades away. Miller, Mack & Fairchild had a woman associate during the war, but she left the firm in 1947 without becoming a partner. "Office girls" were hired to replace young men as messengers and clerks.

The firm was able to secure deferments for several young associates under a selective service provision for firms "supplying technical or managerial services to establishments engaged in war production," which was pertinent to its defense contractor clients.

One associate worked almost full-time during the war advising the First Wisconsin National Bank on emergency loans to war-related industries under the "V for Victory" program. By 1943 most of the firm's young associates had joined or had been drafted into the military.

Members of the firm tried to keep in touch with absent associates and partners. Paul Barnes, who had enlisted in the navy immediately after Pearl Harbor, corresponded regularly with mentor Gilbert Hardgrove, as did many young men whom Hardgrove took under his wing during the turmoil of wartime. Writing to Barnes about current litigation, Hardgrove observed, "Mere law suits must be relatively unimportant from your present viewpoint . . . proximate cause—intervening cause—negligence—damages . . . must all have a diluted sound to a bearded seaman. Yet the review may serve for a time to take your mind away from your more serious occupation."[4]

Barnes responded from the Pacific Fleet: "Your letters are greatly appreciated. I hate to think how far behind I am getting on the law." Many servicemen took advantage of a variety of correspondence courses offered by the armed forces throughout the war. Barnes wrote that he had signed up for a course in legal issues through the University of Wisconsin, but that keeping up with the course from aboard a ship in the Pacific was difficult. "It might take years to finish the course," he wrote Hardgrove.[5]

Writing similar letters to other associates at bases and on ships around the world, Hardgrove kept them posted on the outcome of cases as well as on the atmosphere at the office. He even loaned money to several associates or their families when they were in need. "Consider it a wartime loan, payable only when you are back on your feet at the firm after the war's end," he told one young man.[6]

The firm, too, made an effort to help several associates who were in financial straits. Steven Keane, who entered the service in October 1943 and remained until 1946, recalled that shortly before his departure for the navy, he was asked by Leon Foley whether service pay would be sufficient for the support of his family and aging mother. Although Keane assured him it would, Foley insisted that throughout his time in the service, the law firm would deposit a given amount in his bank account to help him make ends meet. "It created in me a strong sense of loyalty to the firm," Keane remembered. Several other associates—among them Ervin Nemmers,

Marcus Plant, and Herbert Hirschboeck—left for the military or for jobs in defense industries and did not return to the firm at war's end.[7]

The organized bar also felt the pinch of wartime shortages. The American Bar Association wrote its members in 1943: "You are keenly aware of the serious financial situation brought upon us by the war. We have already lost dues of members in service totaling approximately $13,500 and this loss may reach $20,000 before the end of the year." Explaining increased dues of $17 per year, the ABA noted that it had appropriated approximately $45,000 for "essential war work."

Throughout the conflict, both the ABA and local bar associations continued to offer men in uniform the opportunity to take refresher courses by correspondence and launched formal studies of the role of law in a wartime society. The State Bar of Wisconsin, at its midwinter meeting in 1943 chaired by Paul Newcomb, president of the Milwaukee Bar, heard papers on "The President's War Powers" and "The Alien Property Custodian's Relationship to the Public and to the Bar" and a Report on the War Manpower Commission.[8] Similarly, the Milwaukee Bar Association, in conjunction with Marquette University, offered a program of courses early in the conflict that featured sessions conducted by Bert Vandervelde, Leon Foley, J. D. Porter, Fred Sammond, and Herbert Hirschboeck of Miller, Mack & Fairchild on subjects such as "Corporate Records," "Issuance of Securities by Corporations," and "Corporate Taxes."[9]

The National Association of Legal Aid held its annual meeting in Milwaukee in September 1942 and recognized the *pro bono* work of the local bar, led by Paul Newcomb, to aid soldiers and their families in legal matters and to extend the services of lawyers to others who could not pay. Another kind of recognition came when client businesses invited firm attorneys to participate in government ceremonies honoring vital defense work. Several senior partners of the firm participated at a ceremony in May 1943, when the Victory Fleet Flag was presented to the Nordberg Manufacturing Company.[10]

Of the dozen associates who worked at the firm between 1931 and 1945, only half stayed on to become partners following the war. Others went into in-house legal work for corporations, joined other law firms, or entered public service. With the loss of half its associates and with the continuing competition for a short supply of lawyers, the firm shortened the partnership track to seven and a half years. A shorter tenure, it was thought, would help in recruiting associates from national law schools. The firm also tried to ensure that each new associate could become a partner, rather than offering that opportunity to less than one-fifth of new recruits, as did several of the large eastern firms. The partnership track was later shortened by another year, and then lengthened again to eight and a half years in the early 1980s.[11]

While political involvement was no longer a hallmark of firm activity or partner aspiration during the twentieth century, the firm litigated state political issues in the years just before the war. Weary of the La Follette dynasty, Wisconsin voters elected Republican Julius Heil governor by a substantial majority in 1938. Heil and his company had long been clients of the law firm. Heil sought the firm's assistance when Philip La Follette's lame-duck administration maneuvered to deplete the state treasury to embarrass him. La Follette ordered all state reserves transferred from the general fund to the school fund just before he left office, an action that would force Heil to operate without carryover money. On behalf of Heil, the firm sued successfully in the Supreme Court to block the transfer.

Heil was defeated for a third term in 1942 by Orland Loomis, a La Follette progressive. When Loomis died before taking office, Heil petitioned the Supreme Court for the right to name the next governor. Gilbert Hardgrove argued the case for Heil during Christmas week in 1942, but unsuccessfully. The court ruled in favor of Lieutenant Governor-elect Walter S. Goodland, an eighty-year-old, long-time progressive. Heil retired to private life and the firm's political litigation ended for a time. Hardgrove and Heil became close friends; as Hardgrove wrote: "We were in the Supreme Court with Governor Heil when he took office and we were there again when he went out of office."[12]

On September 11, 1942, Miller, Mack & Fairchild celebrated its centennial with a large gathering at the Milwaukee Athletic Club. More than 1,000 people joined in the celebration: fellow members of the city and state bars; members of the Milwaukee business community; leaders of the bar in Chicago, New York, Boston, Washington, and Detroit; leaders in government and directors of government agencies and boards (both state and national); members of the federal and state judiciary; and friends and families of the partners and associates.

The centennial year also marked the loss of the firm's oldest and most esteemed partner, Edwin S. Mack. His unexpected death in April 1942 came as a tremendous blow to the firm, and particularly to Arthur Fairchild, to whom Mack was "more than a partner of four decades, he was also a very close personal friend."[13] Following his 1936 heart attack, Mack had continued to come to the office, but had cut back considerably on the casework he managed. He often lunched at home, then took a midday nap before being driven back to the office for the rest of the afternoon. Unmatched in the firm as an austere and awe-inspiring figure, Mack's presence seemed to fill the corridors. When he was in his office, the atmosphere at the firm was charged.[14]

Associates considered it both a fearsome challenge and a great opportunity to work with Mack. His ability to become fully absorbed in the legal questions surrounding a case was so complete that he appeared at times to be absent-minded. A firm legend recounted a discussion with a corporate client during which, in the midst of pondering out loud about legal issues and possibilities, Mack suddenly stood up, put on his coat, and left the office for the day. The outraged client had to be soothed by Arthur Fairchild, who recounted other, similar stories about Mack's idiosyncrasies. Several lawyers recalled the tension they felt when they were summoned into Mack's office to receive an assignment. One remembered going into Mack's office after submitting a requested memorandum and finding all of the case law he had cited being studiously reviewed. "He was double checking to see whether I had pulled any phony citations." Sometimes Mack would dictate two documents simultaneously, one to Roehr and one to another stenographer.

There were many tales—some true, some apocryphal—about Mack's brilliance and eccentricities. One young associate was startled to find Mack at his office door absently asking him what he was doing. When he truthfully replied, "Nothing, sir," Mack walked on, admonishing him, "Finish it carefully and then report in to see me." But Mack was never so absorbed in large issues that he lost sight of the need for precision. Responding to his doctor's inquiry about whether the pressures at the firm required him to work too hurriedly, Mack replied carefully, "I never work hurriedly, I only work rapidly."[15]

Informality at the office was never accepted, and Mack's interest in the young attorneys never came at the expense of his innate dignity, which kept young men at a distance. "He never called us by our first names," Vernon Swanson recalled. When Mack arrived each morning after everyone else, he would walk down the corridor of office doors toward his own, addressing each associate along the way with a formal "Good morning, Mr. Mooney"; "Good morning, Mr. Swanson"; and so on.

But despite his formality and occasional preoccupation, Mack had a vital and genuine interest in transmitting to the younger men his love of the law and its precision, an interest left over from his days as a law professor several decades earlier. One associate, who later left the firm to teach law, had a memo returned from Mack seven times before it was accepted. (The record for returns from Mack was said to be thirteen.)[16] Mack was also a greatly valued adviser to several Milwaukee business leaders, including Robert Friend of the Nordberg Company and William McGovern of the Wisconsin Telephone Company, who met with him almost every morning.

Mack's growing reputation as a legal scholar and a litigator of overwhelming thoroughness earned him the regard of members of the judiciary as well. The justices of the Wisconsin Supreme Court treated him with high regard. Mack often worked in litigation with another partner, such as Fred Sammond, because "his mind worked so fast that he would jump in his argument, sometimes, from major premise to conclusion and skip over all of the minor premises along the way." It fell to others on the team to fill in the necessary logical steps in the firm's presentation.[17]

By 1941 Mack was spending many weeks away from the office each year, traveling or recuperating at his daughter's ranch in California. He remained interested in the business of the law firm, however, and corresponded regularly with Fairchild and Hardgrove while he was away. Commenting on events in Europe and the Pacific, he wrote, "It is hard to get one's thought off of the war. The present outlook is grim, and I wish I could have more confidence in the ability of those in Washington to deal with the situation." Restless with his emeritus status, Mack discussed AT&T matters with Sammond. He continued to read voluminously. Back at work in early

April 1942, Mack wrote to Hardgrove that he had learned to accept the "delights of laziness as a magic treasure" but that such delights would "evaporate into thin air" when one became absorbed or "imposed upon by the law."[18] Two days later, on April 9, Mack died of a heart attack while visiting the dentist's office a few doors away from the firm.

The reaction of shock and loss amid the ongoing turmoil of the war rocked the law firm. Everyone worried about the effect of the loss on Arthur Fairchild, Mack's partner and friend for more than forty years. The Harvard Club of Milwaukee offered a special tribute, hailing Mack as "erudite in legal lore and a devotee of good literature, exemplar of Harvard's precepts and best traditions, of gracious temperament, beloved at the office and respected by bench and bar."[19]

A member of Mack's 1893 Harvard Law School class wrote that "a distinguished member of the faculty said of Mack that his was the subtlest mind he had ever met at the Harvard Law School." The Wisconsin Bar noted his contributions in the ever-changing field of state regulation: "Modern public utility law was in the process of development in the early years of his practice, and his contribution in that field was exceptional." Longtime friends Frank T. Boesel, Walter H. Bender, and Louis Quarles worked with Fairchild to write the memorial from the Milwaukee County Bar Association. In addition to comments on Mack's exceptional brilliance, which had been noted by so many others, the memorial emphasized his ethical character: "A conscience, both in his professional and in his social life, not doubtful of the ethical limits of action, but instinctively sensing them and always dominating his every human relation."[20]

The firm received hundreds of tributes to Mack from attorneys across the city, the state, and the nation. Members of the state and federal judiciary recalled his presentations in their courts. Chester Morrill, of the Federal Reserve System, commented on the depth of the legal community's loss. Former law students wrote of their memories of Mack during his short tenure as a professor. One remembered, "He left me with a tremendous admiration and inspiration from his exacting thoroughness, untiring industry and enthusiasm in search for the true rule."[21] A committee of justices of the Wisconsin Supreme Court wrote a eulogy and Justice Thomas Fairchild, once an associate at the firm, delivered it.[22]

Following Mack's death, the firm turned to two men of considerable distinction and promise. Joseph E. Rapkin, a partner at Churchill Davis in Milwaukee, came to the firm on July 1, 1943, and became a partner on January 1, 1947. As the second Jewish member of Miller, Mack & Fairchild, he had close ties to several key Jewish leaders in the Milwaukee business community. The second new arrival, James I. Poole, had attended college and law school at the University of Kansas and then had spent several years working in labor negotiations for Phillips Petroleum. He was hired as an associate on October 4, 1943, as the problems exacerbated by the war brought more complexities to the field of labor negotiations. The War Labor Act exacted strict penalties from employers who raised wages excessively in wartime; yet there was so much competition for skilled workers that employers needed expert advice on ways to attract employees without incurring federal penalties. Poole's expertise increased the firm's ability to provide labor counseling to its clients, and he became a partner on January 1, 1947.[23]

Wisconsin emerged from the war with a mature economy, a robust industrial capacity, a well-trained and highly productive labor force, and a booming agricultural sector well-organized for the export of high-quality meat and dairy products. It was poised to enter a period of sustained economic growth and prosperity.

After Mack's death, the leadership of Miller, Mack & Fairchild devolved upon Arthur Fairchild and Leon Foley. Fairchild and Foley, joined later by Lynford Lardner, had a vision for the firm that was both expansive and powerful. Under their direction the firm took steps that heralded extensive changes in its structure and development after the war.

⫷ 15 ⫸

Postwar Growth and
New Directions
1945–1973

The destiny of Miller, Mack & Fairchild after World War II was in the hands of Leon Foley and Lynford Lardner, Jr. Both believed that the firm should expand its partnership and develop a national recruiting policy. Later they decided that the firm should develop practices in other cities and states. That decision recognized that many corporate clients had expanded across state lines and that the federal, rather than the state, government dominated the commercial and legal environment more than ever before. By the early 1970s it became clear that only a large firm could provide attorneys who were highly trained in the specialized areas of law that the New Deal had spawned.[1]

The firm began to recruit veterans promptly after World War II ended in 1945. Starting pay for an associate was $250 per month. Foley widened his reach in 1948 to include the University of Chicago Law School and prestigious schools in the East. He offered starting salaries that competed with Wall Street firms, and emphasized Milwaukee's virtues as a livable city with a healthy family environment. Lardner, who joined in the national recruiting effort, favored Harvard (his alma mater) and Yale.

The new recruiting policy brought in more top associates each year thereafter, leading Allen Taylor to write to his family: "I may not be advancing rapidly toward the top of the firm, but I am moving very swiftly away from the bottom." Foley's idea of offering salaries higher than those on Wall Street and providing a paid trip to Milwaukee for a candidate and his wife proved to be successful. The firm policy of attracting top Jewish attorneys and then of advancing them to partnership was unusual for the time. The only restriction on hiring was that partners' children could not join the firm.[2]

In 1946 a system of two classes of partners—special and general—was set up. The special partners (the first step) were limited to a compensation fixed by the general partners, Fairchild, Hardgrove, Foley, and Sammond. The 1949 partnership agreement detailed the distribution of partnership income: Foley and Sammond received 20 percent each, Fairchild only slightly less, and Hardgrove a little more than 10 percent. Distributions to the junior partners, including Bolliger, Lardner, Poole, and Keane, averaged one-fourth of Foley's or Sammond's.[3]

The two-tier plan was discarded in the 1953 partnership agreement, the first to specify a management structure. Governance was to be in the hands of a self-perpetuating executive committee of five to seven members, with authority by majority vote to offer partnership status, to require a partner's withdrawal or retirement, to terminate the partnership, to fix the distribution of income, to change the partnership name when it was appropriate to do so, and to determine all other policy matters.[4] In practice, the executive committee did what Foley recommended. With Fairchild's gradual withdrawal into an advisory role, Foley's word became law, and he became in fact (but not in name) the chief executive officer. Until he passed the mantle of leadership to Lyn Lardner, Foley ran the firm as something of a benevolent autocrat.

The firm grew from seven partners in 1945 to eighteen in 1958, when there were also twenty associates. With growth came the need for a more organized approach to training. First, a mentor program was tried, with each new associate assigned to a partner according to the senior attorney's specific area of expertise. Soon, however, following the pattern adopted by several New York firms, each associate was assigned to one of several teams. At first each team was known by the name of its leader: "Sammond's Team,"

"Rapkin's Team," and so forth. Later, each came to be known by its area of practice, and there were teams for tax, labor, litigation, trusts and estates, securities, and banking. With the team structure in place, Miller, Mack & Fairchild could offer a breadth and depth of legal counsel competitive with the large firms in Chicago.

Among the partners who carried on the work of the teams and of the firm during these postwar years were James Patrick Brody, Marvin Klitsner, Joseph Barnett, Paul Barnes, David Beckwith, Steve Keane, Theodore "Pete" Bolliger, Allen Taylor, Harold McComas, George Chester, Richard Harrington, James Poole, John Collins, Bernard Kubale, Robert Bradley, Harry Wallace, Herbert Wiedeman, Lyman Precourt, Orin Purintun, Edwin "Ted" Wiley, William Willis, and Lynford Lardner. The emphasis was on the firm's assisting clients through the lawyers that were most expert in the relevant field, not on each lawyer's having his own clients.

Billings grew to $1 million by 1954, steadily increasing each year to reach $2 million by the close of 1958 and $3 million by 1961. The growing demand for legal counsel in the areas of taxation, labor, litigation, estate planning, contracts, insurance, and securities had fully justified Foley's program of recruitment and growth.

Vigorous antitrust prosecutions during the Truman, Eisenhower, Kennedy, and Johnson administrations brought defense work to the firm. The movie industry became an antitrust battleground, with locally owned theaters suing studios for access to new films. The firm's client list of producers and distributors included Paramount, Warner Brothers, RKO, and Twentieth Century-Fox. In one case, the firm prevailed because a new associate—Ted Wiley—found a disappearing comma in the legislative history of a Wisconsin statute of limitations. The firm also represented antitrust defendants in a number of industries, including electrical, optical, water meters, rock salt, and paper.[5]

A number of antitrust cases occupied litigators for years. Another matter that lasted several years resulted from the disastrous 1950 collision of Milwaukee's Speedrail interurban train. Company President Jay Maeder was operating the train on an excursion run for a convention of model railroaders. The excursion train loaded with conventioneers crashed head-on into another train. Ten people were killed and forty-six seriously injured. Maeder's previously unknown color blindness had caused him to overlook a red signal light on the tracks, and other safety measures also failed. Claims against Speedrail and its insurers took years to settle.[6]

Tax law practice, led by Fred Sammond and later by Joseph Barnett, became a growth area after World War II when legislation such as the 1944 excess profits tax and the 1954 federal income tax revision needed application and interpretation. Tax questions sometimes led to litigation against the Internal Revenue Service.[7] The firm represented the Frank Lloyd Wright Foundation of Spring Green, which sued its town government to win a property tax exemption for its Taliesin complex. Wright contended the foundation was either an educational institution or one devoted to the fine arts. But the case foundered because Wright had never relinquished control of the foundation. The trial court decided the foundation didn't meet the statutory definitions of a tax-exempt organization, and the Supreme Court affirmed.[8]

Sammond's prestige as a tax attorney continued to grow. He led an American Bar Association committee on taxation and became a fellow of the American Bar Foundation and a member of the prestigious American Law Institute. One of his most unusual legal challenges occurred in 1954 when he represented Wisconsin's Menominee Indian Tribal Council in drawing a plan of termination from reservation status. The newly created Menominee County and the Menominee business corporation that owned its assets resulted from 1953 legislation and Eisenhower administration policy. Owned and controlled by Menominees, the business corporation tried to develop a tax base and income for the county by the sale of lumber and the development of tourism. However, the county was too poor to succeed without federal assistance, and the termination was reversed in 1974, eight years after Sammond's death. An associate at the firm recalled the respect that the tribal leaders had shown Sammond: He was elected a trustee of the corporation, one of the few non-Indians so chosen. Even Sammond knew, however, that the plan was "a best effort in a doomed cause." Economic independence had been forced on the tribe prematurely.[9]

The work of the securities team often brought the firm before the Securities and Exchange Commission in Washington, where it was aided by the banking and tax teams. The securities team also represented several local stock brokerage houses in securities matters and advised clients on new issues. Occasionally, the firm's leading partners played a pivotal role in the creation of new corporations by obtaining financing or attracting investors. A. W. Fairchild and Leon Foley were particularly effective in bringing potential capital and entrepreneurial talent to a common table.

Administrative law grew in significance after the war. Government regulation meant that corporate finance work could not safely proceed without sophisticated legal counsel. As securities matters became more complex, the firm managed corporate buyouts and related ownership succession questions for several major Wisconsin corporations. Though such work provided a welcome legal challenge, buyouts sometimes resulted in the loss of a local client.

The community was affronted in 1964 when the Milwaukee Braves announced they were moving to Atlanta. Milwaukee County, which had built County Stadium for the Braves in 1953, retained the firm to join the state's antitrust suit to keep baseball in Milwaukee. The Milwaukee Circuit Court held that Wisconsin antitrust law had been violated and ordered baseball's return. But the Wisconsin Supreme Court reversed because, it held, federal antitrust law (which exempted baseball) preempted Wisconsin's. Milwaukee had no more major league baseball until 1970, when an American League franchise was bought and moved here from Seattle.[10]

The corporate, tax, litigation, and securities teams handled most of the firm's work for its large utility clients, which had engaged in so many earlier struggles against state and federal regulations. Electric, gas, and telephone utilities sought advice on tax, regulatory, rate, and securities questions. Several trucking companies sought the firm's services in appearances before a variety of federal and state regulatory bodies. The firm litigated cases involving the Teamsters Union in the 1950s and 1960s. In one case, the firm vindicated on appeal a series of procedural decisions North Central Airlines had made in the course of buying another carrier.[11]

As in the days of Finch & Lynde, the firm's involvement in community affairs was an important factor in attracting new business. The firm was well represented on corporate and civic boards. Sammond was a trustee of Lawrence College, Milwaukee Downer College, and Milwaukee Country Day School, and a member of the advisory council for Marquette Law School, of a Planned Parent-

1. First National Bank building at Water and Mason Streets, location of the firm's offices from 1914 to 1974

2. Arthur W. Fairchild

3. Edwin S. Mack

4. James B. Blake

5. J. Gilbert Hardgrove

6. Paul R. Newcomb

7. Bartholomew Vandervelde

8. Frederic Sammond

9. Leon Foley

10. Theodore C. Bolliger

11. Lynford Lardner, Jr.

12. Joseph E. Rapkin

13. James I. Poole

14. Joseph R. Barnett

15. *In 1928, the firm represented the Milwaukee Gas Light Company in its attempt to raze a speakeasy so it could construct its headquarters building on East Wisconsin Avenue. Contractors excavated around the speakeasy while the firm obtained a court order.*

16. *New First Wisconsin Center where the firm's offices have been located since 1974*

hood committee, and of the State Historical Society of Wisconsin's Board of Curators. He served on the boards of the Milwaukee Auditorium and the Milwaukee Symphony and was a member of the Wisconsin History Foundation. In 1960, the Cosmopolitan Club of Milwaukee awarded Sammond its distinguished service award for outstanding civic contributions. Foley and Fairchild served as directors of a number of major Milwaukee companies and on charitable boards such as Children's Hospital and the Milwaukee Sanitarium. Fairchild's preeminence in Milwaukee social circles was a great asset to the growth of the firm's roster of clients.

Milwaukee widened its cultural base with the Eero Saarinen building, built in 1957 as a war memorial to house the Milwaukee Art Museum, formerly the Layton Art Gallery. Theater was reinvigorated with the establishment of the Milwaukee Repertory Theatre in 1954 at the old Fred Miller Theater building on the east side. Several partners helped create or nurture the Florentine Opera, the Milwaukee Symphony Orchestra, and the Milwaukee Ballet Company in the 1950s. Membership on these cultural boards, as well as on the boards of local charities such as hospitals and the blood bank, became a baton of civic duty passed on from partner to partner.

Other changes in American life after the war affected the practice of law. Real-estate development and the growing commercial base of the city brought new clients to the firm. With commuting by car an accepted way of life, Milwaukee suburbs experienced an unprecedented building boom in both housing and industry. Whitefish Bay, Wauwatosa, and the New Deal Village of Greendale grew rapidly as the postwar baby boom began. Eight new suburbs were incorporated in the Milwaukee area between 1950 and 1957. Milwaukee grew, too, to 637,000 people in 1950 and to 741,000 in 1960, making it the nation's eleventh largest city.[12]

Suburban shopping malls sprang up during the 1950s on land that had once been used for dairy farming. Southgate Mall was the first such development, followed by Capitol Court on the northwest side, Mayfair Mall in Wauwatosa, Bayshore Mall in Whitefish Bay, and then Southridge, Northridge, and Brookfield Square two decades later. Joseph Rapkin represented the Froedtert family interests in the development of both Southgate and Mayfair malls.[13]

The construction of the St. Lawrence Seaway during the 1950s brought international trade to the port of Milwaukee and resulted in new piers and harbor facilities. After the seaway officially opened in July 1959, Milwaukee posted a record number of ocean sailings—261—and the Harbor Commission initiated an $11 million expansion of the port. Within a year, Milwaukee's port traffic had doubled. The city ranked ninth in the country as a manufacturing center, leading the world in the production of diesel and gasoline engines, outboard motors, motorcycles, tractors, padlocks, and beer.[14]

The labor team was in demand in the postwar boom of commerce and industry. In 1949 and 1950, for example, the firm litigated tests of a Wisconsin statute that required arbitration of labor disputes involving utilities and forbade their employees to strike. The Wisconsin Supreme Court upheld the constitutionality of the statute. Later, in an appeal that did not involve the firm, the United States Supreme Court reversed.[15] The firm won labor cases it argued for such clients as A. O. Smith Corporation and the Square D Company in the 1960s.[16] The firm represented Milwaukee in opposing recognition of a union of lawyers employed by the city attorney's office, but lost when the Wisconsin Supreme Court held that the attorneys were not management employees.[17]

Although a Democrat, Hardgrove represented Joseph R. McCarthy in 1946 after he had upset Robert La Follette, Jr., in the Republican senatorial primary. A La Follette supporter had sued McCarthy on the ground that he was disqualified by the Wisconsin Constitution from taking office as a United States senator (and therefore from running for the Senate) during his term as a circuit judge. Hardgrove argued that the laws of the United States and not of Wisconsin controlled the election process for United States senators. Agreeing, the state Supreme Court permitted McCarthy's name to be placed on the November general election ballot.[18] He won the election.

Conservative Republicans were pleased by La Follette's defeat. Only later, after McCarthy's infamous witch hunts, did conservative Republicans like Leon Foley and Arthur Fairchild desert him. Democrats like Hardgrove suspected him of foul play very early, and the *Milwaukee Journal*—which Hardgrove represented—became one of the first newspapers in the country to repudiate him. In 1952, with McCarthy at the height of his power, the *Journal* endorsed his Democratic opponent, Thomas Fairchild, once an associate of the firm. McCarthy won, but two years later was censured by the Senate.

By then he had damaged the careers and lives of many public and private figures.

Thomas Fairchild had left the firm in 1948, when he was elected attorney general. He later became a justice of the Wisconsin Supreme Court and then was appointed to the United States Court of Appeals for the Seventh Circuit. Nevertheless, because of Justice Fairchild's previous political affiliations, Arthur Fairchild frequently took pains to explain that he and the justice were related neither by blood nor by political leaning.

Gilbert Hardgrove exemplified the independent spirit that brought diversity to the law firm. As the first active Catholic partner and the only active Democrat at the time, he relished the differences between himself and his conservative, Republican, and Protestant partners. His Irish heritage enriched his humor and gave fire to his courtroom oratory. He was a father figure and a nurturing presence to the younger men in the office throughout the 1930s, 1940s, and 1950s. His love of the law was contagious, and his mastery of the courtroom was well-known throughout the bar and the judiciary. But he remained outside the firm's circle of power.

By the end of World War II, Fairchild was the only partner with a longer tenure in the firm than Gilbert Hardgrove. When Fairchild first came to the firm in 1905, he quickly earned the respect and trust of both George Miller, his mentor and friend, and the more austere Edwin Mack. Fairchild's contribution to the firm came as much from his personality as from his ability as a business lawyer. He was respected and admired by his colleagues and by the Milwaukee legal and business community for his charm, personal style, business savvy, and humor. His ability to bring the firm's name before business and social leaders attracted as many clients as did the awesome legal talents of Edwin Mack. A deft politician, Fairchild created a sense of mission within the firm that kept the partners working as a team. His talent as a shrewd judge of character and leadership ability was exemplified by his decision to tap Leon Foley as the firm's leader in 1945. His full support gave Foley the backing needed to implement his ambitions for the growth of the firm. Although he worked until his death in August 1956, Fairchild had begun to cut back following a serious heart attack several years earlier. He continued to be an active presence, never completely retiring from practice and supporting Foley when necessary as a peacemaker, mediator, and leader.

Fairchild's example of providing reasonable latitude for the work and opinions of the firm's young associates was adopted by Foley. David Beckwith tested this latitude when he opposed the firm's longtime public support for mandatory membership in the state bar association, a policy first advanced by Edwin Mack in the 1920s. Beckwith argued the junior bar's opposition to the mandatory or integrated bar in a 1955 hearing, one year before the integrated bar was adopted. The freedom to publicly "kick in the traces," as Beckwith put it, was greatly valued by associates.[19]

Fairchild's support for Foley's leadership was crucial when they faced a challenge to the firm's continued use of the names of the dead partners George Miller and Edwin Mack. It was an issue that had been raised by bar associations throughout the country. Some attorneys argued that the continued use of dead partners' names constituted false advertising and was contrary to the spirit of free and open competition. So in 1951, twenty years after Miller's death and nine years after Mack's, the firm became Fairchild, Foley & Sammond. While Arthur Fairchild realized the necessity for the name change and the recognition it brought to the firm's new leaders, he wrote to one client in a nostalgic vein, "This change brings a flood of memories and a resurgence of my deep affection for Mr. Mack and Mr. Miller."[20] It had been Miller, Mack & Fairchild for forty-five years and that name remained in parentheses on the firm's letterhead until 1960, when the name was changed to Foley, Sammond & Lardner. The latter name remained in use until 1969, three years after Sammond's death, when the firm became simply Foley & Lardner. By 1970, bar policy sanctioned the use of deceased partners' names and the name Foley & Lardner has continued ever since.

The firm maintained a ratio of one associate to every partner throughout most of the postwar decades, holding to its intention to promote every qualified associate to partner. The partnership agreed to a "mandatory phasedown" of senior partners at age 65 (age 67 prior to 1985), accompanied by limits on compensation. The message in each team remained strong that attorneys served clients as part of the firm, rather than as individuals, and that all additional fees as trustees, executors, or directors were turned over to the partnership itself.

Support staff also grew in the postwar years. By 1951, the firm employed forty persons to support the thirty-three lawyers. The staff also became more specialized. A full-time librarian joined the firm in 1955 to manage the collection of 12,000 volumes. Storing files also demanded management attention as the firm logged file number 50,000 in 1974. A Secretary's Manual, first published in 1955, and more structured office policies provided absolute rules about lunch hours, vacations, and office dress. The office staff was led by several women who had served the firm for many decades. In addition to Mildred Roehr, who retired in 1975 after fifty years with the firm, there were Irene Seibel, who worked for Leon Foley, Elna Petersen, who had long been Arthur Fairchild's secretary, Harriet Kellner, Sammond's secretary, Elsie Peters, Jennie Hamilton, and Edna Tweeton.[21]

Leon Foley had stepped aside from the full-time management of the firm by the mid-1960s, leaving Lardner to work with the management committee and control the firm's destiny. Since 1921, when the firm was already almost eighty years old, Foley had followed its long-established tradition of serving corporate clients with sound legal advice and astute business judgment. Known at the beginning of his legal career for his outstanding record at Wisconsin's Law School, Foley was the school's first student editor-in-chief of the *Law Review*. His five decades in the practice of law followed in the tradition of B. K. and George Miller as he became an adviser to many of Wisconsin's most powerful corporations, who entrusted him with their business problems. Although he had litigated several cases when he first came to the firm, Foley was an introvert who avoided trial work and used his skills for counseling.

Unlike Mack, who balanced office practice with courtroom expertise, Foley was the exemplar of the twentieth-century corporate lawyer, a counselor and negotiator. Becoming a partner in 1933, just two years after the death of George Miller, Foley rose quickly to a leadership position with the blessing of Mack and Fairchild. Following in the firm's tradition, Foley was active in community service. With his wife and daughter, he was also an active supporter of the symphony and an avid football fan, especially of his alma mater in Madison.

Foley's most important legacy was his plan to build the law firm into a major state and national institution. With Fairchild's blessing and with Lardner's active support, Foley orchestrated the firm's rapid growth and the internal management and organizational changes that growth necessitated. Foley also brought Lardner into an active role in the management of the firm. Memos from the early 1960s about various office matters such as the partners' slowness in billing clients or newly arriving typewriters or copy machines bore the signatures of both Foley and Lardner. By 1966, however, notes to partners and office reminders about administrative details bore the name of the office manager or of Lardner alone. Foley suffered from Alzheimer's disease during his last years, and died in 1978 at the age of eighty-three.

Lyn Lardner's national reputation as a championship golfer and his personal warmth and popularity were invaluable to the realization of Foley's vision. The son of a dentist, Lardner grew up in Oconomowoc, thirty-five miles west of Milwaukee. He attended Harvard during the Depression, earning both a business and a law degree before joining Miller, Mack & Fairchild in August 1940 at the age of twenty-five. From his youth, Lardner had been an avid sportsman, although he hated the water and shunned swimming, even petitioning for permission to graduate from Harvard without passing the mandatory swimming test.

Before 1943, Lardner had won five Wisconsin amateur golf championships. He won his first in 1932 at age seventeen, the youngest winner ever. He qualified for the national amateur tournament five times and once reached the third match round. After a heart murmur kept him out of the service in World War II, he withdrew from state and national competition. However, his lifelong interest in the sport never waned: He was the director of the Wisconsin State Golf Association and in 1972 was elected president of the United States Golf Association.

After joining the firm in 1940, Lardner rose to a position of influence even before he became a partner in 1947. He brought charisma and spontaneity to office gatherings. He was the unquestioned leader of the firm, as Foley had been, and used the management committee largely as a sounding board. Although the period of Lardner's sole management was much shorter than Foley's, his decisions to open offices outside Milwaukee and to move the firm itself into a new downtown location were influential in setting the course of the firm's future in the last quarter of the twentieth century. He was personally involved in the selection and recruitment of every new attorney from 1948 onward.

The firm's offices in the First Wisconsin National Bank Building at 735 North Water Street had been the firm's home since before World War I. By 1970 they had become too crowded despite an extensive expansion and remodeling in 1964. So when First Wisconsin decided to build a forty-two-story tower on the eastern end of Wisconsin Avenue, Lardner agreed to move the firm into its upper floors.

In 1973, at fifty-eight, Lardner was not only highly respected as a businessman and attorney, but was also beloved within the firm, a rare combination of attributes. Lardner enjoyed people and lived life with style and zest. Although plagued with back trouble, he appeared to his partners as a man prepared to meet the challenges of the seventies. But his tenure was suddenly cut short. On Tuesday, October 16, 1973, the firm was rocked by the news that Lardner had drowned that morning in the Milwaukee River, which bordered the west side of the bank building.

After an investigation of the circumstances of Lardner's drowning, authorities dismissed foul play as a cause of death. Mourning partners and Lardner's own wife and four daughters faced the conclusion that he had either fallen or jumped into the river. The partner who had last seen Lardner that morning recalled that he was standing at the river's edge on his way to the office, and that he was seemingly preoccupied. With a worsening back problem, Lardner had been in great pain and faced back surgery which could have left him paralyzed. Although insurers concluded there was insufficient proof of suicide to withhold benefits, suicide was the likely explanation. A few partners believed that a bout with the flu may have resulted in dizziness, causing Lardner to fall into the river, from which, as a nonswimmer, he could not escape. Men who knew him well cited the fact that Lardner was not a person to act impulsively and would have tied up his affairs before committing suicide. His body was found without his wallet, suggesting that he was very confused on the morning of his death.

Lardner's memorial service was held on Friday, October 19, in St. Paul's Episcopal Church, where the rose window given in memory of Asahel Finch illuminated the ceremony. Lardner's family asked for contributions to his favorite causes—the Blood Center,

Children's Hospital or Columbia Hospital, the Golf Association, and the University School of Milwaukee, which he had helped to create with the merger of three competing private schools on the city's east side.[22]

It was difficult to reorganize the firm after such a sudden loss. Unlike Foley, Lardner had left no heir apparent. Meeting immediately after Lardner's death, the management committee, headed by Vernon Swanson, decided against perpetuating one-man rule. In agreeing to overhaul the firm's management structure, the committee wisely yielded to the strong pressure for change exerted by several younger partners who had chafed under the old system and now wanted to be involved in making firm policy. Some partners believed that the very preservation of the 130-year-old partnership was at stake. The firm had outgrown the ability to function well with only one man making all the most important decisions. The committee also added two new members: Allen Taylor and Richard Harrington. They and others who had joined the firm after the war had been instrumental in its growth and success in the 1950s and 1960s.

It was decided that a newly constituted management committee of seven partners would decide all important policy matters, with Swanson, Keane, and Rapkin functioning as an executive committee. The firm appointed Harry Wallace as an administrator to manage day-to-day details of the firm's operation. Management committee members were to be selected by a majority vote of the committee itself, rather than by a vote of all of the partners. A few years later, management committee memberships were limited to nine-year terms.

The new management committee saw an immediate need for a long-range planning study to guide the firm into the end of the century and beyond. Integral to the study's conclusions was a renewed emphasis on national expansion and the recommendation that all books, client accounts, and trust matters be computerized. A technical expert, Colonel A. H. Watkins, who had put a Strategic Air Command base on-line, was hired to bring the firm into the age of computer technology.

In the spring of 1974, the firm's offices were moved to the new First Wisconsin Center. In the three decades since the end of World War II the partnership had experienced tremendous growth as it responded to the increasing need of its clients for legal services. Leon Foley's idea of creating a large firm with teams of experts in specialized areas of law had become a reality. Located at the eastern end of Wisconsin Avenue, the firm's new offices closed a circle, for they looked down on the site of Judge Andrew G. Miller's home where, at an 1839 dinner for Milwaukee lawyers, newcomers Asahel Finch and Charles Lynde had first been introduced to each other.

❦ 16 ❧

Epilogue:
A National Law Firm
1974–1992

By the summer of 1974, Foley & Lardner had reorganized its management and moved into new offices in the First Wisconsin Center at 777 East Wisconsin Avenue. Changing patterns in the local and national economy demanded a new vision for corporate law firms. Implementing an idea that Leon Foley and Lyn Lardner had shared, the management committee decided to establish offices outside Wisconsin. Foley & Lardner thus became the first Wisconsin firm to go national in order to enlarge its client base and better serve clients with nationwide operations.

The firm's first expansion office was founded in Washington, D.C., in 1971, two years before Lardner's death. Early in 1970, Lardner directed Dave Shute to investigate the feasibility of a Washington office. After discussing the idea with friends in other Washington firms and with members of several New York firms that had begun to establish branches there, he gave a positive recommendation based on the apparent opportunity to represent existing clients in their continuing relations with federal agencies.

Before suggesting the expansion to the general partnership, Lardner considered its implications for the firm's internal dynamics. The partnership as a whole had to support the concept of establishing offices outside Milwaukee. It had to be convinced that expansion was consistent with the firm's management style, that it was sound economically, and that it would not harm the firm's internal culture. Leon Foley and several senior partners embraced the plan immediately, while others doubted that the firm could persuade many clients to use such an office. Despite their hesitation, Lardner gave Shute the green light. Shute and an associate from the bank team opened the Washington office in January 1971 in quarters subleased from another firm at 815 Connecticut Avenue, a block north of the White House.[1]

At first, the Washington lawyers concentrated on "portable work," especially assignments that could be done at a distance for the First Wisconsin National Bank and a few other clients. Meanwhile they sought to develop business for Wisconsin firms that needed representation before federal agencies. Attracting new local clients proved more difficult. One early partner recalled, "Being from Milwaukee was not a helpful factor in the climate of Washington, D.C." Shute returned to the Milwaukee office in 1974.[2]

With the hope of increasing its visibility in Washington, the firm made retiring Wisconsin Congressman John W. Byrnes a partner in early 1973. Byrnes had represented Wisconsin's Eighth Congressional District, centered on Green Bay, since 1942, and had retired as the ranking Republican member of the powerful House Ways and Means Committee. Next, Steven Keane and David Beckwith negotiated a merger with the Washington firm of Hollabaugh & Jacobs, effective October 1, 1974. Foley & Lardner brought to the merger the advantages of a full-service firm and a national linkage, while Hollabaugh & Jacobs had a Washington presence as a five-lawyer boutique antitrust and trade-regulation firm. New partners Marcus Hollabaugh and Ephraim Jacobs had practiced in Washington since finishing George Washington University Law School in 1939 and 1942. The merger proved mutually beneficial, and the Washington office grew to twenty-one lawyers in the next five years.

The early 1980s, with its recession and the Reagan administration's curtailment of antitrust enforcement, brought slow times to the Washington office, and the office was cut back to only nine lawyers by the end of that year. However, the office had grown to thirty-five lawyers by 1992. With James Bierman as partner-in-charge, it functioned as a full-service office, with a clientele that for the most part was based in Washington.[3]

Bank team partner Lawrence Bugge opened the firm's second expansion office on September 1, 1975, at the First Wisconsin Bank Center on Madison's Capitol Square. Bugge recalled it was only a "beachhead operation" to begin with, pending a planned merger with a Madison firm. However, Bugge and associate Richard George became responsible for maintaining the office on their own when the merger was delayed and eventually abandoned because of client conflicts.

Working at first on matters for the Wisconsin Housing Finance Authority and for the First Wisconsin National Bank, the two men began to carry out the plan advanced by William Kiernan to develop the firm's reputation in the areas of public finance and corporate underwritings. In 1963 and 1964, Bugge had worked with Bernard Kubale and William Kiernan to write a series of law review articles on the subject of municipal bonds and public debt. Published in the *Wisconsin Law Review*, the articles brought the firm a listing in *The Bond Buyers' Municipal Marketplace,* the "red book," as expert in government finance.[4]

In the early 1970s, the firm had taken an active role in the creation of the Wisconsin Housing Finance Authority, an agency authorized to borrow money for public housing. The firm had won the 1973 WHFA test case, in which the Wisconsin Supreme Court held that the statute creating the agency did not violate the constitutional prohibition on state indebtedness.[5]

Dick George left the Madison office in 1976 to become the executive director of WHFA, leaving Bugge to keep the doors open alone. Bugge brought in two associates from Milwaukee in the same year. Thomas Ragatz came into the office as a partner in 1978, bringing new business and stability to the Madison effort. Editor-in-chief of the *Wisconsin Law Review*, Ragatz had practiced for sixteen years with the Madison firm of Boardman, Suhr, Curry & Field. By 1979, the office had eight attorneys working in the areas of real estate, securities, tax, business, banking, and litigation.

David Walsh and his firm merged with the Madison office in 1986, bringing new clients and new expertise in cable television. Foley & Lardner was the first Milwaukee firm to maintain a full-service office in Madison. With forty-four lawyers in 1992, it was the largest law partnership in the city.

The firm began its expansion into Florida in 1981. Other firms had begun to expand into the sunbelt states as they experienced industrial growth and an influx of retirees. However, the Florida legal climate was even less hospitable to such "carpetbag" offices than Washington had been. The planning and ultimate success of the firm's expansion into the Florida market rested principally on the shoulders of two men, William Kiernan and Gerald Neal.[6] Neal had met Thomas B. Slade III, a long-established Florida attorney based in Jacksonville, in connection with work in Florida for the First Wisconsin National Bank. Slade agreed to an affiliation and opened the firm's first Florida office, Foley, Lardner & Slade, in February 1981, in Jacksonville. That summer, the firm opened a small office in Tampa, on the other side of the peninsula. The office was temporarily located in a rundown neighborhood north of central Tampa, where Neal had to help derelicts off the stairs to open the second-story offices each morning. After this inauspicious beginning, the office moved the next year to the newly built Tampa City Center.

By the middle 1980s it was clear that these two Florida offices could not grow without the local ties that strong indigenous firms had. Three mergers with established Florida firms solidified the firm's Florida operation between 1984 and 1991.

The first merger was with the twenty-year-old firm of van den Berg, Gay, Burke, Wilson & Arkin of Orlando. Egerton K. van den Berg had met Slade and David Beckwith of the Milwaukee office through matters that the firm handled in Florida. A native of Oklahoma, van den Berg had turned down similar merger proposals from New York firms. He believed the values of a midwestern firm fit well with the practice of law in Florida. His great-great-grandmother, Laura Ross Wolcott had been one of Wisconsin's first woman doctors and a friend of B. K. Miller's daughter in the late nineteenth century. J. Gordon Arkin, a Harvard Law graduate who had worked with a New York firm before coming to Orlando, seconded the idea of merging with a midwestern firm.

The Milwaukee team of Allen Taylor, Bernard Kubale, David Beckwith and William Kiernan met with the partners in Orlando and signed a letter of intent in August 1984 for a merger to take effect in

February 1985. The merger brought the firm a strong presence in central Florida. Half of the van den Berg, Gay, Burke, Wilson & Arkin attorneys worked on real estate and construction-related matters for clients such as Disney, the Greater Orlando Airport Authority, Universal Studios, and Busch Properties. Foley & Lardner offered these and other clients a full range of services and the expertise of its teams in each area.

Following the successful Orlando merger, the Tampa office grew with the lateral entries of Daniel Burton and six other attorneys who had practiced in a Tampa firm. Then, in October 1988, the office merged with one of the oldest law firms in Tampa: Hill, Hill & Dickinson. The founder of the fifty-six-year-old Hill firm, Lewis H. Hill, Jr., had come from his native Georgia to Tampa in 1925 during the great Florida land boom. His younger brother, Robert, graduated from Columbia Law School in 1930 and faced a bleak job market in the wake of the crash on Wall Street. "It was possibly the worst year in history to take up law," he recalled.

Urged by his brother, Robert came to Tampa where "there was always plenty of grits and plenty of mullet to survive." There was also plenty of real estate work to do, although not for the wealthy speculators who had flocked there during the 1920s. The new partnership of Hill & Hill kept afloat by working on mortgage refinancing for Roosevelt's New Deal agency, the Home Owners' Loan Corporation, which paid attorneys forty dollars for each new mortgage contract written to save a family's home.

The Hill partnership survived the Depression and prospered with the port activity in World War II and the postwar growth of Tampa. By 1986, the Hill firm practiced in the areas of real estate development, trucking and transportation regulation, cattle ranching, citrus growing, and the resort industry.

The third merger in Florida occurred in Jacksonville. William D. King had joined Foley, Lardner & Slade as a partner in 1982 after practicing for eighteen years in another Jacksonville firm. On February 1, 1985, the office changed its name from Foley, Lardner & Slade to Foley & Lardner, and in August 1986 King became the partner in charge. By the end of 1989 the office had grown to ten attorneys.

King also sought to achieve an attractive merger by talking to two former colleagues who had begun their own partnership, Charles C. Commander III and Mitchell W. Legler. Meetings with the firm of Commander, Legler, Werber, Dawes, Sadler & Howell resulted in a merger on February 1, 1991. Foley & Lardner's expertise in tax, government finance, and intellectual property balanced the strong banking, real estate, and securities practice at Commander, Legler and supported the latter's work with significant clients such as the First Union Bank, SouthTrust Bank, Computer Power, Inc., and Stein Mart, Inc. A year after the merger, the Jacksonville office had thirty-five attorneys and was growing rapidly.

The three successful mergers provided Foley & Lardner with a strong presence in Florida, but the interests of serving clients there demanded even more. Between 1987 and 1988, the firm built on the success of its growing Florida operation by adding offices in West Palm Beach and Tallahassee.

What is now the West Palm Beach office opened in Palm Beach in 1987, at the same time the First Wisconsin Trust Company opened an office in the community. Jack Porter, a trusts and estates attorney in the Milwaukee office, moved to West Palm Beach to open the new location. A member of the Florida bar, Porter operated the office alone for its first full year. The office doubled in size in each of the following four years; by the end of 1991 it had become a full-service office of the firm with sixteen attorneys and an extensive practice in litigation, real estate, estates and trusts, intellectual property, corporations and health care.

The fifth Florida office opened in Tallahassee in March 1988. Bill Bryant, former special counsel to the governor of Florida, had discussed the idea with Kiernan and decided to join the firm. Much of the Tallahassee office's practice was in the area of regulation, agency work, utilities cases, land- and water-usage matters, environmental cases, and matters before the Florida Department of Insurance. The office grew to six attorneys in less than three years. By 1992 Foley & Lardner's 125 lawyers in Florida made it the state's fifth largest law firm.

Following the success of the Florida expansion, Gerry Neal returned closer to home to tap the Chicago market. The firm opened an office in Itasca, Illinois—a western suburb of Chicago—in March

1988, principally to serve the needs of real estate client Trammell Crow. Three months later, Neal and three other attorneys started a Loop office. The Itasca office was closed in 1990. With new clients such as Massachusetts Mutual Life Insurance Company, John Hancock Insurance, First Boston Company, Sears Roebuck, the DeSoto Corporation, and Merrill Lynch, the Chicago operation grew to thirty-one attorneys by early 1992.

The firm also expanded into new practice areas in the 1980s. Although Lynde had taken a patent case all the way to the United States Supreme Court and the firm had always handled some intellectual property matters, Foley & Lardner generally avoided such work because of the business conflicts that it threatened to create among clients. However, the management committee agreed to establish an intellectual property team, principally at the urging of Ted Wiley and Richard Harrington. The team began to function on February 1, 1984.

The practice of intellectual property law grew rapidly during the 1970s, fueled both by changes in law and by the boom in high technology, most notably in electronics. The Patent Cooperation Treaty was signed in Washington in 1970. Nearly all European nations signed the European Patent Convention in 1973, and a second treaty—the Community Patent Convention—was concluded in 1975. The latter will eventually provide a single patent system for the entire Common Market.

However, in the United States lingering New Deal attitudes among the federal judiciary antagonistic toward patent rights hampered effective protection of inventions, particularly in comparison with major foreign competitors, where governments worked in partnership with industry to encourage innovation and protection of the resulting intellectual property rights. The tide changed with the more globally aware and probusiness administrations of the 1970s and 1980s, particularly when the Supreme Court reversed long-standing antipatent attitudes in two landmark cases in the early 1980s. *Diamond v. Chakrabarty* opened the door for inventions in the emerging field of biotechnology to be protected by patents, and *Diamond v. Diehr* set a more receptive course for inventions related to computer software.[7] Throughout the 1980s Congress changed patent law in ways that strongly favored protection for inventions and further stimulated growth in the patent field. Creation of the United States Court of Appeals for the Federal Circuit in 1982 to hear appeals in all patent cases represented another positive development favoring a strong patent system.

The firm's development of an intellectual property team began in 1983 and led to the merger on February 1, 1988, with the Alexandria, Virginia, firm of Schwartz, Jeffrey, Schwaab, Mack, Blumenthal & Evans, comprising fourteen attorneys who specialized in intellectual property law. Foley & Lardner, Schwartz, Jeffrey, Schwaab, Mack, Blumenthal & Evans continued its practice in Alexandria, near the United States Patent Office in Arlington, Virginia. Arthur Schwartz, Peter Mack, David Blumenthal, and Richard L. Schwaab had practiced together since the 1974 merger of two patent firms, Stepno, Schwaab & Linn, and Bacon & Thomas, where Schwartz was a partner. Four years later, the four of them and long-time friend Donald Jeffrey formed their own patent firm and moved to a 200-year-old townhouse in historic Alexandria.[8]

Schwaab and Jeffrey, Wisconsin natives, knew some of the Foley & Lardner partners who had worked to establish the intellectual property team. Foley & Lardner had been canvassing potential merger candidates among intellectual property firms in Chicago and Washington. Its approach to Richard Schwaab in September 1987 was propitious, for the Schwartz partners had just concluded a firm retreat during which they decided to explore merger with a large national firm to gain stronger litigation support and an enhanced domestic presence to balance their predominantly international client base.[9] In 1992 the firm had sixty-five attorneys practicing intellectual property law, nearly fifty of them registered patent attorneys. The firm also had ten registered patent agents in 1992.

In addition, the firm organized teams to practice in the areas of health care and environmental law. In the health-care field, the needs of clients such as Children's Hospital, Froedtert Medical Center, and St. Luke's Hospital grew along with Medicare, Medicaid, and other new federal and state regulation of the health-care industry in the 1970s and 1980s. Established in 1983, the Health Law Department had grown to twenty-six members by 1992.

The Environmental Law Department developed out of Sandy Williams's practice under the federal Clean Air Act of 1970 and the Clean Water Act of 1972. The team grew to two members in 1980, just before the passage of the federal "Superfund" legislation of December 1980 with all of the implications it carried for corporate and real estate clients. By 1992 the Environmental Law Department of the firm numbered sixteen attorneys working in all areas of environmental law.

In late 1990, Foley & Lardner organized GlobaLex, an international strategic alliance with three full-service overseas law firms based in London, Paris, and Stuttgart, with satellite offices in Berlin, Dresden, Singapore, and Taipei. GlobaLex represented a more efficient and cost-effective way to serve the international legal needs of the firm's clients than the more traditional American approaches of either making cross-referral agreements with foreign firms or establishing satellite offices in foreign countries. The objective of GlobaLex was to provide the firm's clients in foreign markets with the same level of service, and the same business and commercial approach to the practice of law as Foley & Lardner provides in the United States.

The firm grew sevenfold in the two decades before its sesquicentenniel, from thirty-five partners in 1970 to 255 in mid-1992. With 197 of Foley & Lardner's 450 attorneys, the Milwaukee office was still the largest, occupying the top seven floors of the First Wisconsin Center and parts of other floors. Although more than half of the firm's attorneys practiced in other cities, most of the department chairmen were based in Milwaukee in 1992, as were eight of the twelve members of the management committee. Support staff totaled 741 persons, half of them—370—based in Milwaukee. Of the employees in Milwaukee, seventy-two were devoted to firm-wide support services. The large international organization of almost 1,200 people was dramatically different from the two-man partnership of Finch & Lynde in 1842. However, there were also similarities. The firm has held to its original mission of serving business clients, whatever their changing legal needs. The substance of the firm's corporate work and the value placed on excellence have roots in the partnership established by Finch & Lynde and are part of a unifying and continuing tradition today.

Appendix I

⊰ Firm Names ⊱

Finch & Lynde	1842–1844
Hubbell, Finch & Lynde	1844–1845
Finch & Lynde	1845–1857
Finches, Lynde & Miller	1857–1890
Miller, Noyes & Miller	1890–1895
Miller, Noyes, Miller & Wahl	1895–1900
Miller, Noyes & Miller	1900–1906
Miller, Mack & Fairchild	1906–1951
Fairchild, Foley & Sammond	1951–1960
Foley, Sammond & Lardner	1960–1969
Foley & Lardner	1969–

Appendix II

⊰ Partners ⊱

Partner	Retired (R) or Withdrew (W)
1842	
Asahel Finch, Jr. *	
William Pitt Lynde *	
1845	
Levi Hubbell *	Aug. 23, 1845 (W)
1857	
Henry M. Finch *	
B. K. Miller, Sr. *	
1886	
B. K. Miller, Jr. *	Feb. 1, 1906 (R)
George P. Miller *	
1890	
George H. Noyes *	Feb. 1, 1906 (R)
1895	
George H. Wahl *	
1905	
Arthur W. Fairchild *	
1906	
Edwin S. Mack *	
1915	
James B. Blake *	
1916	
J. Gilbert Hardgrove *	
1923	
Paul R. Newcomb *	
1933	
Bert Vandervelde *	Jan. 1, 1947 (R)
Leon F. Foley *	
Frederic Sammond *	

* deceased

Partner	*Retired (R) or Withdrew (W)*
1943	
Vernon A. Swanson	Jan. 31, 1976 (R)
1946	
Theodore C. Bolliger *	Feb. 1, 1976 (R)
1947	
Steven E. Keane	Jan. 31, 1989 (R)
Joseph E. Rapkin *	
Lynford Lardner, Jr. *	
James I. Poole *	
1949	
Paul M. Barnes	Feb. 1, 1985 (R)
1953	
Marvin E. Klitsner	Jan. 31, 1988 (R)
1954	
Thomas B. Fifield	Feb. 15, 1962 (W)
1956	
James P. Brody	June 1, 1988 (R)
Joseph R. Barnett *	Jan. 31, 1988 (R)
Richard L. Harrington	Jan. 31, 1984 (R)
Orin Purintun	Dec. 31, 1983 (R)
Allen M. Taylor	
1957	
George M. Chester	Jan. 31, 1987 (R)
1960	
Harrold J. McComas	
Edwin P. Wiley	
Herbert P. Wiedemann	May 31, 1992 (R)
1961	
David E. Beckwith	
Lyman A. Precourt	
William J. Willis	Aug. 1, 1987 (R)
Harry L. Wallace	
1962	
Robert B. Bradley	
1964	
John R. Collins *	
Bernard S. Kubale	
1965	
Edwin F. Walmer	July 1, 1990 (R)
Richard H. Miller	

Partner	*Retired (R) or Withdrew (W)*
1966	
David Shute	Feb. 1, 1981 (W)
James R. Modrall, III	July 1, 1971 (W)
William J. Kiernan, Jr.	
1968	
Eugene C. Daly	Feb. 1, 1988 (R)
Jere D. McGaffey	
Gilbert W. Church	
David H. Fleck	
1970	
Maurice J. McSweeney	
Timothy C. Frautschi	
Lawrence J. Bugge	
James O. Huber	
Robert J. Bonner	
1971	
Robert K. Drummond	
1972	
Robert G. Weber	
Michael S. Nolan	
1973	
John W. Byrnes *	Jan. 31, 1984 (R)
Phillip J. Hanrahan	
Robert A. Christensen	
David W. Croysdale	Aug. 7, 1978 (W)
Harry V. Carlson, Jr.	
John W. Brahm	
1974	
F. Roberts Hanning, Jr.	
Benjamin F. Garmer, III	
Marcus A. Hollabaugh	Feb. 1, 1983 (R)
Ephraim Jacobs	Apr. 30, 1982 (R)
Douglas V. Rigler	Jan. 28, 1985 (W)
John F. Graybeal	May 31, 1984 (W)
Howard W. Fogt, Jr.	
Richard S. Gallagher	
1975	
F. Anthony Maio	
Keith A. Christiansen	
Gerald J. Neal	
Benn S. DiPasquale	

Partner	*Retired (R) or Withdrew (W)*
1976	
Jack A. Porter	
Benjamin J. Abrohams	
Emory Ireland	
David W. Slook	
Ronald L. Walter	
1977	
John S. Skilton	
John R. Dawson	
Michael W. Grebe	
Robert A. Sams	
Allen W. Williams, Jr.	
1978	
David S. Lott	
Richard A. Weiss	
James R. Clark	
Stanley S. Jaspan	
David J. Hase	
Joseph P. Hildebrandt	
Thomas G. Ragatz	
1979	
Thomas L. Shriner, Jr.	
Richard H. Porter	Apr. 15, 1991 (W)
William J. Abraham, Jr.	
James P. Connelly	
James N. Bierman	
Peter B. Edelman	June 30, 1982 (W)
1980	
Richard D. George	Feb. 1, 1982 (W)
Paul D. Braun	
Leonard S. Sosnowski	
Michael D. Fischer	
George D. Cunningham	
Robert A. DuPuy	
Stanley A. Tarkow	
Wayne R. Lueders	
Rodney H. Dow	
W. David Knox II	
Ronald M. Wawrzyn	
Linda H. Kamm	Feb. 1, 1984 (W)
Jack L. Lahr	
Anthony S. Earl	Feb. 19, 1982 (W)
Edwin J. Dryer	Jan. 31, 1987 (R)

Partner	*Retired (R) or Withdrew (W)*
1981	
Michael A. Gehl	
Michael D. Regenfuss	
Ralf-Reinhard Boer	
Michael W. Hatch	
John A. Sanders	
Richard S. Florsheim	
Stephen M. Fisher	
Michael P. Erhard	
Thomas B. Slade, III	Feb. 1, 1992 (R)
1982	
Robert L. Binder	
Carolyn C. Burrell	
Leslie C. Smith	Aug. 31, 1987 (W)
Jeffrey H. Lane	
Greg W. Renz	
Richard H. Casper	
Mark G. Petri	Feb. 29, 1992 (W)
Jon P. Christiansen	
Jay N. Varon	
Michael G. Laskis	
William D. King	
Peter C. Linzmeyer	
1983	
Joan F. Kessler	
1984	
Marsha E. Huff	
Michael A. Bowen	
Luke E. Sims	
Christopher S. Berry	
Jere W. Wiedenman	
Michael M. Biehl	
David A. Baker	Dec. 13, 1991 (W)
Michael A. Lechter	Mar. 15, 1991 (W)
Michael H. Auen	
1985	
Egerton K. van den Berg	
Francis F. Gay	Jan. 31, 1989 (R)
Norman F. Burke	
Jon M. Wilson	
J. Gordon Arkin	
Charles R. Guthridge *	
Christopher C. Skambis, Jr.	

Partner	*Retired (R) or Withdrew (W)*
Paul E. Rosenthal	
Craig B. Ward	Oct. 14, 1988 (W)
David M. Reicher	
Russell J. Barron	

1986

Linda H. Laarman	July 29, 1988 (W)
Joseph B. Tyson, Jr.	
Paul A. Cooney	
Reed Groethe	
Dennis A. Hennigan	Apr. 14, 1989 (W)
James P. O'Shaughnessy	
Samuel H. Weissbard	
Wendy L. Fields	
David G. Walsh	
Robert M. Whitney	
Timothy C. Sweeney	
Daniel N. Burton	
Judith W. Simmons	
Kenneth A. Beytin	
John T. Sefton	
David M. Rieth	
David A. Sacks	

1987

K. Rodney May	
Mark C. Extein	
John P. Horan	
Richard L. Teigen	
Trevor J. Will	
Chauncey W. Lever, Jr.	
Jeffrey J. Jones	
Jane A. Belford	Nov. 1, 1989 (W)
Steven V. Ponto	Jan. 31, 1989 (W)
James M. Landis	
Vance A. Smith	Apr. 16, 1990 (W)
Richard S. Heymann	

1988

Thomas F. Munro, III	
Donald D. Jeffery	
Arthur Schwartz	
Richard L. Schwaab	
Peter G. Mack	
Joseph D. Evans	
David A. Blumenthal	
C. Frederick Geilfuss, II	

Partner	*Retired (R) or Withdrew (W)*
David J. Harth	
Ronald D. Tym	
Nancy J. Sennett	
Mark A. Thimke	
Timothy J. Sheehan	
John J. Feldhaus	
Stephen A. Bent	
Bill L. Bryant, Jr.	
James A. Winkler	
Randall S. Rapp	
Michael L. Weissman	Jan. 2, 1992 (W)
Guy O. Farmer, II	
C. Jeffery Arnold	Dec. 30, 1990 (W)
Jay R. Beskin	Feb. 13, 1991 (W)
Michael B. Carsella	Nov. 30, 1989 (W)
James S. Grodin	
John D. Lien	
Bernhard D. Saxe	
Lewis H. Hill, III	
J. Philip Plyler	
C. Anthony Sexton	Jan. 5, 1991 (W)
Stephen A. Crane	

1989

Robert J. Morris, Jr.	Apr. 13, 1992 (W)
Robert P. Marschall	
William P. Sklar	
Patrick N. Giordano	
Harvey L. Temkin	
George A. Dionisopoulos	
Jamshed J. Patel	
David A. Gatchell	
Charles A. Benner	
Thomas F. Clasen	
Charles J. Steele	
Suzanne S. Dawson	
Jacqueline M. Saue	
Richard O. Gray, Jr.	
Amy S. Rubin	
Steven B. Chameides	
Harvey A. Kurtz	
Joseph C. Branch	
Kathleen M. Rivera	Jan. 31, 1991 (W)
Peter J. Stone	
Thomas C. Ewing	
Donald D. Mondul	

Partner	*Retired (R) or Withdrew (W)*
John C. Cooper, III	
Robert J. Zimmerman	
John M. Olson	
R. Duke Woodson	
Lloyd J. Dickinson	

1990

Harrison K. Chauncey, Jr.	
Leslie H. Gladfelter	Apr. 13, 1992 (W)
Mark M. Schabacker	
Jack B. Siegel	
Philip G. Meyers	
Anne E. Ross	
Richard M. Esenberg	
Kevin D. Anderson	
Michael J. Kelly	
Mary K. Braza	
W. Gray Dunlap, Jr.	
Mark F. Foley	
Charles G. Curtis, Jr.	
Christopher D. Rolle	
William J. Scanlon	
James C. Hauser	Mar. 31, 1992 (W)
Harry C. Engstrom	
Ira C. Wolpert	
Richard A. Durose	
Paul F. Byran	Oct. 31, 1991 (W)
Christopher K. Kay	
Edmund T. Baxa, Jr.	
Peter G. Latham	

1991

Henry A. Gempeler	
David H. Runyan	
Beth Meier Berger	
Christian G. Steinmetz	
Brian W. McGrath	
Maureen A. McGinnity	
David W. Reinecke	
Lawrence T. Lynch	
Keith J. Hesse	
Susan R. Maisa	
Terence J. Delahunty, Jr.	
Michael B. VanSicklen	
Paul R. Monsees	
Martin D. Mann	
Denise T. DiPersio	
Patrick M. Zabrowski	

Partner	Retired (R) or Withdrew (W)
Steven A. Werber	
Charles E. Commander, III	
Mitchell W. Legler	
Michael F. Dawes	
Luther F. Sadler, Jr.	
Charles C. Howell, III	
John M. Welch, Jr.	
Robert E. Meek	
Charles V. Hedrick	
Linda Y. Kelso	
Michael S. O'Neal	
Emerson Lotzia	
Gresham R. Stoneburner	
Andrew Fulton, III	
Robert Brody	
Mark J. Wolfson	
Mark L. Prager	
Sybil Meloy	
John T. Winburn	
Stephen M. Slavin	
George T. Simon	
Edwin D. Mason	
James A. Farrell	

1992

Thomas C. Pence
Michael G. McCarty
Gordon Davenport, III
Timothy J. Radelet
William M. Conley
David M. Lucey
R. Andrew Rock
Wayman C. Lawrence
Edward J. Hammond
Andrew A. Ostrow
Michael E. Olsen
Michael A. Hornreich
Nathan D. Goldman
Thomas F. Maurer
Patrick G. Quick
Ilene K. Gotts
Joseph W. Jacobs
B. Gray Gibbs
Pierre C. Talbert
Kent A. Zaiser
Robert A. Burka
A. Jose Cortina

Appendix III

 Mergers

October 1, 1974	Washington	Hollabaugh & Jacobs
February 1, 1985	Orlando	van den Berg, Gay, Burke, Wilson & Arkin, P.A.
June 15, 1986	Madison	Walsh, Walsh, Sweeney & Whitney
February 1, 1988	Alexandria (and Annapolis)	Schwartz, Jeffrey, Schwaab, Mack, Blumenthal & Evans, P.C.
September 30, 1988	Tampa	Hill, Hill & Dickenson, P.A.
February 1, 1991	Jacksonville	Commander Legler Werber Dawes Sadler & Howell, P.A

Appendix IV

❧ Foley & Lardner Offices ❧

First Wisconsin Center
777 East Wisconsin Avenue
Milwaukee, Wisconsin 53202–5367

First Wisconsin Plaza
One South Pinckney Street
Madison, Wisconsin 53701–1497

Three First National Plaza
70 West Madison Street
Chicago, Illinois 60602–4208

1775 Pennsylvania Avenue, N.W.
Washington, D.C. 20006–4680

1800 Diagonal Road
Alexandria, Virginia 22313–0299

175 Admiral Cochrane Drive
Annapolis, Maryland 21401–7307

The Greenleaf Building
200 Laura Street
Jacksonville, Florida 32201–0240

111 North Orange Avenue
Orlando, Florida 32802–2193

101 North Monroe Street
Tallahassee, Florida 32302–0508

One Tampa City Center
Tampa, Florida 33601–3391

and

Barnett Plaza
101 East Kennedy Boulevard
Tampa, Florida 33601

Phillips Point East Tower
777 South Flagler Drive
West Palm Beach, Florida 33401–6163

GlobaLex Alliance

Foley & Lardner

Nicholson Graham & Jones
25–31 Moorgate
London EC2R 6AR
England

D. de Ricci - G. Selnet et Associes
46 Rue de Bassano
75008 Paris
France

Thummel Schutze & Partner
Landhausstrasse 90
D–7000 Stuttgart 1
Germany

≪ Notes ≫

CHAPTER 1 Beginnings, 1833–1842

[1] For biographical material on Finch, see John R. Berryman, *History of the Bench and Bar of Wisconsin* Vol. 1 (Chicago: H. C. Cooper, Jr., 1898), 443–47.

[2] For details about Finch's years in Michigan, see *Territorial Papers of the United States,* vol. 12, *Michigan Territory, 1829–1837*, 239; *History and Biographical Record of Lewanee County, Michigan*, 86–87; Michigan Censuses, 1710–1830; and *Pioneer History of Ingham County, Michigan,* 1: 498–99.

[3] *Michigan Biographies,* Vol. 1, A–K (1924), 292.

[4] Lawrence M. Friedman, *History of American Law* (New York: Simon & Schuster, 1985), 606–8.

[5] Quoted in ibid., 606.

[6] Carl Frederick Wittke, "The Ohio-Michigan Boundary Dispute Re-examined," *Ohio State Archeological and History Quarterly* (October 1936): 20–21; Helen Wallin, "Michigan's Lost Peninsula," *Michigan Heritage* 2 (Spring 1981): 121–30.

[7] *Journal of the House of Representatives of the State of Michigan 1837* (Detroit: John Bagg, State Printer, 1837), 35–39, 44–45, 54, 55.

[8] William A. Lane, M.D., *Homer and Its Pioneers and Its Business Men of Today* (Homer, Mich.: P. W. Chase, 1888).

[9] Elizabeth Caspar Brown, "The Bar on a Frontier: Wayne County, 1796–1836," *American Journal of Legal History* 14 (1970): 148. A fundamental resource on American legal history is James Willard Hurst, *The Growth of American Law: The Lawmakers* (Boston: Little, Brown, 1950).

[10] For material on the history of Milwaukee, see Harry M. Anderson and Frederick I. Olson, *Milwaukee, At the Gathering of the Waters* (Milwaukee: Milwaukee County Historical Society, 1984); Bayrd Still, *Milwaukee: The History of a City* (Madison: State Historical Society of Wisconsin, 1948); Edwin S. Mack, "The Founding of Milwaukee," in *Proceedings of the State Historical Society of Wisconsin, 1906* (Madison: State Historical Society of Wisconsin, 1907); James S. Buck, *Pioneer History of Milwaukee*, 2 Vols. (Milwaukee: 1876, 1881, revised 1890); John G. Gregory, *History of Milwaukee, Wisconsin*, 4 Vols. (Chicago: 1931); William G. Bruce, *History of Milwaukee City and County*, 3 Vols. (Milwaukee: 1922); and *Memoirs of Milwaukee County*, ed. by Jerome A. Watrous, 2 Vols. (Madison: 1909).

[11] *Blanchard v. Lelands,* Records of the District Court, Milwaukee County, Territory of Wisconsin, in the collection of the Milwaukee County Historical Society (hereinafter referred to as District Court), November Term 1839, Book C, #32, 21.

[12] *Juneau v. Parks;* District Court, November Term 1839, Book C, #58, 29.

[13] *Wells v. Martin,* District Court, November Term 1840, Book C, #19, 129.

[14] Still, 52–68.

[15] *Clark v. Aldrich,* District Court, November Term 1840, Book C, #75, 94.

[16] Still, 54.

[17] J.H. Kennedy, "Bench and Bar of Milwaukee," *Magazine of Western History* 4 (July 1887): 281; and James S. Buck, *Pioneer History of Milwaukee,* Vol. 2, (Milwaukee: 1876), 95.

[18] *Hinman v. Juneau,* District Court, June Term 1842, Book C, #58, 476.

[19] *Bailey v. Steamboat Milwaukee,* District Court, June Term 1842, Book C, #63, 481.

[20] *Whitney v. Hathaway,* District Court, June Term 1842, Book C, 368, 486, was one of hundreds of cases relating to lots along Buffalo and Erie streets that the district court had consolidated. Claimants were represented by Tweedy & Crocker and by other attorneys as well.

[21] Berryman, 340, 443–47.

[22] On William Pitt Lynde and his family, see Hon. Ralph D. Smith, Class of 1827, "Biographical Notices of Yale College Graduates 1816–84; Obituary of Charles James Lynde," in "The Early History of Yale," in Lynde Scrapbooks, Milwaukee County Historical Society; *Milwaukee Sentinel,* June 30, 1840, January 12, 1841, August 17, 1841, August 24, 1841; Mary S. Lynde, "Pioneer Experiences of Milwaukee Women," *Milwaukee Sentinel,* October 16, 1895.

[23] Charles J. Lynde, Letter to John K. Bartlet, New Haven, Conn., December 19, 1840, in Blanchard Harper Papers, Wisconsin State Historical Society, Madison.

[24] Ibid.

CHAPTER 2   Finch & Lynde: Early Partnership, 1842–1848

[1] Bayrd Still, *Milwaukee: The History of a City* (Madison, Wis.: State Historical Society of Wisconsin, 1948), 29, 47, 48; George J. Lankevich, *Milwaukee, A Chronological and Documentary History* (Dobbs Ferry, N.Y.: Oceana Publications, Inc., 1977), 9–10; Mary B. Lynde, as quoted by E. H. Kronshage, "All Around the Town," *Wisconsin News*, August 16, 1929. According to the 1840 census, Milwaukee had a population of 1,712 and Chicago, 4,479. By 1850 Chicago had grown to 29,673; Milwaukee, to 20,061.

[2] Lawrence M. Friedman, *History of American Law* (New York: Simon & Schuster, 1985). In 1991 there were 5,600 lawyers for the 1.4 million residents of the Milwaukee S.M.S.A., only two-thirds as many lawyers per capita as in 1842 when Finch & Lynde opened.

[3] *Statts v. Sanderson*, District Court, November Term 1842, Book D, #16, 16.

[4] *Farmin v. Shelby*, District Court, November Term 1842, Book D, #20, 20.

[5] *Whipple v. Putnam*, District Court, November Term 1842, Book D, #8, 8.

[6] Timothy Walker, "Ways and Means of Professional Success," quoted in Maxwell Bloomfield, "Law vs. Politics: The Self-Image of the American Bar 1830–1860," *American Journal of Legal History* 56 (12), 1968: 318.

[7] Letter to Finch & Lynde, 1845, in John F. Tweedy Papers, State Historical Society of Wisconsin, Madison.

[8] *Eldred v. Dewey*, District Court, November Term 1842, Book D, #53, 59; *Rogers v. Dewey*, District Court, November Term 1842, Book D, #67, 73; *Richardson v. Dewey*, District Court, November Term 1842, Book D, #68, 74, and Book D, #69, 75; and *Mack v. Dewey*, District Court, November Term 1842, Book D, #111, 117; *Finch v. Dewey*, November Term 1844, Book E, #22, 128.

[9] *Blanchard v. Dousman*, District Court, November Term 1842, Book D, #83, 89; *Blanchard v. Dousman*, District Court, June Term 1843, Book D, #85, 91.

[10] *United States v. Gifford*, District Court, November Term 1842, Book D # 87, 93.

[11] *Van Houten v. Smith*, District Court, November Term 1847, Book G, #140, 341.

[12] *Barber and Cronkhite v. Barber*, District Court, November Term 1847, June Term 1849, Book G, #106, 307.

[13] *Cady & Farwell v. Hyde*, District Court, November Term 1843, June Term 1844, Book D, #7, 145; *Farwell v. Lockwood*, District Court, June Term 1845, Book E, #101, 396.

[14] Frank Flower, *History of Milwaukee* (Chicago: Western Historical Society, 1881), 664.

[15] *Chapin v. Jewell*, Circuit Court, June Term 1846, Book F, #98, 229.

[16] See Friedman, 44–45, 95; *Jones v. Barstow*, District Court, November Term 1845, Book F, #101, 173.

[17] *Newhall v. Bullman*, District Court, June 1846, Book F, #111, 241.

[18] *Clark v. Schooner Marvin*, Circuit Court, November Term 1846, Book F, #163, 521. The Wisconsin Marine & Fire Insurance Company was the corporate ancestor of the Marine Bank (now Bank One).

[19] Parker McCobb Reed, *The Bench and Bar of Wisconsin: History and Biography* (Milwaukee: P. M. Reed Publisher, 1882), 458–59; John R. Berryman, *History of the Bench and Bar of Wisconsin Vol. I* (Chicago: H. C. Cooper, Jr., 1898), 96–98.

[20] Reed, 180–81, 654–55.

CHAPTER 3 Political Life in the Wisconsin Territory, 1842–1848

[1] For the material in this chapter on politics and the drive for statehood, see Alice E. Smith, *The History of Wisconsin. Vol. 1: From Exploration to Statehood* (Madison, Wis.: The State Historical Society of Wisconsin, 1973).

[2] "The Lawyer on the Frontier," *American Law Review* 50, no. 27 (1916): 35, 39; *Milwaukee Sentinel and Gazette*, September 18, 1850.

[3] *Sentinel and Gazette*, October 21 and November 26, 1845.

[4] Bayrd Still, *Milwaukee: The History of a City* (Madison: State Historical Society of Wisconsin, 1948), 31–39, 103–8; *Sentinel*, October 20, 1840.

[5] Louis Saxton Gertels, *Anti-slavery Agitation in Wisconsin, 1836–1848*, Master's thesis, University of Wisconsin, 1966, 63, 66, 71.

[6] Frank Flower, *History of Milwaukee* (Chicago: Western Historical Society, 1881), 225, 228–31, 664.

[7] Editorial, *Evening Wisconsin*, April 4, 1883.

[8] Smith, 654–65.

[9] Milo M. Quaife, *The Struggle over Ratification, 1846–1847* (Madison: The State Historical Society of Wisconsin, 1920), 528, 561–63.

[10] Quoted in Quaife, 541–43.

[11] Lynde letter to John H. Tweedy, December 28, 1847. Tweedy papers, Box 2, Madison, State Historical Society of Wisconsin.

[12] B. A. Hinsdale, "Legislation on the Compensation of Members of Congress," *Magazine of Western History* 6 (May 1887): 85–91.

[13] Finch's race against Lynde is described in a number of issues of the *Milwaukee Sentinel and Gazette*. See issues of October 11, 13, 17, 18, 23, 28, 1848, and November 3, 6, 1848; Lynde, Letter to Andrew Elmore, Esq., May 10, 1848, Lynde Collection, Milwaukee County Historical Society.

[14] Ibid., October 31, 1848.

[15] Ibid.

[16] Ibid., October 17, 1848.

[17] Ibid., January 8 and 11, and March 16, 1849.

CHAPTER 4 Law and Early Statehood, 1848–1857

[1] John R. Berryman, *Bench and Bar of Wisconsin*, Vol. I (Chicago: H. C. Cooper, Jr., 1898) 3–4; Karel D. Bicha, "Courts and Criminal Justice: Law Enforcement in Milwaukee County," 145–195, in Ralph M. Aderman, ed., *Trading Post to Metropolis, Milwaukee County's First 150 Years* (Milwaukee: Milwaukee County Historical Society, 1987).

[2] The *Milwaukee Sentinel and Gazette* had a number of articles on the race for the judgeship. See April 1, 1845; December 16 and 30, 1846; January 4, 1847; June 5 and 18, 1848; July 25, 1848; August 2, 4 and 17, 1848; September 1 and 2, 1848; November 28, 1848.

[3] Berryman, 85–86.

[4] *Milwaukee Sentinel and Gazette*, November 28, 1848.

[5] Ibid.

[6] The *Milwaukee Sentinel and Gazette*, August 12, 1851; September 4, 11, 26, 29 and 30, 1851.

[7] John Bradley Winslow, *The Story of a Great Court* (Chicago: T. H. Flood & Co., 1912); *Trial and Impeachment of Levi Hubbell, Judge of the Second Circuit Court* Senate of the State of Wisconsin, June 1853, T. C. Leland (Madison: Beriah Brown, Publishers, 1853); Alfons J. Beitzinger, *Edward G. Ryan, Lion of the Law* (Madison: State Historical Society of Wisconsin, 1960).

[8] George J. Lankevich, *Milwaukee, A Chronological and Documentary History* (Dobbs Ferry, N.Y.: Oceana Publications, Inc., 1977), 16–17.

[9] Robert W. Wells, *This Is Milwaukee* (Garden City, N.Y.: Doubleday, 1970), 58.

[10] *Dictionary of Wisconsin Biography*, 233.

[11] *Eldred v. Ross*, Circuit Court, May Term 1849, Book H, #57, 279.

[12] *Brunette v. Whitney*, Circuit Court, February Term 1852, Book 1, #12, 464; *Whitney v. Brunette*, 3 Wis. 547 (1854) and 15 Wis. 67 (1862).

[13] *Kilbourn v. The Milwaukee and Rock River Canal Company Circuit Court*, February Term 1852, Book J, #114, 334; *Pratt v. Seaver*, Circuit Court, September Term 1849, Book H, #112, 561.

[14] *Kilbourn v. Rock River Canal Co.*, Circuit Court, February Term 1852, Book J, # 114, 334.

[15] *Walker v. Shepardson*, 2 Wis. 282 (1853).

[16] Winslow, 51–53.

[17] Bayrd Still, *Milwaukee: The History of a City* (Madison: State Historical Society of Wisconsin, 1948), 25, 36–37.

[18] *Eble v. The Milwaukee and Waukesha Railroad*, Circuit Court, February Term 1847, April Term 1857, Book 1, #115, 152.

[19] *Milwaukee and Mississippi Railroad v. Comstock*, Circuit Court, May Term 1851, Book 1, #44, 376; *Milwaukee and Mississippi Railroad v. Eldred*, Circuit Court, May Term 1851, Book 1, #45, 377, *Milwaukee and Mississippi Railroad v. Cramer*, Circuit Court, May Term 1851, Book 1, #46, 378; *The Daily Sentinel*, May 26, 1854; *Milwaukee and Mississippi Railroad v. Dousman*, Circuit Court, May Term 1852, Book 1, #14, 554.

[20] *Schwartzburg v. Lundwurm, Milwaukee and Fond du Lac Railroad*, Circuit Court, February Term 1854, Book K, #2, 184; #5, 198.

[21] *Jaeger v. Milwaukee and Fond du Lac and Green Bay Railroad*, Circuit Court, February Term 1854, Book K, #53, 247; *Zoutkie v. Milwaukee and Fond du Lac Railroad,* Circuit Court, February Term 1854, Book K, #56, 251.

[22] Richard N. Current, *The History of Wisconsin,* Vol. 2 (Madison: State Historical Society of Wisconsin, 1976), 31–39; *The Daily Sentinel,* May 26, 1854; Frederick Merk, *The Economic History of Wisconsin During the Civil War Decade* (Madison: State Historical Society of Wisconsin, 1916), 240–43; Lankevich, 18–19.

[23] Lawrence M. Friedman, *History of American Law* (New York: Simon & Schuster, 1985), 467–68, is an excellent source on the development of tort law during the railroad age.

[24] *Stacke v. The Milwaukee and Mississippi Railroad Company*, Circuit Court, April Term 1858, Book P, #48, 51.

[25]*Chamberlain v. The Milwaukee and Mississippi Railroad Co.,* Circuit Court, December Term 1856, September Term 1860, Book M, #30, 145; 7 Wis. 367 (1858).

[26]Friedman, 470, 471, and 473.

[27]*Boyd v. New York and Erie Railroad,* Circuit Court, September Term 1852, Book K, #6; *Ludington v. New York and Erie Railroad,* Circuit Court, September Term 1852, Book K, #7, 7; *Peck v. New York and Erie Railroad,* Circuit Court, September Term 1852, Book K, #11, 11.

[28]*Camp v. Meyer,* Circuit Court, September Term 1856, January Term 1859, Book L, #100, 271; Still, 189.

[29]*Martin v. The Aetna Insurance Co.,* Circuit Court, February Term 1851, Book I, #344, 298.

[30]*Douglas v. Frink,* Circuit Court, February Term 1851, Book I, #51, 305.

[31]Leonard Bayliss Krueger, *History of Commercial Banking in Wisconsin* (Madison: University of Wisconsin Press, 1933), is an excellent source. See especially 41, 56–59.

[32]Alice E. Smith, *George Smith's Money* (Madison: State Historical Society of Wisconsin, 1966), 55; *Pettibone v. Smith,* Circuit Court, September Term 1853, Book K, #18, 157, September Term 1854, Book K, #19, 158.

[33]Current, 105; Krueger, 58–59.

[34]*Globe Bank v. Fillmore,* Circuit Court, September Term 1857, #125, L 470; *Globe Bank v. Juneau,* Circuit Court, September Term 1857, #126, L 471; *Globe Bank v. Lewis,* September Term 1857, #127, L 472; *Globe Bank v. McDonald,* September Term 1857, #138, L 483; *Globe Bank v. Bennett,* September Term 1857, #144, L 1489; *Globe Bank v. Hughes,* September Term 1857, L 490; *Globe Bank v. McKenzie,* September Term 1857, #198, L 543; *Globe Bank v. Noggle,* September Term 1857, #211, L 556; *Globe Bank v. Blodgett,* September Term 1857, 229, L 574.

[35]*The Atlanta Bank v. Cramer,* Circuit Court, September Term 1853, Book K, #9, 148; *Cramer v. Noonan,* 4 Wis. 253 (1855).

[36]Lankevich, 20–21.

[37]Frank Flower, *History of Milwaukee* (Chicago: Western Historical Society, 1881), 1107.

CHAPTER 5 Finches, Lynde & Miller, 1857–1860

[1]J. H. Kennedy, "The Bench and Bar of Milwaukee" (pt. 4), *Magazine of Western History* 6, no. 3 (July 1887): 278.

[2]For material on Matt Finch see John R. Berryman, *History of the Bench and Bar of Wisconsin,* Vol. 1 (Chicago: H. C. Cooper, Jr., 1898), 339, 340,

470–76; and Howard Louis Conard, *History of Milwaukee County from Its Earliest Settlement to 1895* (Chicago: American Biographical Publishing Co., 1895), 397.

[3] For material on B. K. Miller, Sr., see Berryman, 428–30, and Benjamin Kurtz Miller, "Recollections of Early Milwaukee," Miller Papers (Madison: Wisconsin State Historical Society), 1–2.

[4] Emily P. Dodge, "The Evolution of a City Law Office," *Wisconsin Law Review* (1955): 179–80; James S. Buck, *Pioneer History of Milwaukee* (Milwaukee: Swain and Tate, 1876, 1881, rev. 1890), Vol. 1, 57, 94–95, 288–89.

[5] Berryman, 431–32.

[6] Frank Flower, *History of Milwaukee* (Chicago: Western Historical Society, 1881), 1080–81; and *Germania Bank v. Leavenworth*, April Term 1857, #50 L 365.

[7] Otto E. Koegel, *Walter S. Carter, Collector of Young Masters* (New York: Round Table Press, 1953); Robert T. Swaine, *The Cravath Firm and Its Predecessors* (New York: Ad Press, 1946 and 1948) Vol. 1, 3, 587–89, Vol. 2, 1.

[8] *Marshall v. The American Express Company*, 7 Wis. 1 (1858).

[9] *In the Matter of the Will and Estate of Michael Dousman*, December 1857, #165, 1/2 N 425.

[10] *Jones v. City of Milwaukee and Wisconsin Marine and Fire Insurance Company*, Circuit Court, December Term 1858, #386, Q 136; *Reed v. Newhall*, Circuit Court, September Term 1858, #125, P 478; *Treat v. Miner*, Circuit Court, September Term 1858, #131, Q 81; *Hawes v. Stemper*, Circuit Court, April Term 1859, #143, Q 439.

[11] *Hatfield v. Dutcher, Sexton et al.*, Circuit Court, September Term 1859, #113, S 167.

[12] *Terry v. McVicker*, Circuit Court, September Term 1860, #42, T 317; *White v. McVicker*, Circuit Court, September Term 1860, #53, T 335; *Harvey v. McVicker*, Circuit Court, September Term 1860, #61, T 338; *Orvis v. McVicker*, Circuit Court, September Term 1860, #74, T 352.

[13] *The Fifth Ward Gas and Light Company v. Smith*, Circuit Court, February Term 1860, #7, T 514; *Cary v. Rosenwald*, Circuit Court, February Term 1861, #9, T 516; *Shepard v. The Milwaukee Gas Light Co.*, 6 Wis. 526 (1858).

[14] Flower, 1079, 1080, 1085; *State Bank of Wisconsin v. James*, Circuit Court, April Term 1857, L #63, 379; *Peckham v. Rose*, April Term 1857, L #66, 383; *Hale v. Lockwood*, Circuit Court, June Term 1857, L #100, 454; *Peckham v. Vliet*, September Term 1857, L #162, 507.

[15] For material on the railroad debt see Flower, 1085; Leonard Bayliss Krueger, *History of Commercial Banking in Wisconsin* (Madison: University of Wisconsin, 1933), 64–74; Richard N. Current, *The History of Wisconsin, Vol. 2: The Civil War Era 1848–1873* (Madison: State Historical Society of Wisconsin, 1976) 247–48; Frederick Merk, *Economic History of Wisconsin During the Civil War Decade* (Madison: State Historical Society of Wisconsin, 1916); Laurence M. Larson, *A Financial and Administrative History of Milwaukee,* Bulletin of the University of Wisconsin, Madison, No. 242, 1908, 90; Margaret Walsh, *The Manufacturing Frontier, Pioneer Industry in Ante Bellum Wisconsin* (Madison: State Historical Society of Wisconsin, 1972), 178.

[16] Bayrd Still, *Milwaukee: The History of a City* (Madison: State Historical Society of Wisconsin, 1948), 147–49.

[17] For the Lynde-Paine judicial campaign, see John Bradley Winslow, *The Story of a Great Court* (Chicago: T. H. Flood & Co., 1912), 162; and *Milwaukee Sentinel*, February 2; March 5, 8, 9, 21, 22, and 28; April 1 and 15; 1860.

[18] Waukesha *Democrat*, as quoted in the *Sentinel*, April 15, 1859.

[19] See Minutes of the Milwaukee Bar Association, 1858, Area Research Center, University of Wisconsin, Milwaukee; Milwaukee Bar Association File, Records of the Circuit Court, 1858–1860, Milwaukee County Historical Society; Lawrence M. Friedman, *History of American Law* (New York: Simon & Schuster, 1985) 649–50; James Willard Hurst, *The Growth of American Law: The Lawmakers* (Boston: Little, Brown, 1950), 272.

[20] Lee Soltow, *Patterns of Wealth Holding in Wisconsin Since 1850* (Madison: University of Wisconsin Press, 1971), 31, 32; Proceedings of Milwaukee Bar Association 1858.

[21] *State Bank of Wisconsin v. Jackson Hadley*, Circuit Court, April Term 1962, #38, V 564.

[22] *Milwaukee Sentinel*, April 4 and 12, 1860.

[23] George J. Lankevich, *Milwaukee, A Chronological and Documentary History* (Dobbs Ferry, N.Y.: Oceana Publications, Inc., 1977), 27–29; *Milwaukee Sentinel*, June 27, July 13, September 3, and September 27, 1860.

[24] For the *Lady Elgin* disaster, see Still, 153, and *Milwaukee Sentinel*, September 27, 1860.

CHAPTER 6 Milwaukee and the War Years, 1861–1865

[1] Minutes of the Milwaukee Bar Association, 1861.

[2] Gregory Filardo, *Old Milwaukee: A Historic Tour in Picture Postcards* (New York: Vestal Press, 1888), 38.

[3] Minutes of Milwaukee Bar Association, 1861–62, and Albany Building Records, Milwaukee County Historical Society.

[4] Bayrd Still, *Milwaukee: The History of a City* (Madison: State Historical Society of Wisconsin, 1948), 227; George J. Lankevich, *Milwaukee, A Chronological and Documentary History* (Dobbs Ferry, N.Y.: Oceana Publications, Inc., 1977), 28–30.

[5] Lankevich, 30.

[6] Harry M. Anderson and Frederick I. Olson, *Milwaukee, At the Gathering of the Waters* (Milwaukee: Milwaukee County Historical Society, 1984), 44.

[7] *State Bank of Wisconsin v. Newhall*, Circuit Court, December Term 1862, #11, W 78 and #24, W 92.

[8] *Hoyt v. Comstock*, Circuit Court, June Term 1862, #24, W 26.

[9] *Milwaukee Sentinel*, October 24, 1864; Robert W. Wells, *This Is Milwaukee* (Garden City, New York: Doubleday & Company, Inc., 1970), 96–97; Still, 160.

[10] *Milwaukee Sentinel*, November 12, 1862.

[11] Richard N. Current, *The History of Wisconsin*, Vol. 2 (Madison: State Historical Society of Wisconsin, 1976), 244–46.

[12] *Todd v. Lee*, 15 Wis. 400 (1862).

[13] *Quinney v. Denney*, 18 Wis. 510 (1864); *Ruggles v. Marsilliott*, 19 Wis. 173 (1865).

[14] *Milwaukee Sentinel*, February 21, 1863; May 1, 1865.

[15] Burial Records, Forest Home Cemetery, Milwaukee.

[16] Anderson and Olson, 40–42; Lankevich, 30; Wells, 92.

[17] Wells, 95; Anderson and Olson, 44.

[18] *Milwaukee Sentinel*, October 23, 1865.

[19] Lankevich, 27; Leo Soltow, *Patterns of Wealth Holding in Wisconsin Since 1850* (Madison: University of Wisconsin Press, 1972), 33 and 153; Still, 160–61.

CHAPTER 7 Practicing Law in the Gilded Age, 1866–1873

[1] Harry M. Anderson and Frederick I. Olson, *Milwaukee, At the Gathering of the Waters* (Milwaukee: Milwaukee County Historical Society, 1984), 44.

[2] *Gillespie v. Palmer*, 20 Wis. 572 (1866); Anderson and Olson, 44.

[3] George J. Lankevich, *Milwaukee, A Chronological and Documentary History* (Dobbs Ferry, N.Y.: Oceana Publications, Inc., 1977), 32–33.

[4] Ibid, 30–32.

[5] Steven M. Avella, "Health, Hospitals and Welfare: Human Services in Milwaukee County," Ralph M. Aderman ed., *Trading Post to Metropolis, Milwaukee County's First 150 Years* (Milwaukee: Milwaukee County Historical Society, 1987), 196–254.

[6] *Milwaukee Sentinel,* January 13, 1871; July 10, 1877; December 21, 1885; December 22, 1885; December 24, 1885; March 31, 1887; and April 1, 1887.

[7] Frederick I. Olson, "City Expansion and Suburban Spread: Settlements and Governments in Milwaukee County," in Aderman, 27.

[8] Bayrd Still, *Milwaukee: The History of a City* (Madison: State Historical Society of Wisconsin, 1948), 164–65.

[9] *Journal of the Assembly,* March 16, 1866, 632; *Journal of the Senate,* March 2, 1869, 234; January 28, 1870, 103; March 11, 1870, 160, 568; *General Laws,* chapter 35.

[10] *Merriam v. Field,* 24 Wis. 640 (1869).

[11] *Hoth v. Peters,* 55 Wis. 405 (1882).

[12] *Tainter v. Lucas,* 29 Wis. 375 (1872).

[13] Richard N. Current, *The History of Wisconsin,* Vol. 2, *The Civil War Era* (Madison: State Historical Society of Wisconsin, 1984), 417; Robert C. Nesbit, *The History of Wisconsin,* Vol. 3, *Urbanization and Industrialization, 1873–1893* (Madison: State Historical Society of Wisconsin, 1985), 265.

[14] Current, 436.

[15] Ibid, 436, 441–42.

[16] Ibid, 382–84, 590–94; *Long v. The City of New London,* Circuit Court, Eastern District of Wisconsin, 5 F. 559 (1880).

[17] *Journal of the Assembly,* 1866, 632; Nesbit, Vol. 3, 100–107; John W. Cary, *The Organization and History of the Chicago, Milwaukee and St. Paul Railway Company* (Chicago: Cramer, Aikens & Cramer, 1893, reprinted, New York: The Arno Press, 1981); Robert S. Hunt, *Law and Locomotives, The Impact of the Railroads on Wisconsin Law in the Nineteenth Century* (Madison: State Historical Society of Wisconsin, 1958).

[18] *Ackley v. the Chicago, Milwaukee and St. Paul Railway Co.,* 36 Wis. 252 (1874).

[19] Cary; John R. Berryman, *Bench and Bar of Wisconsin,* Vol. 1 (Chicago: H. C. Cooper, Jr., 1898), 443–47.

[20] *Blair v. Milwaukee & Prairie du Chien Railroad Co,* 20 Wis. 267, 276 (1866).

[21]*Delamatry v. The Milwaukee & Prairie du Chien Railroad Co.*, 24 Wis. 578 (1869).

[22]*Hibbard v. The Western Union Telegraph Co.*, 33 Wis. 558 (1873); *Candee v. The Western Union Telegraph Co.*, 34 Wis. 471 (1874); *Heimann v. The Western Union Telegraph Co.*, 57 Wis. 562 (1883).

[23] Still, 333–34; Frederick Merk, *Economic History of Wisconsin During the Civil War Decade* (Madison: State Historical Society of Wisconsin, 1916), 151; Lankevich, 40–41.

[24] Still, 187–89, 333–35.

[25] Berryman, Vol. 1, 428–38.

[26]*Milwaukee Sentinel*, February 12 and April 2, 1872; March 5, 1877.

[27] Berryman, Vol. 1, 428–38.

[28]James Willard Hurst, *The Growth of American Law: The Lawmakers* (Boston: Little, Brown, 1950), 297–98, 303.

[29]*Holden v. Meadows*, 31 Wis. 284 (1872); *Archer v. Meadows*, 33 Wis. 166 (1873); *In re Holden*, 37 Wis. 98 (1875).

[30]*Van Steenwyck v. Washburn*, 59 Wis. 483 (1884).

[31]Asahel Finch, letter to Edward G. Ryan, October 28, 1879, in Ryan Papers, State Historical Society of Wisconsin, and Nesbit, Vol. 3, 250.

[32] Edward G. Ryan, letter to Asahel Finch, Jr., October 24, 1879.

[33] "Incomes of Lawyers," *Albany Law Journal*, Vol. 6, 1872, 249–50.

[34] Berryman, Vol. 1, 428–38.

[35]*Milwaukee Sentinel*, July 19, 1867; January 13, 1871; October 11, 1872; July 10, 1877; August 27, 1878; December 24, 1885; March 31, 1887; April 1, 1887.

[36] Still, 162–64; *Milwaukee Sentinel*, November 26, 1870; January 31, 1871; February 18, 1871; November 13, 1873; November 27, 1873.

[37]*Milwaukee Sentinel*, September 4 and 13, November 2 and 4, 1872.

[38]Nesbit, Vol. 3, 547, 564–66, *Milwaukee Sentinel*, January 18, 1875, and February 8, 1875; Matthew Carpenter, letter to Elisha Keyes, December 27, 1875, and Henry C. Payne, letter to Elisha Keyes, December 24, 1875, and May 31, 1876, in Elisha Keyes Papers, State Historical Society of Wisconsin; E. Bruce Thompson, *Matthew Hale Carpenter, Webster of the West* (Madison, State Historical Society of Wisconsin, 1954), 226, 227, 231, 236; *Congressional Record*, February 6, 1877; Lankevich, 37.

CHAPTER 8   The End of an Era, 1874–1885

[1]*Milwaukee Sentinel*, October 30, 1874.

[2]*Milwaukee Sentinel*, November 4, 1874.

[3]*Milwaukee Sentinel*, November 11, 26, 28, 1874; E. Bruce Thompson, *Matthew Hale Carpenter, Webster of the West* (Madison: State Historical Society of Wisconsin, 1954), 107; *Lynde v. Sentinel*, Circuit Court #4041, Vol. 0, 391.

[4]*Milwaukee Sentinel*, January 16, 1875.

[5] For information on Lynde's record in Congress, see the *Congressional Record*, 44th Congress 1875–1876, Vol. 4, 166, 204, 250, 870; Vol. 5, 752, and the 45th Congress 1877–1878, Vol. 7, 349. See also James Willard Hurst, *The Growth of American Law: The Lawmakers* (Boston: Little, Brown, 1950), 111–12, on the reform in the federal judiciary.

[6] "The Trial of William W. Belknap," *Congressional Record*, 44th Congress, 1876, part 7, Vol. 4, 2158–59; Thompson, 163, 174, 244, 297–98.

[7] Goodell's first application to the Wisconsin bar was denied in a decision written by Chief Justice Edward G. Ryan: *In the Matter of the Motion to Admit Miss Lavinia Goodell to the Bar of This Court*, 39 Wis. 232 (1879). She was admitted four years later after the legislature acted to overrule the decision: *Application of Miss Goodell*, 48 Wis. 693 (1879). For information on Goodell, see Catherine B. Cleary, "Lavinia Goodell, First Woman Lawyer in Wisconsin," *Wisconsin Magazine of History* 74, #4, Summer 1991; Genevieve G. McBride, " 'No Season of Silence,' The Origins of 'Public Relations' in Nineteenth and Twentieth Century Reform Movements in Wisconsin" (unpublished Ph.D. Dissertation, University of Wisconsin, Madison, 1989).

[8] "The *Margaret*," 94 U.S. 494 (1876); *Milwaukee Sentinel*, January 15, 1886, 2.

[9]*Chemung Bank v. Lowery*, 93 U.S. 72 (1876).

[10]*Schumacher v. Cornell*, 96 U.S. 549 (1877).

[11]*Town of Weyauwega v. Ayling*, 99 U.S. 112 (1878).

[12]*Mount Pleasant v. Beckwith*, 100 U.S. 514 (1879).

[13]*Gibbs & Sterrett Manufacturing Company v. Brucker*, 111 U.S. 597 (1884).

[14]*Pope v. Allis*, 115 U.S. 363 (1885).

[15] George J. Lankevich, *Milwaukee, A Chronological and Documentary History* (Dobbs Ferry, N.Y.: Oceana Publications, Inc., 1977), 40–41.

[16] Bayrd Still, *Milwaukee: The History of a City* (Madison: State Historical Society of Wisconsin, 1948), 398–99.

[17]*Wisconsin Telephone Company v. City of Oshkosh*, 62 Wis. 32 (1884).

[18] Still, 488–89.

[19] Ibid., 381, 398, 410, 584.

[20] Ibid., 347.

[21]*Milwaukee Sentinel*, September 21, 1881.

[22] Will C. Conrad, Kathleen F. Wilson, and Dale Wilson, *The Milwaukee Journal: The First Eighty Years* (Madison: University of Wisconsin Press, 1964), 10–16; *Milwaukee Sentinel*, January 22, 1883.

[23]*Milwaukee Sentinel*, April 5, 1883.

[24]John R. Berryman, *History of the Bench and Bar of Wisconsin*, Vol. 1 (Chicago: H. C. Cooper, Jr., 1898), 437, 445.

[25]*Ibid.*, 474, 476.

[26] Records of Forest Home Cemetery, Milwaukee.

CHAPTER 9 The Miller Years, 1886–1890

1 Bayrd Still, *Milwaukee: The History of a City* (Madison: State Historical Society of Wisconsin, 1948), 269–71.

[2]John R. Berryman, *History of the Bench and Bar of Wisconsin*, Vol. 1 (Chicago: H. C. Cooper, Jr., 1898), 628–30.

[3] Robert B. Morris, *Encyclopedia of American History* (New York: Harper & Brothers, Publishers, 1953), 462.

[4] Berryman, Vol. 1, 630–31.

[5] Still, 411.

[6]*Milwaukee Sentinel*, June 3, 1883; July 18, 1888.

[7] Still, 401.

[8] George J. Lankevich, *Milwaukee, A Chronological and Documentary History* (Dobbs Ferry, N.Y.: Oceana Publications, Inc., 1977), 49.

[9] Still, 411.

[10] Robert W. Wells, *Yesterday's Milwaukee* (Miami, Fla.: E. A. Seemann Publishing, Inc., 1976), 84; *Milwaukee Sentinel*, March 4, 1884 and May 31, 1884.

[11]*Milwaukee Sentinel*, November 22, 1885, 4.

[12] B. K. Miller, Sr., letter to Robert Snodgrass, May 27, 1896, in collection of George Chester.

[13] B. K. Miller, Sr., letters to Messrs. Clark and Company, New York, January 28, 1889; to Messrs. Gerbard and Hey, St. Petersburg, Russia, September 20, 1897; to B. Altmann and Company, New York, April 25, 1898; and to Anton Hills, Carlsbad, Austria, September 20, 1897 (Chester Collection).

[14]*Bradley v. Cramer*, 66 Wis. 297 (1886).

[15]*Nellis v. Cramer*, 86 Wis. 337 (1893).

[16]*Merrill v. Wisconsin Female College*, 74 Wis. 415 (1889).

[17] B. K. Miller, Sr., letters to Mrs. John Miller (Margaret) in B. K. Miller, Sr., letter book (Chester Collection).

[18] *Burnham v. Burnham*, 79 Wis. 557 (1891).

[19] *Markwell v. Pereles*, 95 Wis. 406 (1897).

[20] *Burns v. the North Chicago Rolling Mill*, 65 Wis. 312 (1886).

[21] James Willard Hurst, *The Growth of American Law: The Lawmakers* (Boston: Little, Brown, 1950), 342–44; Robert C. Nesbit, *The History of Wisconsin,* Vol. 3, *Urbanization and Industrialization, 1873–1893* (Madison: State Historical Society of Wisconsin, 1985), 118–22.

[22] On the Field Code, see Hurst, 391.

[23] Wayne K. Hobson, "Symbol of the New Profession: Emergence of the Large Law Firm, 1870–1915," in Gerald W. Gawalt, ed., *The New High Priest,* Contributions in Legal Studies #29 (Westport, Conn: Greenwood Press, 1984), 4.

[24] Ibid.

[25] Daisy E. Wright, letter to Mrs. A. G. Miller, October 2, 1899, in B. K. Miller, Sr., letter Book (Chester Collection).

[26] B. K. Miller, Sr., letter to Morris, April 24, 1891 (Chester Collection).

[27] B. K. Miller, Sr., letter to Mary B. Lynde, October 30, 1885 (Chester Collection).

[28] B. K. Miller, Sr., letter to Mary B. Lynde, August 14, 1894 (Chester Collection).

[29] *Tilly and Mary Lynde, defs.*, Circuit Court, 56, #12812, 509.

[30] B. K. Miller, Sr., letter to George Miller, page 1 missing, undated, in letter book pages between May 15 and August 15, 1890 (Chester Collection).

CHAPTER 10 Expanding the Partnership, 1890–1905

[1] John R. Berryman, *History of the Bench and Bar of Wisconsin*, Vol. 2 (Chicago: H. C. Cooper, Jr., 1898), 51–53.

[2] Berryman, Vol. 1, 521–22.

[3] 1894 Partnership Agreement: Firm Archives.

[4] William Ward Wight, *Henry Clay Payne, A Life* (Milwaukee: Burdick and Allen, 1907), 70.

[5] Bayrd Still, *Milwaukee: The History of a City* (Madison: State Historical Society of Wisconsin, 1948), 285.

[6] *Ellis v. The Milwaukee City Railway Co.*, 67 Wis. 135 (1886).

[7] Still, 370.

[8] Ibid, 380–81.

[9] *The State ex rel. The Milwaukee Street Railway Co. v. Anderson*, 90 Wis. 550 (1895).

[10] Accounts of this period can be found in Still, 292–93; George J. Lankevich, *Milwaukee, A Chronological and Documentary History* (Dobbs Ferry, N.Y.: Oceana Publications, Inc., 1977), 42; Richard B. Morris, *Encyclopedia of American History* (New York: Harper & Brothers Publishers, 1953), 522.

[11] *Farmers' Loan and Trust Co. v. Northern Pacific Railroad Co.*, 60 F. 893 (E.D. Wis. 1894).

[12] *Arthur v. Oakes*, 63 F. 310 (7th Cir. 1894).

[13] Some sources for the Milwaukee Electric Railway and Light Company are Joseph M. Canfield, *TM: The Milwaukee Electric Railway and Light Company*, Bulletin #112 (Chicago: Central Electric Railfans Association, 1972), 32–33; Wight, 70; Forrest McDonald, *Let There Be Light: The Electric Utility Industry in Wisconsin 1881–1955* (Madison: The American History Research Center, 1957); Clay McShane, *Technology and Reform: Street Railways and the Growth of Milwaukee* (Madison: State Historical Society of Wisconsin, 1974).

[14] *Milwaukee Electric Railway Co. v. City of Milwaukee*, 87 F. 577 (E.D. Wis. 1898).

[15] *Milwaukee Electric Railway and Light Co. v. Bradley*, 108 Wis. 467 (1901).

[16] *Roberts v. Wisconsin Telephone Co.*, 77 Wis. 589 (1890).

[17] *Wisconsin Telephone Co. v. City of Milwaukee*, 126 Wis. 1 (1895).

[18] Still, 354, 365.

[19] *Ehlert v. Kindt*, 103 Wis. 424 (1899).

[20] *National Foundry and Pipe Works, Ltd. v. Oconto City Water Supply Co.*, 183 U.S. 216 (1902).

[21] *National Foundry and Pipe Works, Ltd. v. Oconto Water Supply Co.*, 113 F. 793, 794 (1902).

[22] *Diamond Glue Co. v. United States Glue Company*, 187 U.S. 611, 614 (1903).

[23] Circuit Court Case Records, 1894, Vol. 60, nos. 14161, 14162, 14164, 14227, 14245, 14332, 14335.

[24] Berryman, Vol. I, 437–38.

[25] Ibid.

[26] Ibid., 630; interview with George Miller Chester.

CHAPTER 11 Miller, Mack & Fairchild, 1906–1917

[1] Edwin S. Mack, Biography, Harvard Transcript; Edwin S. Mack, "Some Incidents in Professional Life," Firm Archives; Frank T. Boesel, "In Memoriam, Edwin S. Mack," Memorial of the Milwaukee County Bar Association, May 21, 1942.

[2] Edwin S. Mack, Obituary, *Evening Wisconsin*, April 10, 1942; James Willard Hurst, *The Growth of American Law* (Boston: Little, Brown, 1950) 255; Kermit L. Hall, *The Magic Mirror, Law in American History* (New York: Oxford University Press, 1989), 258.

[3] Firm Archives.

[4] George J. Lankevich, in *Milwaukee, A Chronological and Documentary History* (Dobbs Ferry, N.Y.: Oceana Publications, Inc., 1977), 49–54, describes Milwaukee in the period before World War I.

[5] Miller, Noyes, Miller & Wahl and Miller, Mack & Fairchild ledger and account books, Firm Archives.

[6] *Kresge v. Maryland Casualty Co.*, 154 Wis. 627 (1913).

[7] *State ex rel. Sperry & Hutchinson Co. v. Weigle*, 166 Wis. 613 (1917).

[8] Richard B. Morris, *Encyclopedia of American History* (New York: Harper & Brothers Publishers, 1953), 660; Bayrd Still, *Milwaukee: The History of a City* (Madison: State Historical Society of Wisconsin, 1948), 405; George Miller letter, "To Pierce Arrow Motor Cars," January 9, 1928, Firm Archives.

[9] Lawrence M. Friedman, *History of American Law* (New York: Simon & Schuster, 1985), 570–71.

[10] Account and ledger books 1890–1910, Firm Archives.

[11] George P. Miller, letter to Messrs. Robert Dun Douglass, Francis E. Minton, and Walter D. Buchanan, February 14, 1911, in Miller Letter Book, Firm Archives.

[12] Interview with Mildred Roehr, 1990.

[13] Ibid.

[14] *Stumm v. Western Union Telegraph Co.*, 140 Wis. 528 (1909); *Sherrard v. Western Union Telegraph Co.*, 146 Wis. 197 (1911); *Slivick v. American Express Co.,*" 176 Wis. 314 (1922).

[15] Still, 315–17.

[16] Brandeis, quoted in Hurst, 381; Robert H. Wiebe, *Businessmen and Reform: A Study of the Progressive Movement* (Chicago: Quadrangle Books, 1962).

[17] Still, 315–17.

[18]*Milwaukee Electric Railway and Light Co. v. Wisconsin Railroad Commission*, 153 Wis. 592 (1913), *aff'd*, 238 U.S. 174 (1915).

[19]*City of Milwaukee v. Milwaukee Electric Railway and Light Co.*, 147 Wis. 458 (1911); *Milwaukee Electric Railway and Light Co. v. City of Milwaukee*, 167 Wis. 384 (1918).

[20]*State ex rel. City of Milwaukee v. Milwaukee Electric Railway and Light Co.*, 165 Wis. 230 (1917).

CHAPTER 12 World War I and the Decade of Prosperity, 1917–1931

[1] Bayrd Still, *Milwaukee: The History of a City* (Madison: State Historical Society of Wisconsin, 1948), 547–48; Harry M. Anderson and Frederick I. Olson, *Milwaukee, At the Gathering of the Waters* (Milwaukee: Milwaukee County Historical Society, 1984), 108; George J. Lankevich, *Milwaukee, A Chronological and Documentary History* (Dobbs Ferry, N.Y.: Oceana Publications, Inc., 1977), 57–58; R. B. Pixley, *Wisconsin in the World War* (Milwaukee: S. and E. Tate Printing Company, 1919), 225.

[2] McAdoo and Chicago and Northwestern entries, firm ledger book 1914–1919; and Joseph M. Canfield, *TM: The Milwaukee Electric Railway and Light Company*, Bulletin #112 (Chicago: Central Electric Railfans Association, 1972), 44.

[3] Records of George Miller, Arthur Fairchild, Firm Archives.

[4] See Biographical Notes, Arthur Fairchild, Firm Archives.

[5] Pixley, 225; Mack Records, Firm Archives.

[6]*Seidel v. The Journal Co.*, Milwaukee Country Circuit Court, Record Book 130, 1919, Case #54028, 75; Lankevich, 61, 63.

[7] Robert C. Nesbit, *The History of Wisconsin*, Vol. 3, *Urbanization and Industrialization, 1873–1893* (Madison: State Historical Society of Wisconsin, 1985), 440.

[8] J. G. Hardgrove, "Does the Eighteenth Amendment Prohibit State Manufacture and Dispensation?", 14 *Marquette Law Review*, 59 (1930).

[9] Lankevich, 62–63.

[10] Lawrence M. Friedman, *History of American Law* (New York: Simon & Schuster, 1985), 683.

[11]*State ex rel. Klefisch v. Wisconsin Telephone Co.*, 181 Wis. 519 (1923); H. Russell Zimmermann, *The Heritage Guidebook, Landmarks and Historical Sites in Southeastern Wisconsin* (Milwaukee: Harry W. Schwartz, 1989), 53; Gregory Filardo, *Old Milwaukee, A Historic Tour in Picture Postcards* (Vestal, N.Y.: The Vestal Press, 1988), 16–17; *Milwaukee Sentinel,*

June 14, 1928; interviews with Mildred Roehr, Vernon Swanson, Allen Taylor, and George Miller Chester, Firm Archives.

[12]*Laws of Wisconsin,* 1929, chap. 439, 593; *Reports of the State Bar Association,* vol. 19, 328–31, 376; Virginia North, "The Family Court," *Marquette Law Review* 18 (1) (December 1933), 241, and 19 (3) (April 1935), 174.

[13] Edwin S. Mack, "Report of the Committee on Professional Standards," *State Bar Association of Wisconsin,* 15 (1924–1925), 59–60; Frank T. Boesel, "In Memoriam, Edwin S. Mack," Memorial of the Milwaukee County Bar Association, May 21, 1942; Laws of Wisconsin, Chapter 314, 1927.

[14] Ledger and accounting records, Firm Archives; the partners remaining at the time of George Miller's death were Arthur Fairchild, 1905; Edwin Mack, 1906; James Blake, 1915; Gilbert Hardgrove, 1916; Paul Newcomb, 1923; Leon Foley, 1933; Fred Sammond, 1933; Bert Vandervelde, 1933.

[15] Miller Files, Firm Archives.

[16] Lankevich, 56–57; "Biography of George Miller," Firm Archives; *Milwaukee Journal,* November 14, December 10, 1930; and June 25, November 21, 1931; Still, 547–48.

CHAPTER 13 Legal Changes in the Depression Era, 1932–1940

[1]*Schwemer v. Fry,* 212 Wis. 88 (1933); *Morris Fox & Company v. Lisman,* 208 Wis. 1 (1931).

[2] For conditions in Wisconsin during the Great Depression, see Paul W. Glad, *The History of Wisconsin, War, A New Era and Depression, 1914–1940,* Vol. V (Madison: State Historical Society of Wisconsin, 1990).

[3]*Will of Church: First Wisconsin Trust Company v. Schultz,* 221 Wis. 472 (1936); *Estate of Fouks,* 213 Wis. 550 (1934).

[4] See Theodore A. Andersen, *A Century of Banking in Wisconsin* (Madison: State Historical Society of Wisconsin, 1954), 159, 161.

[5] Robert C. Nesbit, *Wisconsin: A History* (Madison: University of Wisconsin Press, 1973), 485; Andersen.

[6]*First National Bank of Hartford v. City of Hartford,* 273 U.S. 548 (1927); *Ashland County Bank v. Village of Butternut,* 208 Wis. 90 (1932).

[7]*Banking Commission v. First Wisconsin National Bank,* 234 Wis. 60 (1940).

[8] Interviews with Jeanne Foley, Vernon Swanson, Firm Archives.

[9] Interview with Theodore Bolliger, Firm Archives.

[10] Interview with Allen Taylor, Firm Archives.

[11] Interviews with Vernon Swanson, Theodore Bolliger, Steven Keane.

[12] Bayrd Still, *Milwaukee: The History of a City* (Madison: State Historical Society of Wisconsin, 1948), 478–84

[13] Nesbit, 476, 477.

[14] Firm account and ledger books, Firm Archives.

[15] Firm account book, 1932–1944, Firm Archives; James Willard Hurst, *The Growth of American Law: The Lawmakers* (Boston: Little, Brown, 1950); Marc Galanter and Thomas Palay, *Tournament of Lawyers: The Transformation of the Big Law Firm* (Chicago: University of Chicago Press, 1991), 7–8.

[16] See Frederic Sammond, "Three Common Constitutional Misconceptions of Income Tax Law," 8 *Wisconsin Law Review* 199 (1932).

[17] Lawrence M. Friedman, *History of American Law* (New York: Simon and Schuster, 1985), 655–59.

[18] "Committee on Commissions," *Reports of the Wisconsin State Bar Association*, Vol. 22, 1932, 109–13; Hurst, 427.

[19] *Paramount Publix Corporation v. Hill*, 11 F. Supp. 478 (W.D. Wis. 1932).

[20] Frederic Sammond, "Three Common Constitutional Misconceptions of Income Tax Law," 8 *Wisconsin Law Review* 199 (1932).

[21] *Aluminum Goods Manufacturing Co. v. Commissioner of Internal Revenue*, 56 F.2d 568 (7th Cir. 1932), *aff'd*, 287 U.S. 544 (1933); *State ex rel. Froedtert Grain and Malting Co. v. Tax Commission*, 221 Wis. 225 (1936); *Burroughs Adding Machine Co. v. Tax Commission*, 237 Wis. 423 (1941); *Trane Co. v. Tax Commission*, 235 Wis. 516 (1940); and *Rahr Malting Co. v. United States*, 145 F.2d 867 (7th Cir. 1944).

[22] *Friedmann v. Tax Commission*, 235 Wis. 237 (1940); *Allis v. LaBudde*, 128 F.2d 838 (7th Cir. 1942); *Estate of Hatten*, 233 Wis. 199 (1940); *Will of Kootz*, 228 Wis. 306 (1938); *Cudahy (John) v. Tax Commission*, 226 Wis. 342 (1937); *Cudahy (Michael) v. Tax Commission*, 226 Wis. 317 (1937); *Will of Wehr*, 247 Wis. 98 (1945); and *Will of Prange*, 208 Wis. 404 (1932).

[23] *Will of Nieman: Mack v. Wahl*, 223 Wis. 294 (1936); interview with Therese Mack Goldsmith, Firm Archives.

[24] Richard B. Morris, *Encyclopedia of American History* (New York: Harper & Brothers, 1953), 352.

[25] *Public Service Commission of Wisconsin v. Wisconsin Telephone Co.*, 289 U.S. 67 (1933); *Wisconsin Telephone Co. v. Public Service Commission*, 232 Wis. 274 (1939); interview with Theodore Bolliger, Firm Archives.

[26] Interview with Vernon Swanson.

CHAPTER 14 Partners in Wartime, 1941–1945

[1] *State ex rel. American Legion 1941 Convention Corp. of Milwaukee v. Smith*, 235 Wis. 443 (1940).

[2] *Weisel and Co. v. Bowles*, 156 F.2d 1007 (Ct. Price Controls 1945).

[3] Robert T. Swaine, *The Cravath Firm and Its Predecessors* (New York: Ad Press, 1946 and 1948), Vol. II, 661.

[4] J. Gilbert Hardgrove, letter to Paul Barnes, September 27, 1943, Firm Archives.

[5] Paul Barnes, letter to J. Gilbert Hardgrove, August 4, 1944, Firm Archives.

[6] J. Gilbert Hardgrove letters, Firm Archives.

[7] Interviews with Steven Keane, Theodore Bolliger, Firm Archives.

[8] American Bar Association, letter to J. Gilbert Hardgrove, February 10, 1943, and "Mid-Winter Institute of The State Bar of Wisconsin," January 16, 1943, Firm Archives.

[9] "New Courses for Lawyers," Milwaukee Bar Association Program, 1941–1942.

[10] *The Gavel*, Milwaukee Bar Association, Vol. 5, #1, November 1942, 15; and letter from Miller, Mack and Fairchild, to Robert E. Friend, President Nordberg Manufacturing Company, May 13, 1943, Firm Archives.

[11] Interview with Allen M. Taylor.

[12] Paul W. Glad, *The History of Wisconsin: War, A New Era and Depression, 1914–1940* (Madison: State Historical Society of Wisconsin, 1990), Vol. V, 513, 555–58; Interview with Richard Mooney; *State ex rel Zimmerman v. Dammann*, 229 Wis. 570 (1938); and *Petition of Heil*, 230 Wis. 428 (1938); Nesbit, 527; *State ex rel Martin v. Heil*, 242 Wis. 41 (1942); and J. Gilbert Hardgrove, letter to Plant, February 15, 1943, Firm Archives.

[13] J. Gilbert Hardgrove, letter to Al McCuen, April 20, 1942, Firm Archives.

[14] Interviews with Mildred Roehr, Vernon Swanson, Theresa Mack Goldsmith, Edith Fairchild Frank, Firm Archives.

[15] For personal reflections on Mack, see interviews of Richard Mooney, Theresa Mack Goldsmith, Mildred Roehr, Steven Keane, Vernon Swanson, and Theodore Bolliger, Firm Archives.

[16] Interview with Vernon Swanson, Firm Archives.

[17] Interviews with Theodore Bolliger, Mildred Roehr; Louis Quarles, letter on death of Edwin Mack, April 17, 1942, Firm Archives.

[18] Edwin S. Mack, letters to J. Gilbert Hardgrove, April 14, 1941 and April 7, 1942, Firm Archives.

[19] Harvard University Eulogy on Death of Edwin S. Mack, April 15, 1942, Firm Archives.

[20] Frank T. Boesel, Walter H. Bender, and Louis Quarles, "In Memoriam, Edwin S. Mack"; and Letter of Leon Foley to Chester Morrill, Federal Reserve System, April 15, 1942, Firm Archives.

[21] Letter of Edward C. Higbee to Arthur Fairchild, April 11, 1942, Firm Archives.

[22] The Hon. Thomas E. Fairchild, Eulogy on Edwin S. Mack, Firm Archives.

[23] Interview with Steven Keane, Firm Archives.

CHAPTER 15 Postwar Growth and New Directions, 1945–1973

[1] James Willard Hurst, *The Growth of American Law* (Boston: Little, Brown, 1950); Lawrence Friedman, *History of American Law* (New York: Simon & Schuster, 1985).

[2] Interview with Allen Taylor.

[3] Firm memos dated December 28, 1948, December 31, 1948, December 27, 1949, and December 31, 1949, Firm Archives.

[4] 1953 Partnership Agreement, Firm Archives.

[5] *Grengs v. Twentieth Century Fox Film Corp.,* 232 F.2d 325 (7th Cir. 1956); interviews with Steven Keane, Edwin Wiley.

[6] Gerald Kloss, "1950 Wreck Hastened the Demise of the Interurban Transit Line," *The Milwaukee Journal,* October 30, 1991; interview with Steven Keane; Larry A. Sakar, *Speedrail: Milwaukee's Last Rapid Transit,* (Glendale, Calif: Interurban Press, 1991).

[7] *Rahr Malting Company v. United States,* 157 F. Supp. 803 (E.D. Wis. 1957), *aff'd,* 260 F.2d 309 (7th Cir. 1958); *Consolidated Apparel Co. v. Commissioner of Internal Revenue,* 207 F.2d 580 (7th Cir. 1953).

[8] *Frank Lloyd Wright Foundation v. Town of Wyoming,* 267 Wis. 599 (1954).

[9] Nicholas C. Peroff, *Menominee Drums: Tribal Termination and Restoration 1954–1974* (Norman, Okla.: University of Oklahoma Press, 1982); Interviews with Donald Buzard and George M. Chester; Stephen J. Herzberg, "The Menominee Indians: From Treaty to Termination," *Wisconsin Magazine of History,* Vol. 60, #4, Summer 1977; Ninety-Third Congress, *Hearings Before the Subcommittee on Indian Affairs,* Menominee Restoration Act, May 1973, Serial No. 93–20.

[10] Interview with Steven Keane; *State v. Milwaukee Braves, Inc,* 31 Wis. 2d 699, *cert. denied,* 385 U.S. 990 (1966).

[11] *National Labor Relations Board v. Transamerican Freight Lines, Inc.*, 275 F.2d 311 (7th Cir. 1960); *Hartman v. North Central Airlines, Inc.*, 241 F.2d 859 (7th Cir. 1957).

[12] George J. Lankevich, *Milwaukee, A Chronological and Documentary History* (Dobbs Ferry, N.Y.: Oceana Publications, Inc., 1977), 72, 76.

[13] Harry M. Anderson and Frederick I. Olson, *Milwaukee, At the Gathering of the Waters* (Milwaukee: County Historical Society, 1984), 134–42.

[14] Lankevich, 75–76.

[15] *United Gas, Coke and Chemical Workers of America v. Wisconsin Employment Relations Board*, 255 Wis. 154 (1949); *Wisconsin Employment Relations Board v. Milwaukee Gas Light Co.*, 258 Wis. 1 (1950), *reversed sub nom. Amalgamated Association of Street Electric Railway Motor Coach Employees of America v. Wisconsin Employment Relations Board*, 340 U.S. 383 (1951).

[16] *A. O. Smith Corporation v. National Labor Relations Board*, 343 F.2d 103 (7th Cir. 1965); *Wimberly v. Clark Controller Co.*, 364 F.2d 225 (6th Cir. 1966); *Square D Company v. National Labor Board*, 332 F.2d 360 (9th Cir. 1964).

[17] *City of Milwaukee v. Wisconsin Employment Relations Commission*, 43 Wis. 2d. 596.

[18] *State ex rel. Wettengel v. Zimmerman*, 249 Wis. 237 (1946).

[19] Interview with David Beckwith; Philip Habermann, "History of the Wisconsin State Bar Association," unpublished manuscript (Madison: Wisconsin State Bar Association.)

[20] Arthur Fairchild: Letter to Gilbert Hodges, November 15, 1951.

[21] Interview with Allen Taylor; firm employment records.

[22] *Milwaukee Journal*, October 17, 1973.

CHAPTER 16 Epilogue: A National Law Firm, 1974–1992

[1] For information on the development and growth of the Washington office, see interviews with David Shute, Allen Taylor, Harry Wallace, James Bierman, and Richard Schwaab, in Firm Archives.

[2] Interview with James Bierman.

[3] *Ibid.*

[4] For information on the creation of the Madison office and on the development of the firm's practice in public finance, see interviews with William Kiernan, Thomas Ragatz, Lawrence Bugge, Harry Wallace, and Allen Taylor, Firm Archives; Kiernan, *Wisconsin Municipal Indebtedness: Part 1—The Power to Become Indebted and Its Limits*, 1964 *Wisconsin Law Review* 173;

Kubale, *Wisconsin Municipal Indebtedness: Part 2—Procedures for Issuance of General Obligation Bonds,* at 406; Bugge, *Wisconsin Municipal Indebtedness: Part 3—The Effects of Irregularities in Municipal Obligations and Contracts,* at 549.

[5] *State ex rel. Warren v. Nusbaum,* 59 Wis. 2d 391 (1973).

[6] For information on the development and growth of the Foley & Lardner offices in Florida, see interviews with William Kiernan, Jr., Gerald Neal, Allen Taylor, Harry Wallace, William King, Robert Hill, Lewis Hill III, Egerton van den Berg, John Porter, Gordon Arkin, Charles Commander III, Bill Bryant, Jr., Noreen Fenner, and Mitchell Legler.

[7] *Diamond v. Chakrabarty,* 447 U.S.303 (1980); *Diamond v. Diehr,* 450 U.S. 175 (1981).

[8] For information on the Alexandria office, see interview with Richard Schwaab, Firm Archives.

[9] Interviews with Edwin Wiley and Richard Schwaab.

⋘ Index ⋙

Abbott family, 124
Abolitionists, 23–24, 28, 56, 57
Abraham, William J., Jr., 192
Abrohams, Benjamin J., 192
Academy of Music, 97
Ackley v. Chicago, Milwaukee and St. Paul Railway, 75
Adams, William F., 127
Administrative law, in post-World War II era, 149, 167
Adrian, Michigan, 2
Aetna Insurance Company, 43
Agawann Paper Company, 102
Albany Building, 62
Albany Hall movement, 56, 58, 72
Aldrich, Owen, 7
Alexandria, Virginia, mergers in, 184, 199
Allen-Bradley Company, 84
Allis, Edward P., 63, 79, 88
Allis, Edward P. Co., 79, 123
Allis-Chalmers Co., 63, 88, 102, 123
Allis family, 124, 126, 150
Allis v. LaBudde, 222n
Aluminum Goods Manufacturing Company, 150
Aluminum Goods Manufacturing Co. v. Commissioner of Internal Revenue, 222n
Amalgamated Association of Street Electric Railway Motor Coach Employees of America v. Wisconsin Employment Relations Board, 225n
Amalgamated Street Railway Employees, 112–13
American Bar Association, 138–39, 157, 166
American Bar Foundation, 166
American Express Company, 52, 102, 124, 128

American Federation of Labor, 111, 152
American Law Institute, 149, 166
American Law Review, 121
American Legion Convention (1941), 154
American Motors, 125
American National Bank, 126
American Telephone and Telegraph Company, 97
Anderson, Kevin D., 196
Anneke, Mathilde F., 86
Antitrust law, 149, 165–67, 178
A. O. Smith Corporation v. National Labor Relations Board, 225n
Arbitration panels, 18
Archer v. Meadows, 214n
Arkin, J. Gordon, 180, 193
Armour, Philip, 77
Arnold, C. Jeffery, 195
Arnold, Jonathan, 29
Arthur v. Oakes, 218n
Atlanta Bank, 45–46
Atlanta Bank v. Cramer, 209n
Atlantic and Pacific Tea Company, 89
Auen, Michael H., 193
Automobiles, effect on law practice, 124–25
Auto Parts Manufacturing Company, 125

Bacon & Thomas, 184
Badger State Lumber Company, 102
Bailey, George, 8
Bailey v. Steamboat Milwaukee, 204n
Baker, David A., 193
Banking Commission, 143
Banking Commission v. First Wisconsin National Bank, 221n
Banking House, 32

Banking industry, 44–45
  collection matters, 101
  crisis in, 54–55
  in Depression era, 144
  growth of, 144
  litigation in, 45–46, 51, 144–45
  prohibition on, in constitutional
    referendum, 26–27
  regulation of, 143–44
Bank of Milwaukee, 6
Bankruptcy law, 85
Bank stock, tax on state, 144
Barber, Hiram, 16
Barber and Cronkhite v. Barber, 206n
Barnes, Paul M., xi, 145, 156, 165, 190
Barnett, Joseph R., xi, 165, 166, 190
Barron, Russell J., 194
Bartlett, John K., 9–10
Bartlett, Walter S., 127
Baseball. *See* Cream City Club, Milwaukee
    Braves, Milwaukee Brewers
Baxa, Edmund T., Jr., 196
Bayshore Mall, 168
Beckwith, David E., xi, 165, 171, 178, 180,
    190
Beggs family, 124
Belford, Jane A., 194
Belknap, William W., 86
Bender, Walter H., 161
Benner, Charles A., 195
Bent, Stephen A., 195
Berger, Beth Meier, 196
Berger, Victor, 134, 136
Bernhardt, Sarah, 97
Berry, Christopher S., 193
Beskin, Jay R., 195
Beytin, Kenneth A., 194
Biehl, Michael M., 193
Bierman, James N., 178, 192
Bigelow, F. G., 115
Binder, Robert L., 193
Black suffrage, 71
*Blair v. Milwaukee & Prairie du Chien
    Railroad Co.,* 213n
Blake, James B., 126, 127, 146, 147, 189
Blanchard, Hiram, 5
Blanchard v. Dousman, 205n
Blanchard v. Lelands, 5, 204n
Blatz, Valentin, 43, 85
Blue Star Harness Company, 77
Blumenthal, David A., 184, 194
Boardman, Suhr, Curry & Field, 179
Boer, Ralf-Reinhard, 193
Boesel, Frank T., 161
Bolliger, Theodore C., xi, 145, 146, 165,
    190
Bond Buyers' Municipal Marketplace, 179

Bonner, Robert J., 191
Booth, Edwin, 97
Booth, Sherman, 24, 50, 56, 57
Boston Store, 124
Bouck, Gabriel, 19, 20, 31, 68
Bowen, Michael A., xi, 193
Boyd v. New York and Erie Railroad, 209n
Bradley, Clara Lynde, 84, 105
Bradley, Harry C., 98
Bradley, Justice, 87
Bradley, Robert B., 165, 190
Bradley v. Cramer, 216n
Bradstreet Building, 126
Bragg, Edward, 126
Brahm, John W., 191
Branch, Joseph C., 195
Brandeis, Louis, 101, 130
Braun, John, 43
Braun, Paul D., 192
Braza, Mary K., 196
Breweries, 43, 63, 88, 102, 117, 123, 124,
    137
"Bridge War," 23
Briggs and Stratton, 124
Brody, James P., xi, 149, 165, 190
Brody, Robert, 197
Brown, John, 57
Brown, Samuel, 25
Brumder, George, 117
Brumder Building, 135
Brunette v. Whitney, 208n
Bryant, Bill L., Jr., 182, 195
Buchanan, James, 60
Bugge, Lawrence J., 179, 191
Burka, Robert A., 197
Burke, Norman F., 180, 193
Burlington Mills, 152
Burnham, Daniel, 127
Burnham v. Burnham, 217n
Burns v. North Chicago Rolling Mill, 217n
Burrell, Carolyn C., 193
Burroughs Adding Machine Company, 150
*Burroughs Adding Machine Co. v. Tax
    Commission,* 222n
Burton, Daniel N., 181, 194
Busch Properties, 181
Butler, Benjamin F., 10
Butler, Orange, 2, 3
Butler, Buttrick, & Cottrill, 58
Byran, Paul F., 196
Byrnes, John W., 178, 191

Cady, Linus, 16
Cady & Farwell v. Hyde, 206n
Camp v. Meyer, 209n
Candee v. Western Union Telegraph Co.,
    214n

Capitol Court, 168
Carlsbad health spa, 98
Carlson, Harry V., Jr., 191
Carnegie, Andrew, 125
Carnegie Steel Mill (Homestead, Pennsylvania), 112
Carpenter, Matthew Hale, 82, 84, 90
Carsella, Michael B., 195
Carter, Walter S., 52, 104, 121
Cary, John, 75, 76, 83
Cary v. Rosenwald, 210n
Casper, Richard H., 193
Cass, Lewis, 32
Cassoday, Jolon B., Justice, 89
Centennial Exposition, 85
Central Pacific Railroad, 84
Chamberlain v. Milwaukee and Mississippi Railroad Co., 209n
Chameides, Steven B., 195
Chapin v. Jewell, 18, 206n
Chapman, T. A., and Company, 89, 124
Chapman, Thomas A., 98
Chauncey, Harrison K., Jr., 196
Chemung Bank v. Lowery, 215n
Chester, Alice Miller, 136, 141
Chester, George M., xi, 165, 190
Chicago, expansion office in, 182–83
Chicago, Milwaukee, and St. Paul Railroad, 55, 74, 76, 77
Chicago and Northwestern Railroad, 74–75
Chicago Board of Trade, 102
Chicago, University of, Law School, 126, 163
Chickamauga, battle of, 68
Children's Code (1928), 138
Children's Hospital, 175, 184
Christensen, Robert A., 191
Christiansen, Jon P., 193
Christiansen, Keith A., 191
Church, Gilbert W., 191
Churchill & von Briesen, ix, 117
Cincinnati College of Law, 14
Circuit Court of Appeals Act (1891), 85
City of Milwaukee v. Milwaukee Electric Railway and Light Co., 220n
City of Milwaukee v. Wisconsin Employment Relations Commission, 225n
Civic Auditorium, 90
Clark, James R., 192
Clark v. Aldrich, 6, 204n
Clark v. Schooner Marvin, 206n
Clasen, Thomas F., 195
Clean Air Act (1970), 184
Clean Water Act (1972), 184
Cleveland, Grover, 112
Collections law, 13–14, 49, 63

Collins, John R., 165, 190
Columbia Hospital, 175
Columbia Law School, 181
Commander, Charles E., III, 182, 197
Commander, Legler, Werber, Dawes, Sadler & Howell, P.A., 182, 199
Commercial Bank, 135
Commission of Public Debt for Milwaukee, 67, 72, 82
Computer Power, Inc., 182
Congress of Industrial Organizations (CIO), 152
Conley, William M., 197
Connelly, James P., 192
Conover, O. M., 107
Continental Bank of Illinois, 102
Cooney, Paul A., 194
Cooper, John C., III, 196
Cosmopolitan Club of Milwaukee, 168
Country Day School, 149
Cramer, William E., 45, 46, 99
Crane, Stephen A., 195
Crane Elevator Company, 102
Cravath, Paul, 104
Cravath, Swaine & Moore, 52, 145, 155
Cream City Club, 63
Cream City Railroad, 91
Crocker, Hans, 5, 8, 17
Crosby-Nash, 125
Crosby Transportation Company, 125
Croysdale, David W., 191
Cruiser Motor Car Company, 125
Cudahy, John, 150
Cudahy, Michael, 77, 150
Cudahy, Patrick, 110
Cudahy family, 124
Cudahy (John) v. Tax Commission, 222n
Cudahy (Michael) v. Tax Commission, 222n
Cunningham, George D., 192
Curtis, Charles G., Jr., 196
Curtis, William J., 132

Daily Wisconsin, 46
Daly, Eugene C., 191
Dane, Nathan, 10, 28
Darling, Mason C., 28
Davenport, Gordon III, 197
Davis, Churchill, 162
Dawes, Michael F., 197
Dawson, John R., 192
Dawson, Suzanne S., 195
Deane, Steve, 165
Debs, In re, 112
Delahunty, Terence J., Jr., 196
Delamatry v. Milwaukee & Prairie du Chien Railroad Co., 214n

Democratic party, 4, 12, 97
    antibanking views of, 21, 26
    on constitutional referendum, 26–27
    in 1848 election, 28–32
    in 1859 judicial elections, 56–57
    in 1860 mayoral election, 58–59
    in 1874 congressional election, 83–84
    in Gilded Age, 72, 81–82
    and slavery issue, 23, 50, 56–57
DeSoto Corporation, 183
Deutscher Club, 135
Dewey, Charles, 15
*Diamond Glue Co. v. United States Glue
    Company,* 218n
Diamond v. Chakrabarty, 183, 226n
Diamond v. Diehr, 183
Dickinson, Lloyd J., 196
Dillon, Clarence, 126, 141
Dillon-Read & Co., 126
Dionisopoulos, George A., 195
DiPasquale, Benn S., 191
DiPersio, Denise T., 196
Dixon, Hooker & Palmer, 108
Dixon, Luther, 107
Dixon & Noyes, 108
Dodge, Henry, 21, 22, 25, 28
Douglas v. Frink, 209n
Dousman, George, 15, 18, 53
Dousman, Hercules, 53
Dousman, Michael, 53
Dousman, Talbot, 53
Dow, Rodney H., 192
Downer, Alcie, 99
Downer, Jason, 67
Downer Seminary and College, 22, 99, 149
Drummond, Robert K., 191
Dryer, Edwin J., 192
Dulles, John Foster, 103
Dun, Robert Graham, 126
Dun and Bradstreet, 126
Dunlap, W. Gray, Jr., 196
DuPuy, Robert A., 192
Durkee, Charles, 28–32
Durose, Richard A., 196
Dutcher, Sexton & Company, 53
Dyer, Charles E., Judge, 103

Earl, Anthony S., 192
Eble, Andrew, 40
Eble v. Milwaukee and Waukesha Railroad,
    208n
Edelman, Peter B., 192
Eero Saarinen building, 168
Ehlert v. Kindt, 218n
Eighteenth Amendment, 136
Eisenhower administration, 165, 166
Eldred, Anson, 37

Eldred, Elisha, 37, 59, 98
Eldred v. Dewey, 205n
Eldred v. Ross, 208n
Ellis v. Milwaukee City Railway Co., 217n
Ely, Richard, 125
Emergency Court of Price Appeals, 155
Engstrom, Harry C., 196
Environmental law, 184
Erhard, Michael P., 193
Erie, sinking of, 60
Esenberg, Richard M., 196
European Patent Convention (1973), 183
Evans, Joseph D., 194
Evans, Tim, x
Evening Wisconsin, 24, 45, 49, 99
Evinrude, Ole, 123
Ewing, Thomas C., 195
Excelsior Building, 62
Extein, Mark C., 194

Fairchild, Arthur W., x, 124, 189
    affiliation with firm, 118, 122, 126
    business activities of, 148–49
    contributions to firm, 120, 140, 170–71
    death of, 122, 170
    description of, 170–71
    education of, 122
    leadership of firm, 141, 141, 162, 164, 167
    military service of, 135–36
    social activities of, 148–49
    and tax litigation, 144
    tenure of, 170
Fairchild, Foley & Sammond, 171–72, 187
Fairchild, Hiram O., 122
Fairchild, Thomas, 161, 169–70
Falk, Herman, 141
Falls City Jeans and Woolen Company, 102
Farmer, Guy O. II, 195
Farmers, disputes with railroads, 40, 42,
    55–56, 66, 75
Farmers' and Mechanics' Bank of Detroit, 6
Farmers' and Mechanics' Bank of Homer,
    collapse of, 4–5
Farmers and Millers Bank, 45, 54
*Farmers' Loan and Trust Co. v. Northern
    Pacific Railroad Co.,* 218n
Farmin v. Shelby, 205n
Farrell, James A., 197
Farwell, Leonard, 16
Farwell v. Lockwood, 206n
Federal Deposit Insurance Corporation
    (FDIC), 144
Federal Power Commission, 151
Federal Reserve System, 161
Federal Rubber, 124
Federal Trade Commission, 135
Feldhaus, John J., 195

Feldstein, Janice, xi
Fellow-servant rule, 74
Field, David Dudley, 102
Field Code, 102–3
Fields, Wendy L., 194
Fifield, Thomas B., 190
Fifth Ward Gas and Light Company, 53, 54
*Fifth Ward Gas and Light Company v.
    Smith,* 210*n*
File keeping, 148
Finch, Asahel, Sr., 2, 21
Finch, Asahel, Jr., 189
    abolitionist views of, 23–25, 28–29
    admission to Michigan bar, 3, 4, 5
    admission to Wisconsin bar, 9
    as apprentice, 3
    banking career of, 4–5, 45
    bid for judicial appointment, 19, 25, 36,
        82
    birth of, 2
    business activities of, 2, 73
    in campaign for Congress, 28–32
    in campaign for judgeship, 25, 46, 82
    challenge to reputation, 17
    children of, 5, 22, 23, 32–33, 51
    church activities of, 5, 15, 17
    as city attorney, 35–36
    and Civil War, 65
    courtroom reputation of, 17–18
    death of, 67, 78, 91, 93, 95
    death of children, 17, 33, 67
    defeat in Wisconsin state assembly
        election, 29
    description of, 8
    education of, 2
    election as city attorney, 25
    election to Michigan State Legislature,
        3
    financial fortune of, 72–73
    "Finch's addition," 63
    first marriage of, 2, 5, 32, 46
    in Gilded Age, 72, 73, 78
    home of, 6–7, 54, 91
    impact of 1837 panic on, 4–5
    investments of, 80
    introduction to Charles Lynde, 176
    involvement with railroads, 76
    as justice of the peace, 8
    and labor law, 31
    law partnership with Hubbell, 19
    law partnership with Lynde, 1, 9, 11,
        12–20, 92–93
    law partnership of Wells, Crocker &
        Finch, 5–8
    law partnership of Wells & Finch, 8–9
    as leader in Milwaukee business
        community, 73

    legal education of, 3
    as mentor, 15
    as Michigan state legislator, 3, 4
    move to Michigan, 2
    move to Milwaukee, 2
    as notary public, 8
    political views and affiliations of, 4, 5,
        12, 21–22, 25–27, 30, 31, 57
    political aspirations of, 21, 81
    as president of gas company, 72–73
    public service of, 2, 9–10, 22, 25, 82
    railroad injury of, 76
    and railroads, 40
    second marriage of, 67
    on slavery, 23–25
    on state constitution, 25–27
    as store owner, 2
Finch, Cullen, 49
Finch, Delia, death of, 33, 67
Finch, Elizabeth, death of, 17
Finch, Henry Martyn (Matt), 189
    admission to bar, 49
    apprenticeship of, 49
    association with firm, 46, 48, 49
    birth of, 49
    as collections specialist, 49, 63
    death of, 92, 95
    draft status of, 65
    early career of, 49
    as firm litigator, 78
    home fire of, 59
    investments of, 81, 89
    political affiliation of, 50
Finch, Mary Deforest Bristol, 2, 5, 23, 32,
    46
Finch, Mathilda Douglas, 67
Finch & Lynde, viii, 187
    cases handled by, 13–18, 36, 37–38,
        42–48
    client relationships of, 15–16, 34
    difficulties in Hyde case, 16–17
    expansion of, 46
    fee structure of, 15
    lawsuit against Dewey, 15
    involvement with railroad, 76
    office staff of, 19, 31–32
Finches, Lynde & Miller, 46–60, 187
    appeal cases handled by, 67, 76, 95
    and bankruptcy reform, 50, 51
    case load of, 50, 52–54, 62–67, 73–75,
        77–78
    clients of, 100–102
    growth of, 48, 52, 94–95
    impact of Civil War on, 65–67, 68
    Noyes affiliation with, 108
    offices of, 50–51, 62–63, 67, 89, 103
    office staff of, 50, 104

Finch v. Dewey, 205*n*
Firm offices, 201–202
First Boston Company, 183
First National Bank, 54–55, 97, 126, 127, 128
First Presbyterian Church, 9, 15
First Presbyterian Society of Homer, 4
First Regiment of Wisconsin Volunteers, 19
First Union Bank, 182
First Wisconsin Bank Center, 179
First Wisconsin Corporation, 117
First Wisconsin National Bank, 45, 55, 126, 144, 178–79, 180
First Wisconsin Trust Company, 97, 143, 150, 182
Fischer, Michael D., 192
Fisher, Stephen M., 193
Fitch, Grant, 98, 141
Flambeau Paper Company, 124
Fleck, David H., 191
Florentine Opera, 168
Florida Department of Insurance, 182
Florida, firm offices in, 180–82
Florsheim, Richard S., 193
Fogt, Howard W., Jr., 191
Foley, Lardner & Slade, 180, 181
Foley, Leon F., x, 189
    affiliation with firm, 140, 145, 172
    background of, 147
    as banking specialist, 144
    contributions to firm, 172–73
    death of, 173
    description of, 172–73
    education of, 140
    and leadership of firm, 146, 162, 163, 164, 167
    military service of, 136, 156, 157
    scholarly interests of, 149
Foley, Mark F., 196
Foley & Lardner, 187
    expansion offices of, 178–83
    management structure at, 175, 177
    mergers of, 178, 179, 182, 184
    name change to, 171, 181
    as national law firm, 177
    offices of, 174, 175–76
    reasons for survival and success, xvi–xvii
Foley, Sammond & Lardner, 171, 187
Foley & Lardner, Schwartz, Jeffrey, Schwaab, Mack, Blumenthal & Evans, 184
Ford, Henry, 124–25
Forest Home Cemetery, 91
Fourteenth Amendment, 113
Four Wheel Drive Auto Company, 125
Fox Corporation, 149
Fox River Valley Electric Railway Company, 115

Frautschi, Timothy C., 191
Fred Miller Theater building, 168
Free Banking Law (1852), 44–45
Freedom-of-contract defense, 77
Freeman, 24
Free Soil party, 21, 32
Friedmann v. Tax Commission, 222*n*
Friend, Robert, 160
Frink, Walker & Davis, 43
Froedtert Grain and Malting Co. v. Tax Commission, 222*n*
Froedtert family, 168
Froedtert Malting Company, 124, 150, 153
Froedtert Medical Center, 184
Fugitive Slave Law (1850), 56
Fulton, Andrew III, 197

Gallagher, Richard S., 191
Gallun, A. F., 77
Garfield, James, assassination of, 90
Garmer, Benjamin F. III, 191
Gatchell, David A., 195
Gay, Francis F., 180, 193
Gehl, Michael A., 193
Geiger, Ferdinand, Judge, 141
Geilfuss, C. Frederick II, 194
Gempeler, Henry A., 196
General Mills, 79
George, Richard D., 179, 192
George Washington University Law School, 178
German-American Academy, 135
German-American League, 134
Germania Bank, 51, 117, 135
Germania Building, 135
Gibbs, B. Gray, 197
Gibbs & Sterrett Manufacturing Co., 88
Gibbs & Sterrett Manufacturing Company v. Brucker, 215*n*
Gifford, Joshua, 16
Gillespie, Ezekiel, 71
Gillespie v. Palmer, 71
Gimbel's Department Store, 137
Giordano, Patrick N., 195
Gladfelter, Leslie H., 196
Glass-Steagall Act (1933), 143
Globe Bank of Milwaukee, 45
Globe Bank cases, 209*n*
Globe Transportation Company, 125
Goodell, Lavinia, 86
Goldman, Nathan D., 197
Goldwyn Corp., 149
Gompers, Samuel, 111
Goodland, Walter S., 158
Goodnow, Lyman, 25
Göttingen University, 95
Gotts, Ilene K., 197

Graham, David, 10
Grange Movement, 42
Grant, Harry, 141
Grant, Ulysses S., 68, 82, 90
Gray, Richard O., Jr., 195
Graybeal, John F., 191
Greater Orlando Airport Authority, 181
Grebe, Michael W., 192
Greenback Club, 81
Greene, Howard, 141
Greene, Vroman & Fairchild, 122
Greenleaf, Simon, 10
Grengs v. Twentieth Century Fox Film Corp., 224*n*
Grodin, James S., 195
Groethe, Reed, 194
Guaranty Building, 127
Gilded Age, practicing law in, 70–82
Guthridge, Charles R., 193

Hadley, Jackson, 58
Hadley v. Baxendale, 77
Hale v. Lockwood, 210*n*
Hallows, E. Harold, 146
Hamilton College, 10
Hamilton, Elizabeth, 33
Hamilton, Jennie, 172
Hammond, Edward J., 197
Hance School Building, 2
Hanning, F. Roberts, Jr., 191
Hanrahan, Phillip J., 191
Harbor Commission, 169
Hardgrove, J. Gilbert, x, 189
    affiliation with firm, 126, 145
    background of, 147
    description of, 170
    and Heil case, 158
    and leadership of firm, 140, 156, 164
    opposition of, to prohibition, 137
    as president of Wisconsin Bar
        Association, 149
    representation of Joseph McCarthy by,
        169
    and retail litigation, 124
Harland, Robert, 156
Harnischfeger Company, 102
Harrington, Richard L., 165, 175, 183, 190
Harrison, Benjamin, 112
Harth, David J., 195
Harvard Club of Milwaukee, 161
Harvard Law Review, 121
Harvard Law School, 10, 145
Harvard University, 150, 163
Hase, David J., 192
Haskins, Charles, 38
Hass, Paul, x
Hatch, Michael W., 193

Hatfield v. Dutcher, Sexton et al., 210*n*
Hatten, William, 150
Hauser, James C., 196
Hawes v. Stemper, 210*n*
Hayes, Rutherford B., 86
Haymarket Square, 111
Health Law Department, 184
Hedrick, Charles V., 197
Heil, Julius, 141, 158
Heimann v. Western Union Telegraph Co.,
    214*n*
Hendricks, Claude J., 127
Hennigan, Dennis A., 194
Herman Zoehrlaut Leather Company, 102
Hesse, Keith J., 196
Heymann, Richard S., 194
Hibbard v. Western Union Telegraph Co.,
    214*n*
Hildebrandt, Joseph P., 192
Hill, Hill & Dickenson, P.A., 181, 199
Hill, Lewis H., Sr., 181
Hill, Lewis H. III, 195
Hill, Robert, 181
Hill & Hill, 181
Hinman, Samuel, 8
Hinman v. Juneau, 204*n*
Hirschboeck, Herbert, 156, 157
Hoan, Daniel W., 130, 134, 135, 136, 147,
    154
Hochstadter, Isadore, 63
Holden, In re, 214*n*
Holden v. Meadows, 214*n*
Hollabaugh, Marcus A., 178, 191
Hollabaugh & Jacobs, 178, 199
Holmes, Oliver Wendell, 116
Holton, Edward D., 54
Home of the Friendless, 72
Home Owners' Loan Corporation, 181
Hoover, Herbert, 142
Horan, John P., 194
Horlick, William, 141
Horlick Company, 124
Hornreich, Michael A., 197
Hotel Wisconsin Roof Club, 137
Hoth v. Peters, 213*n*
Howell, Charles C. III, 197
Hoyt, Frank, 141
Hoyt v. Comstock, 212*n*
Hubbell, Finch & Lynde, 18–19, 187
Hubbell, Levi, 189
    and banking industry, 27
    impeachment trial of, 19, 37
    judgeship of, 35, 36
    law partnership with Finch & Lynde, 19
    legal practice of, 52, 63
    retention of, 15, 18–19
Huber, James O., 191

Huebschmann, Francis, 56
Huff, Marsha E., 193
Hurst, James Willard, x
Huston, James L., xi
Hyde, Oliver, 16

Illinois Can Company, 102
Ilsley, Charles, 98
Importers and Traders Bank of New York, 101
Income-tax law, 150
Indian rights cases, 66–67, 86
Industrial exposition (1879), 90
Inheritance taxes, 125
Insull, Samuel, 151
Insull empire, collapse of, 151
Insurance business, litigation in, 43–44
Intellectual property law, 183
Internal Revenue Service, 166
Interstate Commerce Act (1887), 76
In the Matter of the Will and Estate of Michael Dousman, 210n
Ireland, Emory, 192
Iron Block Building, 78
Itasca, Illinois, expansion office in, 182

Jackson, Andrew, 4, 21
Jacksonville, Fla., office expansion/merger in, 180, 181–82, 199
Jacobs, Ephraim, 178, 191
Jacobs, Joseph W., 197
Jaeger v. Milwaukee and Fond du Lac and Green Bay Railroad, 208n
Janesville Road Company, 39
Jaspan, Stanley S., 192
Jeffrey, Donald D., 184, 194
Jenkins, James C., Judge, 112
Jews, prejudice against, 94, 121–22
Johnson Service, 124
Jones, Jeffrey J., 194
Jones v. Barstow, 206n
Jones v. City of Milwaukee and Wisconsin Marine and Fire Insurance Company, 210
Juneau, Solomon, 127
    litigation by and against, 5–6, 8, 23
    as mayor of Milwaukee, 5, 23
Juneau v. Parks, 204n

Kalakaua, King, 84
Kamm, Linda H., 192
Kasten, Walter, 141
Kaumheimer, William, ix
Kay, Christopher K., 196
Keane, Steven E., xi, 145–49, 152, 156, 175, 178, 190
Kellner, Harriet, 172
Kelly, Michael J., 196

Kelso, Linda Y., 197
Kent, Chancellor, 10
Kessler, Joan F., 193
Keyes, Elisha W., 82, 126
Kieckhefer family, 124
Kiernan, William J., Jr., 179, 180, 191
Kilbourn, Byron, 5, 38, 55, 59, 75
Kilbourn v. Milwaukee and Rock River Canal Company Circuit Court, 208n
Kilbourn v. Rock River Canal Co., 208n
King, Rufus, 22, 29, 56, 63, 67
King, William D., 181, 193
Kittredge, Elizabeth, 140
Klitsner, Marvin E., 165, 190
Knox, W. David II, 192
Koch, John, 109
Kresge Store, 124
Kresge v. Maryland Casualty Co., 219n
Kubale, Bernard S., xi, 165, 179, 190
Kurtz, Harvey A., 195
Kurz and Huttenlocher Ice Company, 102

Laarman, Linda H., 194
Labor litigation, 112, 152
LaCrosse and Milwaukee Railroad, 55
Lady Elgin, sinking of, 59, 72
La Follette, Philip, 150, 158
LaFollette, Robert, Jr., 152, 169
La Follette, Robert, Sr., 101, 109–10, 134
Lahr, Jack L., 192
Lakeside Power Plant, 132
Landis, James M., 194
Lane, Jeffrey H., 193
Lardner, Lynford, Jr., x, 190
    affiliation with firm, 145
    death of, 174–75
    education of, 145
    golf interests of, 173
    and leadership of firm, 162, 163, 165, 172, 173–74
Laskis, Michael G., 193
Latham, Peter G., 196
Latus, Scott, x
Lawrence College, 107, 167
Lawrence, Wayman C., 197
Layton, Frederick, 6, 77, 97
Layton Art Gallery, 97, 149, 168
Layton Art Institute, 122
Lechter, Michael A., 193
Legal procedure, reforms in, 102–3
Legler, Mitchell W., 181, 197
Leisure time, 137
Lelands, 5
Lenawee County, Michigan, 3, 4
Lever, Chauncey W., Jr., 194
Liberty Loan drive, 135
Liberty party, 21, 25, 28, 32

Liberty Party Joint Stock Association, 24
Lien, John D., 195
Lilienthal, David, 151–52
Lincoln, Abraham
  assassination of, 69, 90
  election of, 3, 57, 59, 60, 61
  legal education of, 3
  Milwaukee's support for, 65–66
Lines, Spooner & Quarles, ix
Link, Noreen, x
Link Belt Company, 124
Linzmeyer, Peter C., 193
Little River Mills, 44
Little Wagner Act (1937), 152
Lobbying, 114
Long v. City of New London, 213n
Loomis, Orland, 158
Lott, David S., 192
Lotzia, Emerson, 197
Lucey, David M., 197
Ludington, Harrison, 37, 83
Ludington, Nelson, 37
Lueders, Wayne R., 192
Lumber companies, litigation involving,
  37–38, 53, 73–74
Lusitania, sinking of, 135
Lynch, Lawrence T., 196
Lynde, Charles, 5, 7, 10–11, 176
Lynde, Fanny, 33
Lynde, Martius, 84
Lynde, Mary Blanchard, 11, 13, 33, 59,
  71–72, 86, 105
Lynde, Tilly, 105
Lynde, Tilly, Judge, 9, 148
Lynde, Watts, 11
Lynde, William Pitt, 5, 189
  abolitionist views of, 23–25
  admittance to New York bar, 10
  appeal cases of, 87–88
  as attorney general of Wisconsin
    territory, 22
  and banking business, 45, 54–55
  and bar association, 57–58
  birth of, 10
  case load of, 92
  children of, 33
  and Civil War, 65
  in Congressional election, 28–32, 83–84,
    86
  Congressional terms of, 32, 33, 84–86
  death of, 81, 88, 92–93, 95
  and death of brothers, 11
  as district attorney for Wisconsin
    territory, 22
  education of, 10
  and ethics, 90
  as expert on maritime law, 87

  in Gilded Age, 72
  home of, 54
  investments of, 80–81
  in judicial elections, 56–57
  and labor law, 31
  land ventures of, 54
  law partnership with Finch, 1, 9, 11,
    12–20, 92–93
  as leader of political reform, 56
  marriage of, 11, 33, 59
  as mayor of Milwaukee, 59
  in mayoral election, 58–59
  net worth of, 59
  political affiliations and views of, 12, 21,
    30, 56–57
  political interests of, 21, 92
  public service by, 22, 57, 59, 62, 67, 73,
    78
  and railroad litigation, 76
  in the state assembly and Senate, 72–73
  support of, for education, 73
  Supreme Court cases handled by, 33,
    87–88
Lynde, William Pitt, Jr., 81, 92
Lynde family, background, 9

MacChesney & Becker, 52
Mack, Edwin S., ix, x, 140, 189
  affiliation with firm, 118, 121–22
  business activities of, 148–49
  contributions to firm, 120, 124, 159,
    160–61, 170
  death of, 122, 161
  early career of, 121
  education of, 121
  heart attack of, 150–51, 161
  home of, 121
  leadership of firm, 132–33, 135, 140,
    141
  retirement of, 159
  social activities of 148–49
  work habits of, 127–28, 159–60
Mack, Peter G., 184, 194
Mack brothers, 54
Mack v. Dewey, 205n
Madison, expansion of firm to, 179, 199
Madison, Dolley, 33
Madison Regency, 79, 82
Maeder, Jay, 165
Maio, F. Anthony, 191
Maisa, Susan R., 196
Mann, Martin D., 196
Marcus Plant, 156
Margaret case, 87
Marine insurance business, growth in, 18
Markham's Academy, 95
Markwell v. Pereles, 217n

Marquette Law Review, 137
Marquette University, 63, 88, 123, 157
    Law School, 145, 146, 167
Marschall, Robert P., 195
Marshall Field and Company, 102
Marshall v. American Express Company,
    210n
Martin, James, 63
Martin, Morgan, 6, 7–8
Martin v. Aetna Insurance Co., 209n
Mason, Edwin D., 197
Masonic Order, 122
Massachusetts Mutual Life Insurance
    Company, 183
Maurer, Thomas F., 197
May, K. Rodney, 194
Mayfair Mall, 168
MacArthur, Douglas, General, 48
McAdoo, William, 135
McArthur, Arthur, Jr., 48, 68
McArthur, Arthur, Sr., 58
McCarthy, Joseph R., 169–70
McCarty, Michael G., 197
McClellan, George B., 65
McComas, Harold J., xi, 165, 190
McGaffey, Jere D., xi, 191
McGinnity, Maureen A., 196
McGovern, William, 160
McGrath, Brian W., 196
McKinley, William, 122
McSweeney, Maurice J., 191
McVickar and Engleman Company, 53
Meadows cases, 79–80
Meatpacking industry, 77
Medicaid, 184
Medicare, 184
Meek, Robert E., 197
Meloy, Sybil, 197
Menominee County, 166
Menominee Indian Tribal Council, 166
Mentor program, 164
Mergers, 178–81, 184
Merriam v. Field, 213n
Merrill family, 124
Merrill Lynch, 183
Merrill v. Wisconsin Female College, 216n
Metropolitan Museum of Art, 126
Metropolitan Sewerage Commission, 141
Meyers, Philip G., 196
Michael, Best & Friedrich, ix, 117
Michigan, statehood for, 3
Michigan bar, admittance of Finch to, 3
Michigan, University of, Law School, 3
Miller, Andrew, Jr., 48, 68
Miller, Andrew G., Sr.,
    appointment of, as judge, 35, 48
    cases handled by, 14, 16, 56, 64, 98–99

as charter member of Law Institute, 58
    retirement and death of, 8, 91
    and use of arbitration panels, 18
Miller, Benjamin Kurtz, Jr. (Ben), 94, 95,
    115, 118, 139, 140, 189
Miller, Benjamin Kurtz, Sr., viii, ix, 149, 189
    admittance to Wisconsin bar, 50
    as apprentice, 49
    association with firm, 46, 48, 50
    birth of, 49, 95
    case load of, 63, 98–99, 115
    church activities of, 50
    contributions of, to firm, 78–79
    as corporate attorney, 72, 78, 79
    death of, 98, 114, 117–18
    as deputy clerk of court, 49–50
    draft status of, 65
    education of, 35, 49, 95
    as head of firm 94–106
    investments of, 81, 96–97
    land ventures of, 54
    and leadership of firm, 92, 93, 94, 96
    lifestyle of, 98
    management style of, 104–5
    as managing partner, 79
    marriage of, 51, 107
    and Newhall House hotel claims, 91
    and organization of Milwaukee
        Telephone Exchange, 88–89
    political affiliations of, 50
    public service of, 97–98
    retirement from firm, 105–106, 118–19,
        122
    scholarly interests of, 96
    social life of, 50
    ties of, to German community, 117
Miller, George Peckham, viii, 189
    admittance to Wisconsin bar, 95
    association of, with firm, 94
    birth of, 95
    case load of, 88, 92, 98–99, 101, 114,
        115, 121
    children of, 141
    clerkship of, 81
    contributions of, to firm, 121, 141
    corporate career of, 126
    death of, x, 106, 122, 141, 142, 145,
        146, 172
    education of, 95
    investments of, 139
    leadership of law firm, 95–96, 106, 118,
        124, 135, 139, 140
    marriage of, 141
    retirement of, 118–19
Miller, Isabella Peckham, 51, 141
Miller, John, 100
Miller, Laura Chapman, 98, 141

Miller, Mack & Fairchild, ix, 120–33,
    158–59, 187
  billings of, 148, 165
  cases handled by, 125–26, 128–33, 135,
    143, 144–45, 149, 150–52, 165–66
  clients of, 120, 124, 125, 132, 152–53,
    165
  and community affairs, 167–68
  in Depression era, 142–53
  establishment of, 119
  impact of World War II on, 155–57
  leadership of, 162, 163
  as legal advisor and corporate planner,
    123–24
  loyalty to associates during World War II,
    156
  name change of, 171
  offices of, 127, 128, 174
  office staff of, 126–27, 128, 139, 155
  partnership track in, 145, 157–58
  in post-World War I era, 139
  in post-World War II era, 163–76
  salary structure of, 146
  training program, 164
Miller, Madeleine, 107
Miller, Margaret, 100
Miller, Noyes & Miller, ix, 187
  establishment of, 107–108
  expansion of, 118–19
Miller, Noyes, Miller & Wahl, 187
  assets of, 108
  case load of, 110–11, 114–16
  clients of, 112–14
  and death of Wahl, 118
  establishment of, 108
  pay scale in, 108
  and ties with German community, 117
Miller, Richard H., 190
Miller, William, 96–97, 98
Miller Brewery, 137
Miller Building, 78, 127
Milorganite, 141
Milwaukee
  Albany Hall movement in, 56
  breweries in, 63
  as city, 12, 23
  charter ordinance (1900), 109
  commercial growth of, 12–13, 18,
    39–40, 53
  cost of living in, 7
  court system in, 7–8, 13–14, 18, 85
  culture in, 13, 168
  Democratic party in, 21
  draft quota for World War I, 135
  early legal practices in, 5–8, 13
  early ward structure, 22–23
  economic growth in, 37

  effect of Civil War on, 61–69
  fire protection in, 43, 90–91
  as frontier town, 1
  German community in, 29, 31, 54,
    58–59, 117, 134–35, 136
  in Gilded Age, 70–71
  growth of, 122–23
  immigrants in, 13, 63
  impact of Civil War on, 68–69
  impact of Depression on, 147
  impact of World War II on, 154–62
  industrial growth in, 6, 33, 53, 63, 89,
    123, 140–41, 169
  labor movement in, 111–13, 152
  marine insurance business in, 18
  mayors
    Hoan, Daniel W., 130, 134, 135, 136,
      147, 154
    Koch, John, 109
    Lynde, William P., 58–59
    Rose, David, 109
    Seidel, Emil, 128, 136
    Walber, Emil, 108
    Walker, George, 38
    Zeidler, Carl, 154
  municipal services in, 89, 115
  newspapers in, 63
  political parties in, 72–73
  population of, 13, 63, 94, 110–11, 116,
    122, 141, 168
  as port city, 12–13, 18, 168–69
  poverty and homelessness in, 71–72
  progressive movement in, 109–10, 134–35
  and prohibition, 136–37
  real-estate boom in, 110–11
  redistricting of, 90
  smallpox epidemics in, 23, 25
  socialist movement in, 115, 128–29
  suburban growth of, 168
  telephone services of, 88–89
  transportation in, 71, 110, 140
  in World War I, 135
  in post-World War I era, 122–23
  during World War II, 154–55
Milwaukee (steamboat), 8
Milwaukee Academy, 95
Milwaukee, Fond du Lac, and Green Bay
    Railroad, 40
Milwaukee and La Crosse Railroad, 40
Milwaukee and Mississippi Railroad, 40–41,
    55, 66
Milwaukee and Mississippi Railroad v.
    Comstock, 208n
Milwaukee and Mississippi Railroad v.
    Cramer, 208n
Milwaukee and Mississippi Railroad v.
    Dousman, 208n

Milwaukee and Mississippi Railroad v.
   Eldred, 208n
Milwaukee and Northern Railroad, 74
Milwaukee and Prairie du Chien Railroad,
   75
Milwaukee and Watertown Plank Road
   Company, 39
Milwaukee and Waukesha Railroad, 40–41
Milwaukee Art Museum, 97, 168
Milwaukee Art Society, 97
Milwaukee Athletic Club, 158
Milwaukee Auditorium, 168
Milwaukee Ballet Company, 168
Milwaukee Bar Association
   establishment of Law Institute, 58
   expansion of, 104
   fee schedule in, 58
   goals of, 58
   junior bar, 171
   law library at, 62
   officers of, 57, 62, 149
   offices of, 62–63
   office staff at, 103–104
   organization of, 57–58
   on recordkeeping, 104–105
   reforms in, 103
   and wartime training, 157
Milwaukee Blood Center, 174
Milwaukee Board of Public Works, 71
Milwaukee Board of Trade, 33
Milwaukee Braves, 167
Milwaukee Brewers, 63, 167
Milwaukee Building Company,
   incorporation of, 72
Milwaukee Cement Company, 102
Milwaukee Chamber of Commerce, 64, 90
Milwaukee Children's Hospital, 168
Milwaukee City Railway Co., 110
Milwaukee Club, 97, 149
Milwaukee County, schools in, 36
Milwaukee Country Day School, 167
Milwaukee County Historical Society, vii,
   246
Milwaukee County Medical Complex, 68
Milwaukee County Stadium, 167
Milwaukee Courier, 13
Milwaukee Downer College, 167
Milwaukee Downer Seminary, 135
Milwaukee Electric Railway and Light
   Company, 112, 130, 137
Milwaukee Electric Railway and Light Co. v.
   Bradley, 220n
Milwaukee Electric Railway and Light Co. v.
   City of Milwaukee, 220n
Milwaukee Electric Railway and Light Co. v.
   Wisconsin Railroad Commission,
   220n

Milwaukee Exposition Center, 90
Milwaukee Gas Light Company, 46, 53–54,
   72, 114, 124, 130, 132, 138, 151, 152
Milwaukee Journal, 90, 91, 99, 110, 134,
   136, 150, 169
Milwaukee Light Guards, 68
Milwaukee Lyceum, 9
Milwaukee Marine and Fire Insurance
   Company, 95
Milwaukee Medical College, 123
Milwaukee Merchants' Association, 64, 90
Milwaukee Passavant Hospital, 68
Milwaukee Public Library, 78, 89, 97
Milwaukee Repertory Theatre, 168
Milwaukee Sanitarium, 149, 168
Milwaukee School of Engineering, 123
Milwaukee Sentinel, 6, 9, 22, 29, 31, 56,
   83, 99
   libel suit against, 83, 84
Milwaukee's Speedrail interurban train, 1950
   collision of, 165–66
Milwaukee Street Railway Co., 110
Milwaukee Street Railway Co. v. Anderson,
   218n
Milwaukee's Union Stock Yards, 77
Milwaukee Symphony Orchestra, 149, 168
Milwaukee Telephone Company, 88, 89,
   96–97
Milwaukee Theatre Association, 97
Milwaukee Trust Company, 97
Milwaukee University School, 122
Milwaukee Woman's Club, 86
Mitchell, Alexander, 44, 55, 59, 74, 83, 95,
   97
Mitchell family, 126
Mitchell Field, 140
Mix, Edward Townsend, 72, 98
Modrall, James R. III, 191
Mondul, Donald D., 195
Monroe, Vaughn, 137
Monsees, Paul R., 196
Mooney, Richard, xi, 160
Morrill, Chester, 161
Morris, Robert J., Jr., 195
Morris, William, 103, 104
Mount Pleasant v. Beckwith, 215n
Movie-distribution rights, 149
Muller, H. Nicholas III, xi
Municipal League, 109, 114
Munro, Thomas F. III, 194
Music Building, 89

National Association of Legal Aid, 157
National Brake and Electric Company, 125
National City Bank, 101
National Encampment of the Grand Army of
   the Republic, 90

National Foundry and Pipe Works, Ltd., 116
*National Foundry and Pipe Works, Ltd. v.
    Oconto City Water Supply Co.,* 218*n*
National Home for Disabled Volunteer
    Soldiers, 68, 72
National Labor Relations Board, 152
*National Labor Relations Board v.
    Transamerican Freight Lines, Inc.,*
    225*n*
National Park Bank of New York, 101
National Rivet Company, 153
Nazro, John, 63
Neal, Gerald J., 180, 182, 191
Neenah and Menasha Electric Railway
    Company, 115
Negligence cases, 100–101
Nellis v. Cramer, 216*n*
Nemmers, Ervin, 156
Newcomb, Paul R., 127, 144–45, 148–49,
    157, 189
New Deal, 142, 150, 151
Newhall, Daniel, 18, 59, 64
Newhall House, 53, 90–91
Newhall v. Bullman, 206*n*
New York and Erie Railroad Company, 42
New York and Wisconsin Land Company, 8
New York bar, Lynde's admittance to, 10
New York Bottlers Supplies Manufacturing
    Company, 102
New York Life Insurance Company, 124
New York Stock Market, development of
    the, 61
New York, University of City of, 10
    law school of, 9
Nieman, Agnes, 150
Nieman, Lucius, 91, 99, 136, 141, 150–51
Nolan, Michael S., 191
Noonan, Josiah, 46
Nordberg Manufacturing Company, 152,
    157, 160
Normal Institute, 22
North Chicago Rolling Mill Company, 100,
    102, 111
Northern Pacific Railroad, 101, 112
North Point water-intake facility, 115
Northwestern Mutual Life Insurance
    Company, 46, 108, 118
Northwest Ordinance (1787), 3, 39
Noyes, George H., 107, 108, 116, 118–19,
    122, 189
Nunnemacher's Grand Opera House, 97

Ohio, Lenawee County border dispute
    with, 3
Olin, John M., 108
Olmsted, Frederick Law, 98
Olsen, Michael E., 197

Olson, Frederick I., x
Olson, John M., 196
Olwell, Lawrence A., ix
Olwell & Brady, ix
O'Neal, Michael S., 197
O'Neill, Edward, 81
Orlando, Fla., merger in, 180, 199
Orton, Harlow, 93
Oscar Mayer and Company, 124
O'Shaughnessy, James P., 194
Ostrow, Andrew A., 197

Pabst, Fred, 54
Pabst, Gustave, 141
Pabst Brewery, 123, 124, 137
Pabst family, 126
Pabst Theatre, 135
Page, William H., 146
Paine, Byron, 56, 57, 61, 71
Palmer, Henry Lewis, 46, 49, 66, 98, 108,
    118
Panic of 1837, 4–5, 6
Panic of 1857, 42, 45, 48, 51, 55
Panic of 1893, 110
Papendiek, Christopher, 32, 33, 51
Papendiek, George, 32, 33, 51
Papendiek, George, Jr., 33
Papendiek, Mary Finch, 32, 33, 51, 91
Paragon Cigar Manufacturing Company, 102
Paramount Corporation, 149, 165
Patel, Jamshed J., 195
Patent Cooperation Treaty (1970), 183
Payne, Henry C., 110, 112, 113, 115
Payne family, 124
Peckham, George W., 51
Peckham v. Rose, 210*n*
Peet, Stephen, 9
Peim Refining Company, 102
Pemrich, Connie, xi
Pence, Thomas C., 197
Pendleton Act (1883), 109
Pennsylvania College, 95
People's Party, 81
Pereles, Nathan, 54
Peters, Elsie, 172
Petersen, Elna, 172
Petit, L. J., 141
Petri, Mark G., 193
Pfister, Charles, 115
Pfister, Guido, 77
Pfister family, 124
Phillips Petroleum, 162
Plankinton, John, 6, 77
Plankinton-Armour firm, 77
Plankinton family, 124, 126
Plyler, J. Philip, 195
Plymouth Church, 5

Polk, James K., 22, 28, 34, 35
Pollution, 115
Ponto, Steven V., 194
Poole, James I., 152, 162, 165, 190
Pope v. Allis, 215n
Porter, J. D., 157
Porter, Jack A., 182, 192
Porter, Richard H., 192
Potter Law (1874), 75
Pottsville Iron and Steel Company, 102
Poverty, problems of children in, 71–72
Prager, Mark L., 197
Prairie du Chien Railway Company, 75
Prange family, 124, 150
Pratt v. Seaver, 208n
Precourt, Lyman A., 165, 190
Pressed Steel Company, 125
Probate law, 79, 100, 125, 143, 150
Pro bono work, 157
Progressive movement (1886), 101, 109–10, 134
Prohibition, 136–37, 138
Public Service Commission, 129, 130
Public Service Commission of Wisconsin v. Wisconsin Telephone Co., 222n
Public utilities. *See* Utilities
Public Utility Holding Company Act (1935), 151
Pullman railway workers' strike, 112
Purintun, Orin, 165, 190

Quarles, Caroline, 24
Quarles, Charles, ix
Quarles, Joseph V., ix
Quarles, Louis, 161
Quarles & Brady, ix
Quick, Patrick G., 197
Quinney v. Denney, 212n

Radelet, Timothy J., 197
Ragatz, Thomas G., 179, 192
Rahr Malting Company, 150
Rahr Malting Co. v. United States, 222n
Railroad Administration Agency, 135
Railroad Commission, 135
Railroads
    disputes with farmers, 40, 42, 55–56, 66, 75
    funding of construction for, 74–75
    in Gilded Age, 74–75
    importance of, in Civil War, 61, 66
    litigation on, 40–43, 75, 76
    regulation of, 75–76, 135
Randall, Alexander W., 48
Rapkin, Joseph E., 162, 168, 175, 190
Rapp, Randall S., 195
Read, William A., 126

Reconstruction Finance Corporation, 147
Reed, Harrison, 9
Reform Republicans, 79
Regenfuss, Michael D., 193
Reicher, David M., 194
Reinecke, David W., 196
Reinhart, Boerner, Van Deuren, Norris & Rieselbach, ix
Reliance Iron Works, strike at, 111
Renz, Greg W., 193
Republican party, 50
    in 1859 judicial campaign, 56–57
    in 1860 mayoral campaign, 58–59
    in 1860 presidential campaign, 57, 59, 60, 61
    in 1870 mayoral campaign, 81–82
    in 1874 congressional campaign, 83–84
    in Gilded Age, 72
    in 1932 presidential campaign, 142
    in 1946 senatorial campaign, 169
    and slavery issue, 56–57
Richardson v. Dewey, 205n
Rieth, David M., 194
Rigler, Douglas V., 191
Rindskopf, Samuel, 83, 84
Rivera, Kathleen M., 195
River and Lakeshore Railway, 71
RKO, 165
Roberts v. Wisconsin Telephone Co., 218n
Rock, R. Andrew, 197
Rockford Mitten and Hosiery Company, 102
Roehr, Mildred, 127, 172
Rogers, James H., 59
Rogers v. Dewey, 205n
Rolle, Christopher D., 196
Roman Catholicism, 13, 94
Roosevelt, Franklin D., 142, 152, 154
Roosevelt, Theodore, 122
Root, Elihu, 103
Rose, David, 109
Rosenthal, Paul E., 194
Ross, Anne E., 196
Rothe, C. M., 126, 140
Rough and Ready Club, 29, 32
Rubin, Amy S., 195
Rublee, Horace, 56–57
Runyan, David H., 196
Rural Electrification Act (1935), 151
Rusk, Jeremiah, 111
Ryan, Edward G., 19, 31, 37, 80

Sacks, David A., 194
Sadler, Luther F., Jr., 197
St. Lawrence Seaway, 168
St. Luke's Hospital, 184
St. Paul's Episcopal Church, 92, 174
St. Stanislaus Catholic Church, 63, 94

Sammond, Frederic, 189
  affiliation with firm, 140, 145
  apprenticeship of, 140
  background of, 147
  business activities of, 148–49
  education of, 140
  and Indian rights, 166
  membership in scholarly association, 149
  military service of, 136
  social activities of, 148–49
  as tax expert, 150, 157, 166
Sams, Robert A., 192
Sanders, John A., 193
Saue, Jacqueline M., 195
Saxe, Bernhard D., 195
Scanlon, William J., 196
Schabacker, Mark M., 196
Schlitz, Joseph, 123
Schlitz Brewery, 88, 102, 117, 123, 124, 137
Schumacher v. Cornell, 215*n*
Schurz, Carl, 57
Schwaab, Richard L., 184, 194
Schwartz, Arthur, 184, 194
Schwartz, Jeffrey, Schwaab, Mack, Blumenthal & Evans, P.C., 184, 199
Schwartzburg v. Lundwurm, Milwaukee and Fond du Lac Railroad, 208*n*
Schwemer v. Fry, 221*n*
Sears Roebuck, 183
Second Ward Savings Bank of Milwaukee, 126
Securities, in post-World War II era, 166–67
Securities and Exchange Commission, 166
Sedition Law, 136
Sefton, John T., 194
Seibel, Irene, 172
Seidel, Emil, 128, 136
Seidel v. Journal Co., 220*n*
Sellicks's School, 95
Sennett, Nancy J., 195
Sexton, C. Anthony, 195
Sheboygan Chair Company, 102
Sheehan, Timothy J., 195
Shepard v. Milwaukee Gas Light Co., 210*n*
Sherman, William Tecumseh, 66
Sherman Anti-Trust Act (1890), 112
Sherrard v. Western Union Telegraph Co., 219*n*
Shriner, Thomas L., Jr., xi, 192
Shute, David, 177, 191
Siegel, Jack B., 196
Simmons, Judith W., 194
Simon, George T., 197
Simonson, Judy, x
Sims, Luke E., 193
Skambis, Christopher C., Jr., 193

Skeeles, Nelson D., 2
Skilton, John S., 192
Sklar, William P., 195
Slade, Thomas B., III, 180, 193
Slavery, sentiment on, 23–25, 28–29, 56–57
Slavin, Stephen M., 197
Slivick v. American Express Co., 219*n*
Slook, David W., 192
Smallpox epidemics, 23, 71
Smith, A. O., Company, 153, 169
Smith, Abigail, 16
Smith, Abram D., 49, 56
Smith, Clement C., 8, 44, 98, 141
Smith, Israel, 16
Smith, James, 18
Smith, Leander, 82
Smith, Leslie C., 193
Smith, Madeleine Miller, 98
Smith, Vance A., 194
Smith, William E., 86
Smith Company, A. O., 125
Socialist labor organization, 109
Socialist movement, 109, 115
Socialist party, 109, 128–29, 134, 136
Solomon, Edward, 54
Sosnowski, Leonard S., 192
South Trust Bank, 182
Spencerian Business College, 104
Sperry and Hutchinson Co., 124
Spooner, John C., ix
Square D Company, 169
Square D. Company v. National Labor Board, 225*n*
Stacke v. Milwaukee and Mississippi Railroad Company, 208*n*
Starkweather, John C., 19–20, 31, 68
State Bank of Wisconsin v. Jackson Hadley, 211*n*
State Bank of Wisconsin v. James, 210*n*
State Bank of Wisconsin v. Newhall, 212*n*
State ex rel. City of Milwaukee v. Milwaukee Electric Railway and Light Co., 220*n*
State ex rel. Klefisch v. Wisconsin Telephone Co., 220*n*
State ex rel. Martin v. Heil, 223*n*
State ex rel. Sperry & Hutchinson Co. v. Weigle, 219*n*
State ex rel. Warren v. Nusbaum, 226*n*
State ex rel. Zimmerman v. Dammann, 223*n*
State Historical Society of Wisconsin, vii, x, 92, 108, 168
Stats v. Sanderson, 205*n*
Steele, Charles J., 195
Stein Mart, Inc., 182
Steinmetz, Christian G., 196
Stepno, Schwaab & Linn, 184

Stone, Peter J., 195
Stoneburner, Gresham R., 197
Story, Joseph, 10, 73
Stumm v. Western Union Telegraph Co.,
    219*n*
Sturgeon Bay Canal, 85
Sullivan & Cromwell, 101, 103, 132
Superfund legislation, 184
Swaine, Robert T., 155
Swanson, Vernon A., xi, 145, 146, 151,
    152–53, 175, 190
Sweeney, Timothy C., 194
Sylvester Marvin (schooner), 18

Tainter, Andrew, 74
Tainter v. Lucas, 213*n*
Talbert, Pierre C., 197
Tallahassee, Fla., expansion office in, 182
Tallmadge, Nathaniel, 22
Tampa, Fla., office expansion/merger in,
    180, 181, 199
Tanning industry, 77–78
Tarkow, Stanley A., 192
Tax law practice, 149, 166
Taylor, Allen M., xi, 164, 165, 175, 190
Taylor, Zachary, 29, 32
Teamsters Union, 167
Technology, 123
Tecumseh, Michigan, 2
Teigen, Richard L., 194
Temkin, Harvey L., 195
Temperance movement, 9, 25–26, 31
Terry v. McVicker, 210*n*
Tesch, John, 58, 59
Thimke, Mark A., 195
Tilden, Samuel, in 1876 election, 86
Todd v. Lee, 212*n*
Trade-union movement, 112
Trammell Crow, 182
Trane Co. v. Tax Commission, 222*n*
Trane Company, 150
Treat v. Miner, 210*n*
Trostel, Albert O., 77
Turnverein Club, 88
Tweedy, John, vii, 8, 17, 26, 29, 56
Tweeton, Edna, 172
Twentieth Century-Fox, 165
Tym, Ronald D., 195
Tyson, Joseph B., Jr., 194

Uihlein, Joseph, 141
Uihlein family, 117, 126
Union College, 19, 20
Union of Presbyterian and Congregational
    Churches, 24
Union Pacific Railroad, 84

Unions, 152
*United Gas, Coke and Chemical Workers of
    America v. Wisconsin Employment
    Relations Board*, 225*n*
United States Conference of Mayors, 147
United States Golf Association, 173, 175
U.S. Sanitary Commission, 68
United States Steel, 102
United States Supreme Court, 33, 87–88,
    150, 151–52, 158
United States v. Gifford, 205*n*
Universal Studios, 181
University Club, 149
University School of Milwaukee, 135, 149,
    175
Usinger family, 126
Utilities. *See also specific utility*
    litigation on, 53, 167
    public ownership of city, 114
    regulation of, 109, 119, 129–33

Van Buren, Martin, 10, 32
van den Berg, Egerton K., 180, 193
van den Berg, Gay, Burke, Wilson & Arkin,
    180, 199
Vandervelde, Bert, 127, 145, 147, 148–49,
    157, 189
Van Dyke, George, 141
Van Dyke, John, 98
Van Dyke, W. D., 141
Van Houten, Elizabeth, 16
Van Houten, John, 16
Van Houten v. Smith, 206*n*
Van Sicklen, Michael B., 196
Van Steenwyck v. Washburn, 214*n*
Varon, Jay N., 193
Veterans Administration Center, 68
"V for Victory" program, 156
Victory Fleet Flag, 157
Villard, Henry, 110, 112, 132
Vliet, Garret, 54
Vogel, Fred, Jr., 77, 141
Vogel family, 124
Volksfreund, 31
von Briesen & Purtell, ix, 117

Wagner Act (1935), 152
Wahl, Frederick R., 127
Wahl, George H., 108, 118, 189
Walber, Emil, 108
Waldo, Otis H., 58
Walker, Brown & Wahl, 108
Walker, George, 38, 41
Walker, Timothy, 14
Walker v. Shepardson, 208*n*
Wallace, Harry L., xi, 165, 175, 190

Walmer, Edwin F., 190
Walsh, David O., 179, 194
Walsh, Walsh, Sweeney & Whitney, 199
Walter, Ronald L., 192
Ward, Craig B., 194
War Industries Board, 135
War Labor Act, 162
War Labor Board, 135
Warner Brothers, 165
Washburn, Cadwallader, 79–80
Washington College, 49
Watkins, Colonel A. H., 175
Waukesha *Democrat,* 57
Wauwatosa citizens, protest over trolley
    fares, 113
Wawrzyn, Ronald M., 192
Weber, Robert G., 191
Wehr Corporation, 124, 150
Weisel and Co. v. Bowles, 223n
Weiss, Richard A., 192
Weissbard, Samuel H., 194
Weissman, Michael L., 195
Welch, John M., Jr., 197
Wells & Finch, 8–9
Wells, Crocker, & Finch, 5, 6, 8, 53
Wells, Daniel, 31
Wells, Horatio N., 5, 24–25
Wells Fargo, 124
Wells v. Martin, 204n
Werber, Steven A., 197
West Bend Aluminum, 124
Western Union Telegraph Company, 77,
    102, 128
West Palm Beach, Fla., expansion office in,
    182
West Side Street Railway Company, 91
Weyauwega v. Ayling, 215n
Wheat industry, litigation in, 64, 65
Whig party, 5, 12, 21, 23, 50
    and constitutional referendum, 26–27
    in election of 1848, 28–32
    leaders of, 31
Whipple v. Putnam, 14, 205n
White Rock Mineral Spring Company, 102
Whitney, Abel, partnerships with Finch, 2
Whitney, Robert M., 194
Whitney v. Brunette, 208n
Whitney v. Hathaway, 8, 204n
Whiton, E. V., 31
Wiedemann, Herbert P., 165, 190
Wiedenman, Jere W., 193
Wiley, Edwin P., xi, 165, 183, 190
Will, Trevor J., 194
Williams, Allen W., Jr., 184, 192
Willis, William J., 165, 190
Will of Nieman: *Mack v. Wahl,* 222n
Wilmot Proviso, 23

Wilson, Jon M., 193
Wilson, Woodrow, 135, 136
Wimberly v. Clark Controller Co., 225n
Winburn, John T., 197
Wineke, Susan, xi
Winkler, Flanders, Bottum, Smith & Vilas,
    ix, 117
Winkler, James A., 195
Wisconsin
    constitution for, 19, 25–27
    governors of, 16, 83
        Goodland, 158
        Heil, 158
        Loomis, 158
    immigrants to, 74
    statehood for, 12, 28, 34–47
    territorial status for, 13, 21, 22, 25–28
Wisconsin Anti-slavery Society, 28
Wisconsin Assembly and Senate, 46
Wisconsin Banking Commission, 144
Wisconsin Bar Association, 86, 138–39,
    149, 157, 171
Wisconsin Board of Immigration, 74
Wisconsin Central Railroad, 101
Wisconsin Club, 135
Wisconsin court system
    early judges in, 36–37, 48
    establishment of separate appellate body,
        35
    judicial elections for, 34–35
    judicial terms in, 35
    organization of, 27–28
    partisan battles in, 35
Wisconsin Electric Power Company, 132
*Wisconsin Employment Relations Board v.
    Milwaukee Gas Light Co.,* 225n
Wisconsin Enabling Act (1869), 75
Wisconsin Fair Labor Board, 152
Wisconsin Female College, 99
Wisconsin Gas Company, 152
Wisconsin Gas Light Co., 138
Wisconsin History Foundation, 168
Wisconsin Housing Finance Authority, 179
Wisconsin Idea, 123
Wisconsin Law Review, 140, 172, 179
Wisconsin Marine and Fire Insurance
    Company, 44, 95, 101
Wisconsin Marine Bank, 18, 45
Wisconsin Power and Light Company, 151
Wisconsin Public Service Commission, 143
Wisconsin Railroad Commission, 129,
    130–31
Wisconsin Securities Commission, 143
Wisconsin State Golf Association, 173
Wisconsin State Journal, 57
Wisconsin Supreme Court, 41, 56, 161
    justices of, 19, 107, 146

Wisconsin Telephone Company, 97, 104,
  129, 151–52
  litigation involving, 89, 114, 130, 132,
  138, 152, 160
*Wisconsin Telephone Co. v. City of
  Milwaukee,* 218n
Wisconsin Telephone Co. v. City of Oshkosh,
  215n
Wisconsin Territorial Anti-slavery Society,
  24
Wisconsin, University of, 107, 108, 123
  Board of Regents of, 108
  Law School at, 3, 81, 121, 145, 146, 172
Wolcott, Laura Ross, 180
Wolfson, Mark J., 1979
Wolpert, Ira C., 1968
Women
  admission to Wisconsin bar, 86
  education for, 22
  impact of World War II on, 155

legal rights of, 16, 66, 103
  voting rights for, 86
Wood, Edgar L., ix
Wood, Warner, Tyrrell & Bruce, ix
Woodson, R. Duke, 1968
Workmen's Compensation Act (Wisconsin),
  137
Wright, Daisy E., 104
Wright, Frank Lloyd, Foundation, 166

Y ale University, 10, 163
Yates, Peter, 17
Young Men's Association, 89, 97

Z abrowski, Patrick M., 196
Zaiser, Kent A., 197
Zeidler, Carl, 154
Zimmerman, Robert J., 196

Acknowledgments for Photographs
Following page 69:
Foley & Lardner: 11
Courtesy of Milwaukee County Historical Society: 1, 2, 3, 4, 5, 6, 7, 8, 9, 10, 12, 14, 15, 16, 17, 18
University of Wisconsin–Milwaukee Area Research Center: 13

Following page 119:
Foley & Lardner: 1, 3, 9, 10, 11, 12
Courtesy of Milwaukee County Historical Society: 2, 4, 5, 6, 7, 8, 13, 14, 15, 16, 17, 18, 19

Following page 167:
Foley & Lardner: 2, 3, 4, 5, 6, 7, 8, 9, 10, 11, 12, 13, 14
Courtesy of Milwaukee County Historical Society: 1
First Wisconsin National Bank: 16
Wisconsin Gas Company: 15